# PRIZE

## Anne & Isaac Orkin Memorial Cup

awarded to

**Libbi Yehood**

for

Secular Progress

ArtScroll Series®

*by*
Yair Weinstock

*translated by*
Libby Lazewnik

Published by
Mesorah Publications, ltd

**A famous novelist retells classic stories with passion and spirit**

FIRST EDITION
*First Impression … April 2003*
*Second Impression … October 2004*

Published and Distributed by
**MESORAH PUBLICATIONS, LTD.**
4401 Second Avenue / Brooklyn, N.Y 11232

*Distributed in Europe by*
**LEHMANNS**
Unit E, Viking Business Park
Rolling Mill Road
Jarow, Tyne & Wear, NE32 3DP
England

*Distributed in Australia and New Zealand by*
**GOLDS WORLDS OF JUDAICA**
3-13 William Street
Balaclava, Melbourne 3183
Victoria, Australia

*Distributed in Israel by*
**SIFRIATI / A. GITLER — BOOKS**
6 Hayarkon Street
Bnei Brak 51127

*Distributed in South Africa by*
**KOLLEL BOOKSHOP**
Shop 8A Norwood Hypermarket
Norwood 2196, Johannesburg, South Africa

---

**ARTSCROLL SERIES®**
**TALES FOR THE SOUL 4**
*© Copyright 2003, by* MESORAH PUBLICATIONS, Ltd.
*4401 Second Avenue / Brooklyn, N.Y. 11232 / (718) 921-9000*

---

**ALL RIGHTS RESERVED**
*The text, prefatory and associated textual contents and introductions*
*— including the typographic layout, cover artwork and ornamental graphics —*
*have been designed, edited and revised as to content, form and style.*

**No part of this book may be reproduced**
**IN ANY FORM, PHOTOCOPYING, OR COMPUTER RETRIEVAL SYSTEMS**
**— even for personal use without written permission from**
**the copyright holder, Mesorah Publications Ltd.**
*except by a reviewer who wishes to quote brief passages*
*in connection with a review written for inclusion in magazines or newspapers.*

**THE RIGHTS OF THE COPYRIGHT HOLDER WILL BE STRICTLY ENFORCED.**

ISBN:
1-57819-732-5 (hard cover)
1-57819-733-3 (paperback)

Typography by CompuScribe at ArtScroll Studios, Ltd.
Printed in the United States of America by Noble Book Press Corp.
Bound by Sefercraft, Quality Bookbinders, Ltd., Brooklyn N.Y. 11232

# Table of Contents

| | |
|---|---:|
| Stolen Property | 9 |
| Tale of a Tallis | 16 |
| A Rabbi's Courage | 24 |
| The Curse | 33 |
| R' Shmelke's Extraordinary Visitors | 38 |
| A Jar of Snuff | 47 |
| A "Cold Shoulder" from the Rebbe | 56 |
| Four Missions in One Night | 63 |
| He Who Succors the Poor | 72 |
| Unnecessary Questions | 79 |
| Three Wondrous Coins | 88 |
| The Curse of Money | 97 |
| I Will Speak to Him in a Dream | 103 |
| A Public Outcry | 110 |
| A First-Class Ticket | 117 |
| Rashi's Learning Partner | 128 |
| The Keeper of Promises | 137 |
| The Scales of Heaven | 143 |
| The Rebbe in Vienna | 151 |
| Of Chicken Soup and Cholent | 157 |
| A Long-Ago Intifada | 163 |
| The Power of Shabbos Clothes | 171 |

| | |
|---|---|
| A Gaon in Sefer Devarim | 180 |
| The Astonishing Arab Merchant | 186 |
| Three Who Cried | 194 |
| The Man Who Conquered the Ox | 202 |
| "Do Not Be Afraid" | 210 |
| "A Tzaddik Will Be Rescued" | 218 |
| Sweetening the Judgment | 227 |
| What R' Elisha Learned | 230 |
| Fifty Secret Signatures | 238 |
| By the Light of the Bonfire | 246 |

# Stolen Property

THE TOWN OF VILEDNIK, IN THE UKRAINE (ON THE BORDER with White Russia), was a more important place than its size might have indicated. Though small in area, the roads to Vilednik were always busy.

Vilednik was the home of the holy Rebbe, R' Yisrael Dov, author of *Sh'eiris Yisrael* and known throughout Eastern Europe as the Tzaddik of Vilednik. He had been a student of R' Mordechai of Chernobyl and R' Levi Yitzchak of Berditchev.

Even in a generation rich with great and holy men, R' Yisrael Dov of Vilednik shone with a special light. He could discern how a man had spent his life, from childhood until that moment. Even more — when an animal would pass beneath his window, R' Yisrael Dov would know at once all about its *master's* life!

The blessings he bestowed upon the people were effective, bringing an astonishing number of extraordinary results in their wake. It was said that anyone who came to him — even if his hand did no more than touch the doorknob of the Rebbe's room — found the salvation he was seeking. Emulating his Creator, he was filled with compassion for everyone, sharing in another's pain as if that person were his dearest friend. He loved every Jew as if that Jew were his only son.

It was R' Yisrael Dov's greatest desire to sway people's hearts to return to their Father in Heaven. Speaking privately with every person who came to see him, he would explain just how the visitor's actions had been punished with the specific illness or suffering that afflicted him. In short, R' Yisrael Dov was a giant in a generation of giants.

He was responsible for making penitents out of thousands of Jews in his time, whether they came seeking his advice and blessing, or to beg his Divinely assisted help in finding lost valuables. This group included *agunos* who came to see if the Rebbe could search throughout the world with his inner eye and find their missing husbands.

Our story is about one of these unfortunate women, an *agunah* who came to Vilednik one morning to seek the Rebbe's help.

"Lock the door immediately and don't let anyone come in. Do they think I stand in Hashem's place? Do they think I can fulfill every person's wish? I cannot help her at all!"

This explicit instruction was delivered to the Rebbe's *gabbai* in a clear, loud voice. Knowing that the Rebbe was able to see things that others could not, the *gabbai* knew that the order had some reason behind it. Since the Rebbe had mentioned that he could not "help her at all," the *gabbai* surmised that a woman visitor had come to Vilednik — probably a woman embroiled in an unusually difficult or complex situation. The compassionate Rebbe, pained by any Jew's plight, knew that this time it would be extremely difficult for him to help the unfortunate newcomer.

The *gabbai*, however, also knew that the Rebbe's orders of this kind never lasted long. When he witnessed the visitor pleading for entry, the Rebbe would open the doors himself, and gesture for the *gabbai* to admit all those waiting to see him, however painful their stories.

Just as the *gabbai* had surmised, that very morning an *agunah* had arrived from Lithuania, seeking help for her very difficult situation. Her husband had abandoned her nineteen years earlier, leaving her with four small children. Hearing many tales of wondrous salvations wrought by the Tzaddik of Vilednik, she had spent her money and energy to travel for two full years, from her hometown in Lithuania through the wilds of the Ukraine, until she reached Vilednik at last.

By the time she had reached her lodgings in town, the Rebbe already sensed her arrival and knew why she had come, and had instructed the *gabbai* not to allow anyone in. The *gabbai*, however, merely closed the door, but did not lock it.

Hardly had the Rebbe entered his room than the *agunah* hurried to his house. She pushed open the door and chased away the *gabbai* — who feebly attempted to stop her. Like a wounded lioness, she burst into the Rebbe's room.

"Rebbe!" she wailed. "I can't bear it any longer! My troubles have overflowed their limit. Please rescue me from my suffering!"

The Rebbe's expression changed. Before the woman had entered his room, his look had been severe. Now, as he listened to her pain-racked cries, his face softened with deep pity. The *gabbai* was very familiar with this sight. He knew, too, that the Rebbe's compassion was no ordinary emotion. When the Rebbe shared in another's pain, he was stealing away bits and pieces of his own health. People thought that the Rebbe pulled "miracles" out of his sleeve, as it were — effortlessly. The *gabbai* knew that every "miracle" had its price, and that the one to pay it was the Rebbe.

"What is the trouble?" R' Yisrael Dov asked softly.

With an effort, the woman stifled her sobs. "Nineteen years have passed since my husband ran away, abandoning me and our four children. I have lived with the pain, the shame, and the humiliation all this time. To feed my little ones, I strained myself to the utmost! Now I just can't do it anymore. The children have grown, and now that they have reached marriageable age, not only do I lack the money to marry them off, but lately I have begun to lose my strength as well. I can no longer work as hard as I used to, so there is not enough to support us. I have been traveling for two years! Rebbe! I have come from Lithuania because I have heard wonderful things about you. Only you can save me!"

As she talked and wept, the Rebbe sat staring at the ground. His ears were always sealed to praise. The woman's distress, however, deeply pierced his heart.

Despite the way he felt inside, the Rebbe's outward expression was hard and angry. Suddenly, he turned to the *gabbai* and berated him, "You *batlan!* Why didn't you lock the door when I told you to? Why did you let her in? Now send her out at once!"

The *gabbai* stood stupefied.

The *agunah* herself burst into heartrending wails. "*Gevald!* Holy Rebbe, what are you doing to me? I've spent two years traveling here from my home — and now you throw me out without even hearing my story? Holy Rebbe, save me! Have pity on me and on my four children. If it's money you want, I will pay. I am prepared to hand over everything I have — five rubles!" Her hand went to the small, knotted bundle at her side.

The Rebbe smiled. "You have six rubles in there, not five."

Shocked into speechlessness, the *agunah* fell silent. People had told her that the Viledniker Rebbe's eyes saw all, and now she had seen evidence of this with her own eyes.

"The Rebbe is right," she whispered. "All right. You can have all six rubles."

"Plus another 25 kopeks," the Rebbe laughed. "Teach your tongue to speak the truth."

"True again," the woman acknowledged. She spoke in a dazed fashion. "In my bundle are exactly six rubles and 25 kopeks. But I cannot give the Rebbe the kopeks. I need them for my traveling expenses."

Still smiling, the Rebbe said, "I don't want even one cent! On the contrary, I would like to give you a few more coins for your sustenance."

The woman remained silent, defeated. The Rebbe instructed her, "Keep the six rubles for your expenses. I will give you several silver kopeks [as opposed to copper kopeks, which were not worth much, silver kopeks were very valuable]. Use the silver coins to buy large pretzels of dough. Sell these in the market square on market day. With the profits you make, buy new pretzels and continue to sell them. Perhaps in this way *Hashem Yisbarach* will help you to support yourself and marry off your children."

When he finished speaking, he opened a drawer in his desk and took out 25 silver kopeks. He gave them to the *agunah*, who thanked him warmly and took her leave.

Bright and early the next morning, the woman went to the bakery to buy her pretzels. She discovered that, with the money the Rebbe had given her, she had enough to purchase some cakes as well. Loaded down with a considerable quantity of both items, she directed her footsteps toward the market square.

She immediately realized the fruits of the Rebbe's blessing. No sooner had the *agunah* set up her wares than customers came swarming around. All that day she worked busily, and by evening she had sold every last pretzel and cake. Counting her profits, she realized that she had enough to buy double the quantity on the following day.

The work was hard. Standing all day long in the snow selling her wares was no easy task. Her fingers grew red and chapped, and finally blue, from the cold. From time to time she would blow on them to warm them. But her inner satisfaction was great. She would do the same thing again the next day, despite the hardships!

Early the next morning, she proceeded once again to the bakery, returning to her stall in the marketplace with heavy baskets. She spread out the freshly baked goods so that their tempting aroma spread far and wide. Again the customers flocked around, giving her no peace even for a minute's time. Her large trays emptied at a rapid clip. With each passing hour, she saw the Rebbe's blessing coming true.

Toward evening, a customer approached the *agunah's* stall. The corpulent gentile hungrily examined her wares. "I hear that you sell tasty pretzels. Give me thirty kopeks' worth."

Happily, she gathered together all the pretzels remaining on her tray. The man took a large purse from his pocket from which to pay her. He handed the *agunah* one ruble.

She handed him his change, seventy kopeks, which he immediately transferred to a second purse that held his small change.

As the man turned, his larger purse fell into the deep snow.

It was only a few moments before the man was back, and he began searching on the tray for his lost purse.

"Where is my money?" he demanded loudly, when he failed to find it. "Just a little while ago, I left my purse here. There was a large sum of money in it. You must have seen it and hidden it somewhere. Return my money now!"

"Purse?" the *agunah* repeated innocently. "You took your purse, sir. You put your change inside and left."

"I had two purses!" the gentile shouted. "I left the larger one here. You've stolen it. Give me my money, you thief!"

"Liar!" the woman shrieked back. "I did not steal any purse!"

The man's face turned brick red with rage. He nearly lifted his stick to hit her, but restrained himself at the last moment. Instead, he went to find a policeman. Bringing the officer back to the woman's stall, he poured out his story.

The officer was at a loss. The man claimed, "I left my purse here and she stole it from me." The woman denied the whole story.

"Listen to me," the officer advised. "We are in Vilednik, not Moscow. We have a holy rabbi living among us, a man whose eyes see everything. Both of you go see him. If the woman really did steal the purse, the rabbi will know, and he will not have mercy on her because she is his coreligionist. Your money will be returned to you, down to the last kopek!"

The gentile insisted that she accompany him to the Rebbe at once. Unafraid, the *agunah* went along. She was confident that the Rebbe would find her innocent and send the gentile away from her.

Standing before the Rebbe, the gentile told his story, and the woman denied any knowledge of the purse.

14 / TALES FOR THE SOUL

The Rebbe eyed them both carefully. "Come back here tomorrow afternoon, at 3 o'clock," he said, "so that I can consider the case."

The next morning the woman returned to her post, once again laden with delicious fresh baked goods, but as she was setting out her wares, she stumbled. Looking down, she saw what seemed to be a purse — probably the purse for which the gentile was searching. She opened the bag and was shocked to find that it contained the staggering sum of 10,000 rubles.

She was unsure of what to do. Certainly the gentile would never believe what had happened and would drag her to the police charging her with theft. In the meantime, she dropped the purse into her bag, awaiting what would transpire at the Rebbe's house.

At the appointed hour, the disputants appeared once again before the Rebbe. Before the woman could say anything, the Rebbe began to interrogate the gentile about his purse. Were there any identifying marks on it? How much money did it contain, and in what kind of bills?

The man began to answer, but the Rebbe cut him off before he'd completed the first sentence.

"Why are you babbling at me in Russian?" he scolded. "Can't you speak Yiddish?"

The gentile's face was blank with incomprehension. He continued to describe his purse in Russian.

The Rebbe turned to the *gabbai*. "Go fetch the broomstick and give this fellow a few good smacks. Let's see if he really doesn't know any Yiddish."

The *gabbai* ran to the next room to bring the stick. Frightened, the gentile shrank back, then began to speak rapidly in Yiddish, as fluent as any Jew's.

"You wicked man!" the Rebbe cried in a terrible voice. "Why did you abandon your wife for nineteen years? This woman standing here is your wife! How long can you be so cruel to her?"

STOLEN PROPERTY / 15

The blood drained from the man's face. His eyes bulged from their sockets and he leaned against the table as though he needed its support in order not to collapse. The woman stared at the "gentile," thunderstruck. Suddenly recognizing her long-lost husband, she, too, nearly fainted.

"What cruelty!" the Rebbe continued to berate the man. "Why did you abandon your children for so many long years? Do you not have an obligation to support them? Must your abandoned wife carry the full burden for their support as well as marry them off all by herself?"

The husband, who had worn the mask of a gentile for years, broke down completely. He confessed to what he had done, and expressed remorse and readiness to compensate his wife for her nineteen years of suffering.

That very week, the husband gave the *agunah* a *get* in the Vilednik *beis din*. Apart from this, he left her nearly all his money. One thousand rubles was all he kept for himself.

With the remaining 9,000 rubles, the woman was able to support herself and her children respectably. It was just as the Rebbe had blessed her: "Perhaps, in this way, *Hashem Yisbarach* will help you to support yourself and marry off your children."

# Tale of a Tallis

COMMOTION OUTSIDE THE HOME OF TZEMACH, THE TAILOR of Ostraha, drew the attention of passers-by. A small crowd gathered in the street outside the house in the noonday sun, talking animatedly.

"What's going on?"

"Tzemach the tailor is ill."

"What kind of illness? Is it serious?"

"I just saw a famous doctor leave the house with a very sober face. He told Tzemach's son that all hope was lost. There is nothing left for him to do."

"Well, he deserves it!"

These were no joking words. The Jews of Ostraha truly detested Tzemach the tailor.

Tzemach had been raised among gentiles from an early age, and he resembled the worst of them. A coarse, earthy man, he was uneducated and ignorant. Had these been his only "virtues," however, the people would have been ready to accept him. But Tzemach was not content to merely stray from the path of righteousness; he went further by actively pursuing a wicked and wanton lifestyle. An expert tailor, he was much in demand by the local gentry and hobnobbed with counts and government officials as though he himself had been born a gentile. When he broke bread with these acquaintants, he partook of their nonkosher delicacies with gusto and delight.

At home, too, he transgressed all the Torah's mitzvos and prohibitions. His eyes reflected the pollution of his soul. He made sure not to associate with the Jewish community in any way, rebuffing attempts by Jews to befriend him, and ultimately the townspeople responded in kind.

They kept their distance from Tzemach and many tried to avoid doing business with him. Occasionally, someone would try to defend him on the grounds that he was a *tinok shenishba*, an orphan who had been raised among gentiles without a Jewish father to teach and guide him, but this argument fell on deaf ears. The Jews continued to regard him with a baleful eye.

That was why no one grieved when news of Tzemach's illness became known.

It was not long afterward that wails erupted from the tailor's house. They came from Tzemach's wife and children. Outside, the people of Ostraha were satisfied that Divine Justice had finally been served. "It's a sign that Hashem does not overlook sinners," they said.

It was a long-standing custom in Ostraha that when a member of the community passed away, the *shamash* would go from door to door rattling a *tzedakah* box and proclaiming, "*Tzedakah tatzil mimaves!*" ("Charity saves from death"). Everyone would give something, while the *shamash* informed them who had died and when they might pay their last respects.

On the day of Tzemach the tailor's death, the *shamash* picked up his *tzedakah* box and began his usual route among the houses. But this time, in contrast to a sorrowful tone, his voice had a bit of a lilt.

He reached the door of the *Av Beis Din* of Ostraha, the *tzaddik* R' Pinchas Shapiro, later to become known as the great chassidic luminary R' Pinchas of Koritz. Knocking on the door, he called out laughingly, "*Tzedakah tatzil mimaves!*"

The *Av Beis Din* came out and inquired, "Who passed away today?"

"Better that the Rebbe does not ask for that wicked one's name, may it be blotted out," the *shamash* replied.

"Tell me his name anyway," the Rebbe persisted. "I want to know."

"Well — if the Rebbe insists — The Rebbe probably does not know Tzemach the tailor, a man who never passed up an opportunity to sin. A man who followed all of his desires, who moved among the *poritzim* and learned from their dissolute ways." The *shamash* ended by giving Tzemach's address.

To his total stupefaction, R' Pinchas's face grew very pale. He seized the *shamash's* hand emotionally and pleaded, "When they carry the body to the cemetery, make sure you let me know. I want to participate in the funeral."

The *shamash* left, his head spinning. *Since the day he first arrived in our city, the Av Beis Din has never participated in a funeral. Everyone knows that the Rebbe does not follow the body as it is carried along on its bier. And now, at the funeral of such a wicked man, he wants to come? What an astonishing thing, to be sure!*

He walked along, preoccupied and troubled, until acquaintances stopped him to ask what was wrong. The *shamash* told them of the startling new development.

Now his surprise began to spread to others. No one could understand R' Pinchas. Anyone who violated the kinds of serious trans-

18 / TALES FOR THE SOUL

gressions that Tzemach had could not possibly be one of the world's thirty-six hidden *tzaddikim*. What was the Rebbe thinking?

Then came another surprise, hard on the heels of the first. The *shamash* burst out of the home of the holy R' Yeva, the *Maggid* of Ostraha, to whom he had related the whole story.

"And do you know what R' Yeva said?" the *shamash* exclaimed in wonder. "He said, 'I do not understand R' Pinchas's reasoning. But if R' Pinchas is planning to attend the funeral, then I'm coming, too!' "

The news spread as if on wings: Both the *Av Beis Din* and the *Maggid* were planning to attend the funeral of Tzemach the tailor. And if those two were going, who would not go along with them? And so it came about that all of Ostraha came out to pay their last respects to the man whom they had despised during his lifetime.

When the tailor's body was carried out of his home, the *shamash* ran to summon the *Av Beis Din* and the *Maggid* to the funeral. R' Pinchas put on his overcoat, picked up his walking stick, and led the procession of mourners to the cemetery. As he walked, he kept waving the stick as though to ward off troublesome creatures. The expression on his face frightened all who saw it. At the gravesite, he stood unmoving until the body had been completely interred.

When the procession returned from the cemetery, the *Maggid*, R' Yeva, approached R' Pinchas and asked humbly, "What is the reason for the honor that the Rebbe gave to the deceased man — an honor greater than he has given to any other person in our city? What gives this man preference over all others?"

R' Pinchas turned to R' Yeva, and to all the listening crowd. "Listen, and I will tell you the whole story. Then you will know what it was that gave the dead man this great merit."

Tears of joy and of sorrow mingled in the bride's house.

It was late for a wedding: nearly midnight. But everything and everybody was in place. The *chasan*, the *kallah*, and their parents were there; the four-poled *chupah* was ready; candles, wine, and a goblet were waiting. The bride's father held an old *kesubah* in his hand, which he dictated slowly, word for word, to the town scribe, who copied the words quickly with his goose-feather quill on thick brown paper.

The *kesubah* was duly completed, and two witnesses were called forth to sign their names to it. The two sets of parents embraced with radiant faces. Emotionally, the bride burst into tears beneath her veil and prayed fervently. The wedding party and the invited guests prepared to leave the house for the shul courtyard, where the ceremony would take place.

Both the bride and groom were from very poor families. Most of the townspeople were sound asleep at this hour; only a small number had come to join in the festivities.

All eyes turned to the city's *Av Beis Din*, the holy R' Pinchas Shapiro. It was no secret that, if not for his direct hand, the young couple would not have reached this happy juncture. Their engagement had lasted a full twenty-four months before it came to R' Pinchas Shapiro's attention. The *Av Beis Din* was told that the engaged couple and their families were destitute. There was not enough money between them to cover even the most essential expenses, such as wedding clothes for the *chasan* and *kallah*. An apartment and furniture were out of the question.

R' Pinchas was shaken to the core. Horrified, he asked, "How is it possible that a young man and woman are engaged for two full years, and no one pays them the slightest attention?" At once, he began to circulate through the town in person, collecting funds for the couple. Concerned about the damage to the Torah's honor, community activists hurried to take the Rebbe's place, and they did not stop until they had collected a sufficient amount to cover all necessary expenses. Only then did R' Pinchas calm down. He summoned the young couple's parents and joyfully informed them that they could set a date for the wedding. He had all the money they needed.

And now, at last, the great day had come. The troubled times were over, the joyful ones about to commence. The small crowd prepared to leave the *kallah's* house to proceed to the *chupah*.

There was a sudden commotion. The bride nearly fainted. Her mother burst into bitter tears. Her father paled and the *chasan's* father stood speechless.

The *chasan* was adamant. "I am not going to the *chupah*!"

"What is it? What's the matter?" the bride's father asked, thunderstruck.

Angrily, the *chasan* said, "When we got engaged, you promised me heaven and earth — but you did not fulfill any of it. Had it not been for the holy Rebbe who hastened to help us, your daughter and I would have been forced to wait until our hair turned white. I forgave you for everything. But you're going on your merry way, with no intention of keeping even a tenth of what you promised."

The *kallah's* father wiped beads of perspiration from his brow. He asked the furious *chasan*, "And what was I supposed to do, when I had not even so much as a kernel of wheat to give you? Why are you ruining the *simchah*? Do you intend to humiliate everyone here?"

The young man was unmoved. Calmly, he asked, "What about the *tallis* you promised to buy me?"

The bride's father hung his head. The *chasan* was right. Even that small promise had not been kept.

"Look, my dear son-in-law," he urged. "Let's go to the *chupah* now and not spoil the *simchah*. There are still hours to go before morning. Meanwhile, something will be done. We'll get hold of a *tallis* somehow. I'll give you mine — It'll be all right, don't worry."

The young bridegroom had had a bitter education in disappointment and broken promises. Quietly, he said, "If I don't get a new *tallis* right here and now, I am not going to the *chupah*!"

The *kallah* shed copious tears, while various people tried to appease the stubborn *chasan*. But he would not change his mind. He would get his *tallis* — or the wedding was off!

R' Pinchas, the *Av Beis Din*, was at the center of the efforts to talk sense to the young man. "It's the middle of the night," he said. "All the stores are closed. I promise you that, in the morning, I will personally bring you a *tallis*."

But the *chasan* was as obstinate as a mule. He would not budge from his position.

The *Av Beis Din* was a practical man. While others continued to trade words, he leaped into action. He went in search of a generous man to provide a *tallis* for the *chasan*.

~✦~

R' Pinchas walked the dark streets, eyes darting left and right searching to find a candle burning in a window, a sign that someone was still awake. He walked a long time. Never letting despair gain the upper hand, he continued to prowl the streets of Ostraha. And, at last, his efforts were rewarded. He saw a light in a window. Without hesitation, R' Pinchas approached the house.

His sensitive nose detected the stench of contamination: It was Tzemach the tailor's house. Ignoring the pervasive aura of sin, R' Pinchas knocked on the door.

The tailor was busy cutting out a piece of cloth when he heard the knock. He ran to open the door. To his utter shock, standing on his doorstep was none other than the city's rabbi!

"Wh-what does Your Holiness want at such an hour?" he wondered.

R' Pinchas told him of the poor *kallah* whose marriage, after two difficult years of waiting, hung by a thread. "If I don't buy him a new *tallis* tonight, the wedding will be canceled, and the unfortunate girl will have to return to her father's home, humiliated."

Tzemach the tailor was a sinner, but he had a compassionate heart. "Pity the bride who cannot stand under the wedding canopy. I am prepared to participate in the cost of a *tallis*."

He took out a half-ruble coin — no negligible amount in those days — and graciously handed it to the Rebbe. Thanking him, R' Pinchas went in search of further funds.

He had not gone far when he heard footsteps running after him on the dark street. Turning, he saw that it was none other than Tzemach the tailor, trembling with excitement.

"Holy Rebbe," he cried, "if I give you the entire price of the *tallis*, can you promise me a share in the World to Come?"

R' Pinchas could have enumerated the lengthy list of the tailor's sins — but that would have taken days. Time was of the essence. He

22 / TALES FOR THE SOUL

answered at once, "Yes! If you give me money to buy the *tallis* I guarantee you a share in the World to Come."

The tailor thrust a large sum of money into the Rebbe's hand. It paid for a beautiful new *tallis,* which R' Pinchas managed to purchase after running around some time longer through the sleeping streets. At long last, the *chupah* took place just before dawn rose in the sky.

That was how Tzemach the tailor had spared this Jewish daughter further humiliation.

"All this took place only last week," R' Pinchas told the *Maggid*, R' Yeva, as the crowd stood by, listening raptly. "That was why I was so moved when I heard that he had died. I knew that the merit of the charity the tailor performed was great indeed, and I came to pay him my last respects.

"When I came to the funeral, I saw Tzemach wrapped in the mitzvah of the very *tallis* for which he had so generously paid. Thousands of destructive agents danced around him, trying to get to the tailor and harm him — but the mitzvah of the *tallis* that he had donated protected him on every side.

"When the funeral procession started out toward the cemetery," R' Pinchas continued, "I saw huge destructive angels running after him, determined to exact payment for all the sins he had committed. None of them, however, could come near Tzemach, because of the mitzvah of the *tallis* that protected him. I waved my stick at them and scattered them. They will never be able to approach the tailor again."

# A Rabbi's Courage

WHEN R' DOVID TEVEL, AUTHOR OF *NACHALAS DOVID* and the volume of responsa *Beis Dovid*, was proposed for the position of rabbi in Stopitz, a town in Lithuania, the people turned to his Rebbe, the holy *gaon* R' Chaim of Volozhin, to ask if he was fit for the position.

"The rabbinate of Stopitz?" R' Chaim asked incredulously. "My student, R' Dovid Tevel, could be chief rabbi even of Minsk!"

The warm recommendation left no room for doubt. R' Chaim of Volozhin never uttered an extraneous word, and he was not prone to exaggeration. If he said that R' Dovid Tevel could serve as rabbi of the great city of Minsk, then it must be so. As word spread, the community activists of Minsk began to envy their neighbors in Stopitz for having the privilege of such a spiritual leader.

R' Dovid Tevel was duly appointed to the post, and he served Stopitz in tranquility. Though he hated the status of chief rabbi, he very much enjoyed the work. Life moved pleasantly along, like the placid rivers that flow through Lithuania. R' Dovid Tevel used every moment wisely and did not waste much time in sleep. Before dawn, he was already up and about, learning *Gemara* or the *Shulchan Aruch* by flickering candlelight.

Life continued peacefully, until the famous *din Torah* came along. To hear the people of Stopitz discuss it, there was not, and had never been, any other such case in history.

What was the nature of the *din Torah* that caused such turmoil in the placid town of Stopitz?

Gavriel HaLevi was a prominent member of the Stopitz community. From his small hometown, he managed a branching business empire that spread worldwide. Good fortune dogged his every move.

Whenever he sniffed out a commodity that was selling cheaply but about to rise, he would snap it up at half-price — only to see it soon swell to many times its former value.

Two sons were born to Gavriel: Shimon, the firstborn, and his brother, Yochanan, who was younger by one year. The brothers grew up together and were taught by the same teachers, but from early childhood it was clear that Shimon, the *bechor*, was destined for great things, while Yochanan would need Heavenly help just to grow into a decent Jew.

The signs were clear and easy to read. Young Shimon was a diligent student who was careful not to waste his time. Every free moment was used for Torah study. The good women of Stopitz would whisper to his mother, Matilda, that the boy was growing up just like R' Dovid Tevel. Listening, Matilda's heart would swell with joy. Bowing her head modestly, she would murmur, "*Baruch Hashem.*"

About Yochanan, the consensus was far different.

"Yochanan is diligent, too," the town's jokesters would quip. "Diligent at finding new ways to be wild!"

Yochanan spent every spare minute in games and wild antics. Slipping away from his tutor, he ran to the marketplace to tickle the noses of the oxen waiting to be sold. The oxen began to bellow, sending the entire place into an uproar. By the time order was restored, Yochanan was long gone. The next day he strolled through the market with an innocent face, while "accidentally" overturning a vegetable cart and performing various other pranks.

Neither his father's scoldings nor his mother's pleas had the slightest effect on the boy. His tutor's exhortations fell on deaf ears. Yochanan remained as wild as ever.

By the time his younger son reached the age of 13, Gavriel accepted the fact that Yochanan would not be the next *Vilna Gaon*. The boy lacked all motivation to learn Torah and seemed incapable of sitting and learning for more than two minutes at a time. Gavriel thought about taking him into the family business, but was advised against it. Yochanan had a negative reputation in town, and no one would place much trust in him. It was better to send him away and give people a chance to forget his wild antics.

A RABBI'S COURAGE / 25

Gavriel asked an old friend, Zundel, a merchant in Vilna, to take in his son and educate him in the ways of the business world. This plan would keep Yochanan from idleness, and was also a way for Gavriel to fulfill his obligation to teach his son a trade.

Yochanan was duly dispatched to Vilna, capital city of Lithuania. Zundel welcomed him warmly into his home, where he taught him the business and incidentally slipped in a few nuggets of Torah alongside — a saying of *Chazal* here, a *vort* there — so that the youth would not grow up completely ignorant.

At first, Yochanan continued playing his pranks. He would overturn market stalls, or pour water into the shoes of men coming to the bathhouse, or tie together the fringes on the *talleisim* of men absorbed in their *davening*. But time began to work its changes. Gradually, Yochanan was weaned from his childish antics. Torah study, however, was not yet on his agenda. After a day's work, Zundel would scan his accounts quickly and then make for the local shul, where he would snatch the opportunity for a bit of *Tehillim, Ein Yaakov, mishnayos,* and sometimes learn a page of *Gemara* together with a partner — all this while young Yochanan passed the time in idle talk, waiting for supper.

By the time Yochanan was 18, he had become Zundel's right-hand man. Zundel taught him the art of accounting and how to keep accurate books, thus paving the road to an independent business.

While Yochanan was making strides in the business world, his brother, Shimon, was achieving great strides in his Torah study and spiritual growth in the Volozhiner Yeshivah. Diligent as ever, he had gained much wisdom and was greatly respected by all.

One day, Yochanan received a letter from his mother:

> *Hurry home quickly. The business is about to go under! Father has become very weak due to heart disease. He has to spend most of his time in bed, and his recovery will be a long one. I have been managing the business myself, and my strength is running out. Please come home quickly and help me.*

Yochanan consulted with Zundel immediately. Zundel told him to hurry home and support his parents in their hour of need. He sent the young man off with a warm farewell and a handsome gift.

Shimon received an identical letter. Going to his *rebbei'im* for advice, he was told that he should remain in the yeshivah. Hashem, in His mercy, would help.

And so, Shimon remained in yeshivah while his brother, Yochanan, went home to run the family business alone. For a time, their father, Gavriel, lay feebly on his bed. When he had recovered somewhat, he grew angry at his firstborn son.

"Is this a *ben Torah?* How can he leave a sick man and his family in distress like this?"

Refusing to listen to explanations or justifications from the people in town who offered them — especially the rabbi — Gavriel decided to punish Shimon. He wrote a will in which he left everything he possessed (a considerable fortune) as a gift to Yochanan. When Gavriel's time came, Shimon would get nothing.

The years passed. Yochanan married and settled in Stopitz, close to his father's house. Shimon remained in Volozhin. When he married, his family was conspicuously absent from the festivities. They had shunned him in anger years before.

Heartbroken, Shimon sent his father a placating telegram. He received no answer.

Presently, Shimon was appointed the *dayan* of a small Lithuanian town. His friends predicted that this was only the beginning — the first modest sprouting of what was destined to grow into a glorious tree.

After five years of silence, Shimon the *dayan* received an urgent letter from his brother: *Father is very ill. He wishes to see you before he dies.*

Shimon set out for Stopitz that very day, a road he had not traveled for many years. He went straight to his father's house and directly to his father's bed.

"Father is asleep," whispered Yochanan. "Wait a while until he wakes up." He left the room.

As Shimon stood by the bed, his entire life seemed to pass before his eyes. He saw his pleasant childhood years in Stopitz, when he was a paragon for all the other children in town. Then, he had stood in the center, while Yochanan had been the wild and unruly one. Now their places seemed to have been entirely reversed. He, Shimon, was the shunned one, while Yochanan had become a wealthy and respected gentleman.

"Shimon, my son," he heard his father say weakly. "Is that you?"

He tore himself from his thoughts and bent over his father. Gavriel had opened his eyes and was gazing emotionally at his oldest son.

"Shimon, my son!" Gavriel cried, tears streaming down his sunken cheeks. "I am very close to the World of Truth. I regret what has passed between us. Please forgive me for pushing you aside. Blinded by the material world, I did not see the eternal value of our holy Torah. Can you forgive me?"

Choking back his own tears, Shimon nodded his head, "Yes."

"I wish to rescind the will I wrote in favor of Yochanan," the sick man continued. "I want to have a portion in your Torah. Perhaps that will stand in my favor when I stand before the Throne of Glory. There, in the World of Truth, they must certainly value you, the *talmid chacham*, more than your unlearned brother." He paused, gasping for breath. "Hurry, Shimon. Run out to the street and bring me two kosher witnesses."

Shimon raced into the street to find two men prepared to co-sign his father's signature, rescinding the gift he had originally deeded to Yochanan.

Shamai, the elderly *gabbai*, was strolling in the fresh air in the company of Leibel Polanski, a rich Jew from Minsk. Shimon hesitated before calling out to them. Leibel was a prominent figure who frequently passed through Stopitz on his various business affairs. Coming up behind them, Shimon eavesdropped on their conversation. Shamai, the *gabbai*, was trying to persuade Leibel to donate money for the purpose of shoring up the shul's aging walls. Leibel protested that he had donated a new *bimah* for the shul just two months before, as well as a new *paroches* for the old Ark.

Shimon cleared his throat. "Excuse me. May I interrupt for a moment?"

The discussion stopped as though sliced with a knife. Both men turned to Shimon curiously.

"Forgive my intrusion. My father is lying in bed, very ill. He asks you to step in to serve as witnesses for his signature."

"And who are you?" They did not recognize him.

Shimon introduced himself.

"*Oy!*" the *gabbai* clutched his head. "This is Shimon, Gavriel's *tzaddik* of a son!

"Do you hear?" he asked Leibel, smiling broadly. "I remember him and his brother when they were children. Yochanan was a wild one, always playing 'accidental' pranks like spilling all the money out of the *tzedakah* boxes. And who was the one who always offered to help me pick up the coins? None other than Shimon *Hatzaddik*! Ah, how the time passes…. Little lambs grow into sheep — and here he stands before us now. Shimon, I didn't recognize you. You left our town a youth and now your beard is so long."

With some urgency, Shimon cut short the *gabbai's* reminiscences and asked the two men to accompany him to his father's house.

They listened as Gavriel rescinded the will he had made in Yochanan's favor, and then willed a double portion of his assets to his firstborn son Shimon, according to Torah law. Shamai and Leibel signed the document as witnesses. Shimon asked them not to publicize the matter, as he did not want to anger Yochanan, who believed that the entire inheritance was to be his own.

Gavriel Halevi passed away two days later. All of Stopitz turned out to pay their last respects to the upright and generous merchant.

The following day, Stopitz was stunned by the news of Shamai the *gabbai's* sudden death. For the second consecutive day, the townspeople attended funerals of two of its most upstanding citizens.

As the week of mourning wound to a close, Yochanan asked Shimon when he was planning to leave "my house."

To Yochanan's shock, Shimon produced his father's last-minute will, and showed his brother that their father had changed his mind about the old gift deed and had instead bequeathed a double portion of his assets to Shimon, his firstborn.

That very day, the two brothers appeared at the *beis din*. Each held a document in his hand. Yochanan waved his gift deed, and Shimon the deathbed will.

"It's a forgery!" Yochanan exclaimed, pointing to Shimon's document. "Everyone knows whom our father shunned and to whom he bequeathed all his worldly goods."

R' Dovid Tevel, the *Av Beis Din*, had a difficult time adjudicating the case. He declared that the two witnesses must come forward and confirm the second document by re-signing it. But the first witness, Shamai the *gabbai*, had just died. Leibel Polanski refused to come to Stopitz from Minsk, claiming that he had no idea what they were talking about and that he did not know Shimon at all.

Shimon refused to give up. He asked several people in Stopitz to come forward and confirm that Leibel's signature was genuine. It was here that he discovered the enormity of his problem. Leibel was a wealthy and powerful man who intimidated everyone. No one dared come forward to confirm his signature, because no one wanted to become entangled with the powerful Leibel Polanski of Minsk.

Mourning and empty handed, Shimon was forced to return to his home without a single penny of his father's inheritance. Yochanan, now a wealthy man, did not waste any time. He immediately sold off his father's business and other assets and emigrated to America. That was the last anyone in Stopitz heard of him.

One day, two businessmen came to settle a dispute at the *beis din* in the town where Shimon served as *dayan*. Noticing the dark cloud hanging over Shimon, whom they had known for some time, they begged him to tell them what was wrong. Finally, Shimon poured out his heart, and showed them his document.

At once, both men cried, "We know Leibel's signature very well. We are prepared to testify to that in court!"

30 / TALES FOR THE SOUL

Without delay, the three traveled directly to Stopitz. To Shimon's joy, Leibel happened to be in town that day. Without delay, they went to R' Dovid Tevel's *beis din*, where the two businessmen confirmed that Leibel's signature was genuine.

Word spread throughout Stopitz: The rabbi and *Av Beis Din* had summoned Leibel Polanski to a *din Torah*.

Stopitz was abuzz with the news. The people whispered, speculated, and wondered aloud. Who dared bring the mighty Leibel Polanski to a *din Torah*? And what, exactly, was Leibel's crime?

The *din Torah* was all the people could talk about. They decided that the young rabbi would never dare lift a hand in judgment against the powerful Leibel Polanski. Even if the defendant was guilty, the rabbi would find a way to exonerate him.

Not many days passed before R' Dovid Tevel issued his verdict.

"I told you!" the news-spreaders crowed. "Leibel was acquitted."

"But what kind of acquittal?" others protested. "He was acquitted of human punishment, but remains guilty in the eyes of Heaven. The rabbi said that Leibel had transgressed the injunction of, 'He who knows testimony about his fellow man and does not testify on his behalf.'"

"What does that matter? The main thing is that the rabbi found a masterly way to break the barrel and preserve the wine. In one fell swoop, he managed to find Leibel both guilty and innocent."

The verdict was still fresh when a new thunderbolt fell. After R' Dovid Tevel acquitted Leibel of wrongdoing against human law, the rich man rose to leave.

"Wait," the rabbi called sternly. "You are not going anywhere."

"What?" Leibel demanded, furious. "I've been acquitted!"

"Acquitted of breaking a human law — but guilty by Heavenly standards. I am not letting you go until you fulfill your obligation under Heavenly law!"

Leibel was no ignoramus. "How can you do that? You can't force a person to pay a Heavenly account!"

"When the defendant is a rich man and the plaintiff is poor, we do force him," R' Dovid Tevel answered in a ringing voice.

And he did not permit Leibel to leave the *beis din* until he had paid Shimon for the damages he had caused him — a considerable sum.

A RABBI'S COURAGE / 31

The townspeople were astonished at their young rabbi's courage and integrity. But they were also fearfully certain of one thing: Leibel would surely find some way to revenge himself on R' Dovid Tevel.

R' Dovid Tevel served as rabbi of Stopitz for 32 years. At the end of that time, a delegation arrived from Minsk, requesting that he head their rabbinate.

R' Dovid gave his answer at once. He had never forgotten that his Rebbe, R' Chaim Volozhiner, had confidently stated that R' Dovid was capable of serving as rabbi of Minsk. Now those words would come true.

"I have always known of my Rebbe's greatness," R' Dovid Tevel said. "He never spoke idly. If he said that I was capable of serving in Minsk, it means that he wanted me to serve there."

All of Stopitz was broken hearted when they learned that their beloved rabbi was leaving them. At the same time, they rejoiced at the honor being bestowed upon him. Minsk was a large city, and the position of rabbi there held great stature.

But the people of Stopitz were surprised. Where was Leibel Polanski's revenge? Leibel was one of Minsk's most prominent figures. How had he not opposed R' Dovid Tevel's appointment?

Gradually, the facts came to light.

So impressed had Leibel been at the young rabbi's courage at his, Leibel's, *din Torah*, that not only had he not stood in the way of his appointment as rabbi of Minsk, but had actually been one of its strongest supporters. When the Jewish leaders of Minsk gathered to discuss the search for a new rabbi, Leibel told them the story of his judgment. "A rabbi like that, who did not try to curry favor with me and who did not allow me to leave without paying my obligation by Heavenly law — who is better fit to be spiritual head of our city?"

It was due to Leibel's story that R' Dovid Tevel was accepted as rabbi of Minsk. After witnessing the rabbi's unswerving commitment to what was right, R' Dovid's greatest potential adversary was transformed into his greatest friend and supporter.

# The Curse

THEY SAY THAT ERETZ YISRAEL IS EARNED THROUGH SUFFERING, and that was one thing that was never lacking in the life of R' Moshe Mordechai, the Rebbe of Lelov. He was destitute. Even as a young man, his family was hungry for bread. With sorrow in his heart, the Rebbe decided to travel to Poland in search of salvation. Before he set out, he went to see the old Rebbe of Rachmastrivka, R' Nachum, for a blessing.
"Do you know how to 'make' money?" R' Nachum asked. Without waiting for an answer, he added, "My father, R' Yochanan, *zt"l*, knew how to 'make' money. Listen, and I'll tell you the story ..."

From every corner of Russia, *chassidim* flocked to R' Yochanan of Rachmastrivka's court. Some came to learn from him, others simply to bask in his holy presence. And, of course, there were numerous Jews who sought the Rebbe's support in their personal lives. Into his attentive ears they poured their stories — age-old tales of sickness, financial difficulty, or *shidduch* troubles.

The Rebbe did not wait for his *chassidim* to leave their far-flung villages and towns and travel the many kilometers to Rachmastrivka. Instead, he traveled himself, spending a Shabbos in this village and a few days in that one, showering light and renewed life wherever he went: a sprinkling of spirituality in the midst of the harsh daily grind.

Every few months, his travels took him to a certain Polish town, home to several score of his *chassidim*. One of these *chassidim* happened to be a very prosperous man, owner of fields and vineyards, flour mills and taverns throughout that part of the country. Many Jews in the area earned their living working for his various enterprises.

This wealthy gentleman had one serious fault: He was extremely miserly, loath to part with the smallest coin. He never gave charity. The town's poor, having despaired of receiving any help from him, steered clear of his stately mansion. Those unfortunate beggars coming from distant places who knocked unwittingly on his door were unceremoniously thrown out on their ear by the rich man's servants.

The miser was a devoted *chassid* of R' Yochanan's. But much as he loved to be in his Rebbe's presence, he was always afraid that he would be asked to part with some of his beloved money if he met with the Rebbe during the week. Therefore, it was his custom to join the Rebbe only after Shabbos had begun, when no money could change hands and nobody was likely to bring up financial matters.

He came to shul and then to the Rebbe's *tisch* on Friday nights, and appeared in shul again on Shabbos morning, when he was honored with a respectable *aliyah*, as befit his position. He even showed up at the third meal of the day, a meager repast. As he sat among the other *chassidim* and sang energetically along with them, his nervousness increased with each passing minute. Every nerve was attuned to the window, which showed the darkening sky outside.

When full darkness had descended, he would hastily mumble the Grace after Meals and slip out under cover of night. He did not stop to wonder what his friends — or even the Rebbe himself — thought of this behavior. At the moment, his mind was fully caught up in his one great fear: that they would *daven Ma'ariv* and make *Havdalah*, after which the Rebbe would crook a finger to summon him closer, and ask, "Why is your name always absent from the list of 'gift-givers'?" And what would he answer then? He'd be left with no option. Against his will, he'd be forced to go home and return with his purse, from which he would have to pull out a large bill and hand it over!

A cold sweat broke out on the *chassid's* brow as he hurried away in the darkness. His breath came in ragged gasps until he'd reached his own doorway and the safety of his beautiful home.

This, then, was the rich *chassid's* custom whenever the Rebbe came to town. It was the object of much laughter and mockery among his neighbors — to the point where, as the third Shabbos meal wound to a close, they would clear a path for him to leave and send him off with scornful comments such as, "Running scared, eh?" and "Don't forget to make *Havdalah!*"

Once, this reaction had not bothered him in the least. Lately, however, he had begun to feel upset. A strong desire gripped him, at such moments, to be like all the others, to stay for *Ma'ariv* and hear the Rebbe's *Havdalah*, and to part from him with a warm handshake. But the unhealthy and overpowering fear was still too strong.

R' Yochanan saw all, and understood all. The man's wounded soul cried out to him. R' Yochanan sought a way to release his loyal follower from the curse of his terrible miserliness. He was waiting for the right moment. Maybe, one Shabbos, the *chassid* would miraculously stay for *Havdalah* — or perhaps he would come see the Rebbe at his lodgings on a Friday.

The Rebbe waited a long time for the miracle to happen. But, so far, nothing.

One Sunday morning, after *Shacharis*, the Rebbe parted from his *chassidim* and climbed into his carriage. The horses had not trotted far down the road when R' Yochanan suddenly signaled the coachman to turn around and return to the town they had just left.

Directing the coachman along a winding side road, the Rebbe brought the coach to the rich man's property. His *gabbaim* and helpers were unable to stifle their cries of wonder at the landscaping. Beautiful and lovingly tended gardens spread out behind the property's high walls, multicolored flower beds interspersed with lines of fruit trees in full bloom. In the exact center of the garden sparkled a pretty blue lake, on whose waters glided a number of proud swans. The *chassidim* feasted their eyes on the loveliness around them. It was clear to see how the miser chose to spend his money.

The Rebbe wasted no time on the landscaping. He went right up to the front door and knocked loudly.

The servant who answered the knock was startled and awed at the sight of R' Yochanan standing on the doorstep. Standing respectfully back, he let the illustrious entourage pass before him into the house.

The rich man had very mixed emotions upon finding his revered Rebbe in his home. On the one hand, there was great and genuine joy — and, on the other, distress and shame. It seemed as clear as the noonday sun that the Rebbe had not troubled himself to visit on a weekday without some definite purpose. This visit would cost him dearly.

The man and his sons sat beside the Rebbe in the ornate living room, waiting nervously for R' Yochanan to speak.

The Rebbe was in no hurry. In leisurely fashion, his gaze swept the room. He took in the expensive crystal chandelier suspended from the ceiling, even now, in broad daylight, illuminating the room with blazing light. He noted the silver and gold ornaments gracing the cabinets, and the priceless rugs spread out at their feet. As for his host, the rich man's nerves were being stretched to the breaking point. A thousand thoughts jostled for prominence in his mind as, in a frantic hurry, he tried to devise suitable answers to the many questions he might be asked. And still, the Rebbe did not speak.

At last, the *chassid* found his own voice. "Rebbe, bless me!"

"Is it a blessing you want? And what will you give in return?"

"Rebbe, I — I will give 100 gold coins!" The rich man's hand, heavy as lead, went to his purse.

"A hundred whole gold coins?" the Rebbe repeated mockingly.

"N-no. Not a hundred," his host retreated, his face already bathed in perspiration. "I will give 200." It was difficult for him to pronounce the words — as though it was his own living heart that he was offering on a tray to the *tzaddik*.

"Two hundred?" the Rebbe repeated, angrily this time. Then, to his host's stupefaction, the Rebbe began to curse him roundly. He cursed the man, his wife, his sons, and his daughters with every sort of catastrophe and untimely death.

Had the *chassid* dared glance into the Rebbe's face, he would have noticed a small smile lurking in his eyes. But his confusion at the angry outpouring blinded him. His heart sank and an anguished cry escaped his throat.

"What does the Rebbe want from me?" he sobbed. "Just tell me, and I will give it."

"If you want the curse removed from you, hand over all your property to me," R' Yochanan ordered.

The *chassid* sprang to his feet and began running through the house like a man possessed. In every room he gathered up great armfuls of precious objects and treasures, things made of gold and silver, diamonds and precious gems. R' Yochanan was not yet satisified. "Bring it all — now!"

In the end, the rich man wrote out a deed transferring all of his considerable property to the Rebbe, to dispose of as he saw fit.

The deed was duly handed over to the Rebbe. Humbly, the *chassid* stood waiting to hear what would come next.

"Take the deed," said R' Yochanan, his compassionate and loving gaze caressing his faithful *chassid*. "Take all your money. I don't need even a penny from you."

Astonished and confused, the *chassid* stared at the Rebbe to see if he was joking, or if his own ears had misled him.

The Rebbe explained: "Know this, my friend. All of your property was in the hands of the Evil One. He held complete dominion over your money and belongings, which was why you were unable to give so much as a penny to *tzedakah*. Now that you have handed all your property over to me, the polluted forces no longer have power over you. From here on in, the money is your own, and you will give much to charity."

It is said that, from that day forward, the *chassid* was a different man. He began inviting hordes of guests into his home from all over the area, and he scattered money to those in need with a most liberal hand. But he reserved the largest sums for his Rebbe, R' Yochanan of Rachmastrivka.

"There you have it," concluded R' Nachum to his visitor, the Rebbe of Lelov. "That's how my father knew how to 'make money.'"

[Author's Note: I heard this story from my esteemed father, R' Shlomo Menachem Weinstock, *shlita*, who heard it from the Rebbe of Lelov.]

# R' Shmelke's Extraordinary Visitors

THE LARGE NIKOLSBURG *BEIS MIDRASH* WAS FILLED TO THE rafters. Every bench was occupied and there was no passing room even in the aisles. It was Shabbos afternoon, but the atmosphere in the shul did not reflect the usual Shabbos tranquility. Normally, at this time of day, people would be strolling the city's streets calmly, unhurriedly, enjoying the day's peaceful rhythm. But there was no calm or peace in the big shul this afternoon. The very air was charged with expectancy, as all awaited the arrival of the new rabbi.

He was the holy *gaon*, R' Shmuel Shmelke Horowitz, who had recently served as rabbi and *av beis din* in the city of Shiniva, and before that in the city of Ritshval. Now he had been appointed *rav* and *av beis din* of Nikolsburg.

Nikolsburg was a city of contradictions. It had its share of awesome Torah scholars, who awaited the *rav* now with anxious anticipation, to hear his sermon and analyze it down to the minutest detail.

38 / TALES FOR THE SOUL

On the other side of the coin, the winds of the so-called Enlightenment had begun to blow through Nikolsburg of late. These winds had already started spreading foul seeds through the city. Proponents of this movement were sitting in the audience, too. They were also awaiting the new rabbi's sermon. They wished to see if he was a complete "fanatic," or if there was room for flexibility in his approach. Their attitude toward him would depend on what they found today; either they would declare total war, or would declare an uneasy truce.

A respectful hush fell suddenly over the crowd. The new rabbi entered the hall, wrapped in his *tallis*. With a brisk stride he climbed the steps to the *aron kodesh*, reverently kissed the *paroches* [curtain] in front of it, turned, and launched into his sermon.

There was only one man in that room who knew the *rav's* secret. He was R' Shmelke's beloved student, R' Moshe Leib of Sassov, who had accompanied R' Shmelke from Shiniva to Nikolsburg. On the way, they had spent Shabbos in Cracow. The dignitaries there had invited R' Shmelke to speak in their shul, and in their honor he had delivered the very sermon that he had prepared for Nikolsburg. Since several householders from Nikolsburg had been present in Cracow that Shabbos, and had heard the sermon, it was impossible for him to deliver the same one now. All the way back to Nikolsburg, these men had animatedly discussed the brilliant talk with R' Shmelke, never knowing that it had been originally intended for their own community and had only been delivered in Cracow out of sheer politeness.

"What shall I do?" R' Shmelke had asked his student.

"Prepare a new *derashah* [sermon]," R' Moshe Leib had replied.

But on the road, R' Shmelke had no chance to prepare the talk. Friday night, he had sat down to review a *sugya* by the light of an especially tall candle that R' Moshe Leib had prepared for him, hung against the wall before Shabbos. But the candle had inexplicably flickered out, leaving the *rav* sitting in darkness.

And so, when he walked into Nikolsburg's big shul that Shabbos afternoon, R' Shmelke had no *derashah* prepared!

The rabbi's gaze swept the enormous crowd. Some were sitting in attitudes of reverence, signaling that they had already accepted R' Shmelke as their *rav*. Others sat as though poised for battle, flashes of lightning darting from their eyes. And some watched him with frankly critical expressions, for his appearance bespoke a decided "fanaticism."

The *shtender* before R' Shmelke was bare. He summoned the *shamash*. "Please bring me a gemara."

"Which *maseches* [tractate]?" the *shamash* asked.

"Whichever comes to hand first."

An astonished whisper began to pass like a wind through the packed *beis midrash*. Wondering, the *shamash* went to the bookcase and pulled out a thick volume of gemara without checking to see which one he'd chosen. Silently, he placed the volume before the *rav*.

R' Shmelke opened the gemara, scanned the first page, and then began to learn it out loud in a pleasant voice, discussing the view of *Rashi* and *Tosafos*. As he spoke, he began to erect a tower of questions.

The learned men in the audience proceeded to bat around answers. One raised a solution; another brought a supporting text; a third shot it down. R' Shmelke, meanwhile, stood silently listening to the cut and thrust of their dialogue. At one point, he raised his *tallis* over his head and murmured a low prayer for clarity of thought, so that he might not be humiliated.

When his silent prayer was finished, R' Shmelke lowered the *tallis* from his head and began to summarize the questions that he and the other scholars had raised on the *sugya*. The total came to 130 questions in all!

And then, before the stupefied gaze of the assembled throng, he proceeded to reconcile all the questions and contradictions in a dazzling manner that provided no less than 72 answers!

The scholars in the crowd sat with their mouths hanging open, stunned. Brilliance of this magnitude was something they had never seen. As though oblivious to their reaction, R' Shmelke began to speak on topics in *aggadah*, discussing the verse "Behold, Hashem rides on a light cloud ["*av kal*"]" (*Yeshayahu* 19:1). He played on the

40 / TALES FOR THE SOUL

numerical values of "*av*" [cloud], which is 72, and "*kal*" [light], which is 130 — in other words, 72 answers to 130 questions!

Even the skies contributed their share to R' Shmelke's triumph. For months before his coming, there had been no rain. The ground was hard and parched and the sky bright as metal. But on the day R' Shmelke came to town, it was as if the very skies had opened, and an abundance of blessed rain had fallen. It was clear to the meanest intelligence that the new *rav* had brought blessings along with him.

His talk finished, R' Shmelke noticed a number of sullen faces in the crowd. The faces belonged to the Enlightenment supporters, and R' Shmelke knew that if he did not win them over at once, they had the power to make his life bitter indeed.

He implemented a plan: On each of the next seven Sabbaths, right after discussing the Torah portion in his sermon, the *rav* spoke about an area of science and Torah. In this way, he won over the hearts of those who had been ready to reject him. They saw that the new rabbi was not only great in Torah, but also well versed in all knowledge.

On the eighth Shabbos, when he'd completed his sermon, R' Shmelke saw fit to explain his actions to Nikolsburg's religious community, which had been taken aback by this unusual step.

"It is written, 'It is better to heed to a wise man's rebuke than a man listening to the songs of fools,'" he began. "Is this not something we could have figured out on our own? Do we not understand that a wise man's rebuke is more worthy of being heeded than a fool's song?"

Then he explained. "It does not say, 'It is better to heed a wise man's rebuke than fools' songs.' The actual words are, 'It is better to heed a wise man's rebuke than *a man listening* to the songs of fools.' In other words, people are more willing to accept a wise man's rebuke when he is also versed in the songs of the fools — that is, if he is versed in the wisdom and science of the world at large."

As long as R' Shmelke remained removed from community affairs, the proponents of the Enlightenment left him alone. The moment he began to involve himself, however — making rules aimed at spiritually strengthening the community— these men flared up in anger. Forgetting their admiration for his worldly wisdom, they set out to battle the rabbi in earnest.

If his new enemies believed R' Shmelke a coward, they were mistaken. Not only did he not back down from his position, but he also accurately pinpointed the source of the trouble. There were those community leaders who fervently believed in the ideals of the Enlightenment. Others, however, supported the movement only out of fear of being called primitive and old-fashioned.

On the following Shabbos, R' Shmelke began to let loose his criticism of the community leaders who had gone astray in their beliefs. "The people of this city see their leaders becoming lax in the performance of the mitzvos, those people in whose hearts fear of Heaven no longer resides. Therefore, the people say, 'Mah ha'avodah hazos lanu?'" (i.e., "Why are we ourselves doing this work?")

The community leaders were stunned. They were not at all accustomed to being addressed in this fashion.

"Know this!" thundered R' Shmelke from the pulpit. "If you do not change your behavior, I will follow the example of Israel's rabbis of old against those who breach our fences!"

It is difficult to describe the storm that erupted after this talk. As might be expected with such a controversial issue, the community was split into two factions. On one side stood those whom the rabbi had publicly rebuked, those rich and powerful community leaders who had been infected by the Enlightenment. Alongside them stood some Jews whose views were to the left of mainstream Judaism. This group loudly demanded that the rabbi be removed from his post because of his overly Orthodox opinions.

On the opposing side was the rest of the community, its majority of pious Jews who were appalled at the things being said about their *rav.* "Are you not ashamed to speak that way about our holy rabbi, from whose eyes greatness shines?" they cried out in pain.

The debate raged furiously. Gradually, the pious ones pulled ahead. The rabbi would not be deposed.

Before long, however, R' Shmelke began to rebuke the community leaders again. This time, they decided to act.

That very night, a group of them met in the home of Mordechai (Marcus) Tuckler, a well-known communal figure, to pen a fiery letter of dismissal to the *rav.* In degrading language they let him know that he must leave the rabbinate of their city — immediately!

Now a small problem arose. Which courageous soul would dare deliver the letter to R' Shmelke?

The men glanced uneasily at one another. One complained of a headache, another of a pain in his stomach. A third announced that he would not set foot in the rabbi's house as a matter of principle.

All eyes turned to their leader, Marcus Tuckler. He picked up the letter, scanned it as though seeing it for the first time, and suddenly whined, "Why do you do things without asking me? There is a limit to the amount of time I have to devote to communal affairs. I need to get some rest now."

In the end, the unsavory job was handed — as usual — to Zeidel the *shamash*, who often served as scapegoat for the others. Though already an old man, he was always ready to do his community's bidding. "He won't be afraid of the rabbi," the leaders decided. "On the contrary — the rabbi is obligated to honor the elderly *shamash*!"

The *shamash* was summoned at once to Tuckler's home, and the sealed envelope was placed in his hands.

"And what does the letter say?" Zeidel asked curiously. Zeidel was no fool.

They told him how the rabbi was constantly persecuting them, and what a mitzvah he would be doing in delivering the letter of dismissal.

Zeidel's reaction was completely unexpected.

"I will not do this!" he shouted, eyes wide with terror. "It will never happen!"

The leaders were taken aback. "Why are you so afraid?" they asked in surprise.

Zeidel looked around at them, breathing deeply to calm himself. At last, he spoke.

"As you know, among my other communal tasks I have the job of waking people up for morning services," Zeidel said. "I go around rapping on shutters, as regularly as the sun itself comes up in the morning. I know that if I were to skip this job, the people could go on sweetly sleeping until the middle of the morning.

"I had never found a person who wakes before me — until the new rabbi came. When I would come to his house to rouse him, I would find the candle lit in his room and the rabbi sitting at the table learning Torah — he had apparently been doing so for several hours already.

"What especially drew my attention," the *shamash* continued, "was his learning partner. He was a man with holiness radiating from his face, but unfamiliar to me. Clearly, he is not from these parts. I know everyone in Nikolsburg from childhood, and I have never seen that man.

"This is how it's been from the rabbi's first day."

Zeidel paused for a moment before continuing. "I asked the *rav* who his visitor was, but he avoided giving me a direct answer. But when he saw that it was no one-time incident, but that I actually was able to see the fellow every morning, he told me that the visitor is none other than Eliyahu *Hanavi*, come to learn Torah with him every day!"

"I became accustomed to seeing R' Shmelke's guest," Zeidel said, as the others listened in amazement. "Then, one day, I came to the rabbi's house before dawn and saw him walk outside with Eliyahu Hanavi, to welcome a second visitor whose face shone with a royal glow and who wore a golden crown on his head. When I asked who the man was, and the *rav* realized that I had seen him, he told me that he was none other than Menashe, king of Yehudah!

"I was almost paralyzed with amazement, just as you are now. When I'd collected my wits, I asked in a trembling voice, 'Eliyahu Hanavi comes to learn with the *rav* — that I can understand. But why King Menashe?'

"And this is what R' Shmelke answered:

"'In a small town not far from Nikolsburg lived a pious young man who worked hard to earn a living while laboring over the Torah during every spare hour. He was known throughout the town as a good man.

"'One night, a zealous spirit seized him. He got up and sneaked into the local church by breaking down its aging door, and he began to break all the statues and crosses he found there. His action was discovered the next morning, and it created a furor. The Christians claimed that the Jews had had a hand in the matter. As proof, they pointed out that not a single item of gold or silver, nor any precious gem, had been stolen from the church!

"'Though the priest and his assistants did their best to find the perpetrator, it was like seeking out a single tree in a forest. They got nowhere with their investigation.

"'Seeing that he had not been found out, the young Jew decided to repeat his performance in another town. He broke into a second church and wreaked similar havoc there. Then, a few days later, he did the same in a third church.

"'The area police figured that a man who had committed a crime three times was likely to commit a fourth. They placed stakeouts at other churches, and waited. On the Jew's fourth attempt, he was captured red-handed.

"'The Jew admitted openly that he was the one responsible for all the destruction. He assured the police that he had acted alone, without help, for he did not wish any other Jew to be harmed because of him.

"'The Jew was arrested and brought to prison that very day — and was promptly executed.'

"As you know," Zeidel continued the tale he had heard from R' Shmelke, "when a young man dies leaving behind a widow and orphans, the community starts a fund for them, to prevent them from starving. The widow of the young man who had 'smashed the idols' came to ask for community support for herself and her six children.

"But the community leaders reacted angrily. Is it not enough that the man, by arousing the wrath of our Christian neighbors, nearly caused all of our blood to be spilled? Must we also support that suicidal madman's children?'

"But the rest of the community opposed this opinion, saying, 'Is it possible? Even the simplest fellow deserves to have his family supported by the community after his death! But this holy individual, who gave his life for the sanctification of Hashem's Name — is he not worthy of such consideration?'

"The argument raged until it reached our own great rabbi. R' Shmelke was asked to resolve the dispute.

"'That is why King Menashe came to visit me,' R' Shmelke confided to me. 'And this is what he told me: "Know this. *I* was the young man who was killed. Because I sinned and worshiped idols during my lifetime, it was decreed that my soul return to this world to set right the scales by smashing idols."'

"It was King Menashe's personal intervention that led the *rav* to rule in favor of the widow. He declared that the community must support the widow and six young children, because all this had been Divinely orchestrated and is beyond our comprehension!"

Zeidel the *shamash* fell silent.

His listeners' ears rang for a long time with the strange and moving story. No one knew what to say. Finally, Zeidel stood up, took the letter of dismissal for R' Shmelke, and tore it into shreds. He met with no opposition.

Eyes flashing, he faced the group of community leaders. "We have such a rabbi, who merits meeting with Eliyahu Hanavi every night and to whom King Menashe came from the upper world. This is the man you wish to fire?"

The holy rebbe R' Simcha Bunim of Peshis'cha used to tell this story, adding, "The fact that R' Shmelke merited meeting Eliyahu Hanavi every night does not amaze me. What moves me greatly is the simple *shamash* of Nikolsburg, who displayed such a marvelous, holy purity. Here is a man who also saw Eliyahu every morning, yet it did not occur to him to boast about it, even a little.

"There is no one like the simple Jew of old. Such men no longer exist!"

# A Jar of Snuff

WINTER HELD THE LAND FAST IN ITS ICY GRIP WHEN R' Naftali Hakohen Katz, author of the *Semichas Chachamim*, came to visit his follower, Zalman the Innkeeper. Zalman lived in a small village near Pozna. From time to time he would travel to see R' Naftali, who — apart from his genius in Torah — was one of the foremost Kabbalists of his time, and his practices were accorded with the guidelines of this esoteric area of study. R' Naftali lived before the era of *chassidus* — at the time of his death, the Ba'al Shem Tov was still a young man — yet many of R' Naftali's customs were similar to those later practiced by great rebbes.

Zalman the Innkeeper leased a large inn from the local *poritz* (landowner), from which he dispensed food, drink, and hospitality to passing Jewish travelers. There was a tavern for the local gentiles as well, who came after a hard day's work to slake their thirst with whiskey. When Zalman's soul grew thirsty for spirituality, he would make the trip to Puzna to bask in R' Naftali's presence until he felt at peace.

R' Naftali's personal visit to Zalman's inn surprised the innkeeper greatly. The great man was so busy with his schedule of learning and devotions that he hardly had time for far more important matters than visiting his followers.

But Zalman's surprise did not keep him from welcoming his illustrious guest with every honor and attention. He put R' Naftali in the inn's best bedroom and hovered solicitously about him all that day, ready and eager to satisfy his rebbe's every need.

Toward evening, Zalman prepared a bowl of barley soup for R' Naftali and stood by to serve him. Suddenly, R' Naftali's face became shadowed. Something, it was clear, was disturbing his peace. For several minutes he sat lost in thought. Then he turned to the innkeeper and said, "Zalmanke, do you want to make me happy? Please get me a jar of snuff."

Zalman was stupefied. *Snuff?* R' Naftali was not known to have ever indulged in that habit. Why this sudden craving for snuff on such a frigid winter's night?

"The closest tobacco shop is in a village several kilometers from here," he said in a low voice. "There is a snowstorm raging outside. It's been snowing steadily for hours."

R' Naftali did not answer. He merely tapped his finger sharply on the table. That was enough for Zalman. Summoning his gentile servant, he bade him hitch the horses to the carriage. They would set out on the errand at once.

The worker could hardly open the door. A powerful wind howled outside, pressing against the door and making it nearly impossible to push open. It was only with great effort that he managed to fight back the strong gusts and step outside. He returned a few minutes later, face crimson with the cold and teeth chattering uncontrollably.

"It's impossible to remain out of doors for even a minute," he complained, shivering violently. "And you want me to go on a long trip with you?"

"Stay, then," Zalman said at once. His heart told him that if his rebbe wanted him to go out on a night like this, there must be something behind it — some secret that was not for a gentile to know. He put on his leather boots and wrapped himself in his fur cloak, then went outside to hitch up the horses himself.

As the horses began to clip-clop their way slowly into the storm, Zalman sat lost in a reflective mood. He was a devout believer. It was not a jar of snuff that R' Naftali wanted, but something else. He let the horses lead. There was a higher Power in the world, and He would show them where to go.

The frenzied wind howled. Snowflakes whirled wildly on every side, obscuring everything. His worker, Zalman thought, had been right: The cold penetrated his very bones. All the layers of clothing he wore were useless, hardly better than layers of paper in the face of the freezing wind. What he would not have given to be lying safe and warm in his own bed beneath his thick feather quilt!

Then, steeling himself again, he plowed on. If the Rebbe had sent him, there was no questioning or doubting his orders.

The horses continued to plod slowly through the fresh snow, leaving a trail of hoofprints in their wake. Had the beasts been able to speak, Zalman suspected that they, too, would have expressed a preference for their stable instead of plodding through the deep snow on this icy night.

At that moment, a sound reached Zalman's ears. It seemed to be the echo of a piercing cry. He halted the horses, listening intently. Had he really heard something, or was it just his imagination, fueled by the shrieking wind?

The scream came again. "Help!"

In a flash, Zalman turned the horses toward the voice and set them galloping. A brief ride brought the carriage to the shore of a small, shallow pond. A horrifying sight met Zalman's eyes.

In the center of the pond stood a carriage, water covering its wheels. Two horses crouched there, in the shallow, ice-coated water. They were clearly near death. Inside the carriage itself sat two soaked and sodden men. One was the wagon driver, still grasping his useless whip. Beside him sat another man. It was the *poritz* Andrei Lundsberg, a nobleman who was also a high-ranking army officer. Spotting Zalman, he shouted hoarsely, "Help us!"

Zalman did not hesitate for a moment. Approaching the pond cautiously, he stepped out onto the ice and unhitched the two dying horses from the half-sunken carriage. Then he harnessed his own two fresh horses to the nobleman's vehicle. A few strong tugs, and the carriage with its passengers emerged from the pond.

"I — I have no words with which to thank you!" gasped the *poritz*. "You came here like an angel sent from Heaven. I was certain I would freeze to death here!"

"What happened?" Zalman asked.

"We saw the frozen pond," Lundsberg said, "and thought that we could cross it, as we've done many times in the past. Tragically, the ice split suddenly and we sank into the freezing water. Had you not happened by, we would surely have died on this spot, my driver and I."

The words emerged with difficulty. The *poritz* was blue with cold and shaking from head to toe. His driver did not look much better. When Zalman suggested that they return to his inn, which was not far away, Lundsberg jumped at the idea.

As he entered the inn with the nobleman and his driver behind him, Zalman knew that this was the "jar of snuff" he'd been sent to fetch. There was a definite look of satisfaction on R' Naftali's face as he regarded the two violently shivering guests in their sodden clothes.

The next hour saw Zalman working frenziedly. He found dry, clean clothes for his new guests, seated them by the blazing fire, fed them a hot meal, and offered them a drink. When they had eaten and drunk their fill, he prepared two beds and covered them with thick quilts. Tucked up warmly, the *poritz* and his driver offered grateful smiles that warmed the innkeeper's heart. Zalman picked up the small oil lamp and quietly left the room.

R' Naftali was sitting at the table with a *sefer*. He twinkled at Zalman. "You have taken care of all their needs?"

"Yes."

"You did well," R' Naftali said warmly. "Give them a good meal tomorrow morning, too. When the *poritz* Lundsberg wants to pay you, give him a detailed bill for everything you did for him in this inn. But don't agree to accept a cent. If he persists and asks what you want as reward for saving his life, say that you want nothing."

"The Rebbe's words are holy to me," Zalman the Innkeeper replied humbly.

As he turned to leave the room, he remembered that the Rebbe had never asked him about the jar of snuff he'd been sent to buy.

Early the next morning, Zalman accompanied R' Naftali to the small village shul and *davened Shacharis* with him. On their return to the inn, he served his Rebbe breakfast before going to rouse his two other guests, who were still sleeping soundly.

The morning meal completed, the time for payment had arrived. The *poritz* looked very different now than he had the night before. His clothes had dried. His thick hair was neatly combed. Color had returned to his cheeks, and his eyes sparkled with life. Turning to Zalman, he said, "I'd like to pay you for all your goodness to us."

"Certainly." Zalman went to a drawer where, as per his Rebbe's instructions, he had prepared an itemized bill. As Lundsberg read the bill, he looked perplexed. "I don't understand."

"It couldn't be simpler," said the innkeeper. "Here you are: supper for two, beds for two, breakfast for two. Total: 20 zlotys."

"But that's small change. We owe you far more than this!"

"What do you owe me?"

The *poritz* exclaimed, "You saved two lives — mine, and my driver's! Had you not happened by the pond last night, they would have found our frozen bodies weeks or months from now! Apart from that, you rescued my carriage, which cost me a pretty penny."

"Well, what do you want to give me?" Zalman asked.

Lundsberg held up a bag filled with coins. "Stick your hand in and take as much as you want."

For an instant, the temptation nearly overpowered Zalman. Had the Rebbe not warned him on the previous night not to take anything, he would have reached in and grabbed a wealth of coins.

Instead, he spread his arms at his sides. "I do not wish to take anything. Only 20 zlotys, my regular fee."

The *poritz* peered at him. "Jew, why do you torture yourself? Take! I give you with a full heart!"

"The Master of the Universe will pay me for my good deed," Zalman said calmly.

"I don't believe it," Lundsberg cried. "And these are the people whom they claim are so greedy for money?"

The nobleman was astounded. For a long moment he stood riveted to the spot. Stirring at last, he said, "At least write down for me your name, together with the names of your family, as a souvenir. I will engrave it on my heart."

The innkeeper had no objection. He wrote down his name and those of his family and handed the list to Lundsberg, who promised to copy them into his personal notebook the moment he got home.

As he watched the two men leave his inn, Zalman understood the Rebbe's intention. Here was a *kiddush Hashem!* His own noble behavior had caused a sanctification of Hashem's Name before the two gentiles.

Two years later, in the winter of 5509 (1749), R' Naftali Katz left for Eretz Yisrael, leaving Zalman the Innkeeper bereft of a rebbe and guide. Then, some eight years after that, his financial situation began to worsen.

The descent from prosperity was a gradual one. Fewer and fewer customers came to the inn, and its income dwindled accordingly. At year's end, Zalman did not have enough money to pay the inn's yearly rental fee. The local *poritz* from whom he leased the building granted him another year in which to pay, but when that time came Zalman's situation was even worse than before. His family was dressed in tatters and there were no profits to speak of. When the time arrived for paying his debt, Zalman had nothing.

All the explanations and excuses in the world did not avail him now. It was up to the *poritz* to decide whether to be just or merciful. He chose justice.

That same day, he had Zalman and his entire family arrested and locked up in jail. A speedy trial was instituted, at which the judges handed down an even speedier verdict. The Jewish family was condemned to death.

The means of execution was left in the *poritz's* hands. He strained his mind to find a suitable revenge for his former tenant, who had lived rent-free on his property for two whole years. At last, he decided to put off the execution until an upcoming Christian holiday. The neighborhood would be filled with visiting noblemen then. What better entertainment for his guests than watching the spilled blood of an entire Jewish family?

Languishing in their prison cell, Zalman and his family knew that their doom would soon be upon them. Unless a miracle happened, they would shortly be executed.

With all their might, they seized on the ancient "weapon" of Yaakov Avinu. They prayed and said *Tehillim* from memory. They cried out to *Hakadosh Baruch Hu* to arouse His mercy for their plight and rescue them.

The wind carried their crying voices to a nobleman passing not far from the jail. He had been traveling on the high road with no intention of stopping in the village, when he realized that he had no small bills with which to pay his expenses on the rest of the journey. His old friend, the local *poritz*, always had an ample stock of bills and coins of every denomination. The nobleman made a detour and entered the village.

The bitter cries aroused his curiosity. He wished to follow them to their sources, but time was pressing. He went directly to the home of the local *poritz*.

The *poritz* greeted him warmly. After he'd supplied his guest with the necessary bills and coins, the visitor asked, "I heard awful cries on my way here. They seemed to come from the cellar of a building. What were they?"

Gleefully, the *poritz* related the story of the Jew who had reneged on payment of his rent, and how he'd been sentenced to death along with his family. "In ten days, on our holiday, we will take them out to be executed. It is my pleasure to invite you to watch along with us."

"In ten days?" The visiting nobleman considered. "I am on my way to Kiev now. On my way back, I will pass this way and will accept your invitation."

To Andrei Lundsberg's credit — for that was the nobleman's name — his mouth and heart were not in accord. He had an entirely different intention in mind — to investigate the matter at closer quarters. He wanted to see for himself the unfortunates whose cries had pierced his heart. By making haste, he managed to complete his business affairs in half the time he had originally planned.

A JAR OF SNUFF / 53

On his return from Kiev, he entered the village without fanfare and surreptitiously approached the cellar from which he had heard the voices.

The voices were still crying out as before. Moving close to the window, he called softly, "Jews!"

Complete silence fell.

"Jews," called Andrei Lundsberg again. "I want to help you."

Zalman the Innkeeper stepped close to the barred window, or as close as he could with iron shackles around his ankles. "Who are you?" he heard the nobleman ask.

"I am Zalman the Innkeeper."

A stirring of memory went through the nobleman. The name seemed familiar.

Suddenly, he remembered. Ten years had passed since the winter's night when he had nearly frozen in the pond. Urgently, he whipped his notebook from his pocket and flipped back through its pages to the older entries.

Yes, there it was — Zalman the Innkeeper, from this very village. He was the man who had saved him that night, but had declined to accept a penny in reward. Wishing to be certain, Lundsberg called softly, "Tell me the names of your family members."

Without understanding the strange request, Zalman reeled off the names.

"I'll be back soon," Lundsberg promised.

Zalman's eyes watched the other man's hasty retreat. "Do not trust great men," he murmured to himself. Yosef *Hatzaddik* had pinned his hopes on a human being, asking the minister to remember him to the king. For that lack of faith, two years were added to his imprisonment in Egypt.

The Egyptian minister took two years to remember Yosef. Andrei Lundsberg was much better than that: He did not waste a minute.

Lundsberg, as has been noted, was not merely a nobleman; he was also a high-ranking army officer. Twelve hours after he left the village, he was back with a troop of soldiers under his command. Should the local *poritz* put up resistance to his plan, Lundsberg intended to fight him until he had his way.

54 / TALES FOR THE SOUL

In the end, however, there was no need for arms. The village was asleep when he entered, and no one stopped him and his men from breaking down the prison door and freeing the innkeeper and his family.

A closed carriage awaited the family that had been saved from the lion's very jaws. They were taken swiftly to the distant town where Lundsberg reigned. He handed them over to a Jewish innkeeper with whom he was acquainted, with orders to care for all their needs.

A full month passed while the family regained its strength. Then Lundsberg gave Zalman a new inn of his own. He would not be satisfied until he had also supplied Zalman with a lifetime supply of whiskey, at no charge.

Zalman accepted this bounty in stunned silence. Why was he being accorded this outstanding treatment? He was afraid to ask. It seemed to him that he was asleep and dreaming. All too soon, morning would come and he would be back in his dank prison cell, awaiting the *poritz's* cruel punishment.

Lundsberg noticed the Jew's confusion. Smiling, he asked, "Do you remember me?"

Zalman peered closely at the nobleman's face. The difficult intervening years had erased many things from his memory.

"Ten years ago," Lundsberg said, "you came on a freezing, snowy night to a pond whose thin layer of ice had cracked. A *poritz* and his driver were stuck in the water. You saved them from certain death and refused to take so much as a penny in reward. Now do you remember?"

The memory came flooding back. Zalman nodded, speechless.

"I am the *poritz* you saved," Lundsberg said. "I praise my Creator for giving me the opportunity to return the favor to the man who helped me!"

Zalman saw it all clearly now. At the time, he had thought he understood his Rebbe's intention, but it was only at this moment that he truly plumbed the depths of R' Naftali's prescience. His Rebbe had prepared the cure — ten years before the blow fell.

# A "Cold Shoulder" from the Rebbe

THE HOLY REBBE, R' YAAKOV YITZCHAK HOROWITZ, WAS known by the illustrious title of the "Chozeh of Lublin" because his eyes saw from one end of the world to the other. He was the Rebbe of rebbes, leader of thousands of Jews, and wise shepherd to his considerable flock. With only one glance, he knew a person to the depths of his soul, and knew also what that person needed to do to repair any fault in himself.

In his youth, the famous Rebbe, R' Yissachar Dov of Radoshitz, spent some time with the Chozeh of Lublin. From the Chozeh he learned a lifestyle that went beyond intellect. He purified himself with tears and heartfelt pleas to his Creator to show him the path by which he might serve Him best. Though it was obvious to all that the young man had no thought or feeling that was not dedicated to Hashem, everyone called him, simply, "Berel." People were not quick to lavish praise or titles of honor in those days. It took much time and repeated tests until one earned the title of "Reb" — let alone "Rebbe."

Young Berel had lodgings together with Reb Meyer, known as R' Meyer'l of Stavnitz. The difference between their respective rooms was as great as the gap in their respective statures. Berel slept in the attic, on a thin, hard pallet that someone had optimistically called a mattress, and on which he scarcely managed to snatch a few hours of sleep. R' Meyer'l, on the other hand, occupied a spacious, comfortable room below. While still a *chassid* of the Chozeh of Lublin, R' Meyer'l already led his own flock as Rebbe in Stavnitz. On his visits to his own Rebbe, the Chozeh, he was accorded royal treatment. Following the lead of the *Chozeh* himself, the *chassidim* treated R' Meyer'l with great respect. His status was high, and his aspirations even higher.

56 / TALES FOR THE SOUL

Berel, on the other hand, had not even earned the title "Reb" preceding his name. Not that he thirsted for titles and honor; any student of *chassidus* will tell you that arrogance and the quest for honor are a person's greatest enemies. No, Berel did not run after honor. Instead, his heart broke at the realization that, where R' Meyer of Stavnitz was galloping at a pace of a thousand yards a minute on his quest for spiritual acheivement, he himself was only limping along.

"Who will give me wings like a dove?" Berel quoted to himself, all afire to draw closer to his Creator. If being called "Rebbe" would help him reach his goal more quickly — if that would lend him the wings he craved so ardently — then it was worthwhile being a Rebbe!

In other words, Berel tried to put last before first. In the process, he earned a stern rebuke from his master and teacher, the Chozeh of Lublin. Here is how it happened.

One morning, Berel climbed down the ladder from the attic. At the foot of the ladder he encountered R' Meyer'l, who had just stepped out of his own room and was about to descend to the floor below. Berel looked into R' Meyer'l's face, and sighed.

R' Meyer'l sensed that the sigh had come from the depths of the young man's pure soul. It was not a sigh of pain, or of any material distress, but a silent cry over a spiritual need.

"Berel, why are you sighing? Do you need anything?" he asked. "After all, we find ourselves in a virtual *Gan Eden* here, in the presence of such a great rebbe. Why do you sigh?"

Berel's answer was another sigh. "How can I not sigh?" he asked R' Meyer'l. "Whenever there is anything special to be done, who does the Rebbe choose to do it? Rebbe Meyer'l of Stavnitz! 'Please *daven* for the *amud*.' On Shabbos, 'Please sing us a *zemer*.' Compared to that, Berel is a spiritual beggar, dog-paddling in the shallows. When does anyone remember Berel? At the marriage of two orphans or a pair of paupers, then the Rebbe tells me, 'Berel, go to the wedding and make them laugh!' And Berel never hesitates. He enthusiastically fulfills the Rebbe's every command, telling jokes just like any empty-headed fool to the unfortunate *chasan* and *kallah*. I know that humility is the most desirable quality — but why am I so far behind in Hashem's service?"

Tears trembled at the corners of Berel's eyes as he spoke.

R' Meyer'l was taken aback at what he'd just heard. "And I thought you were satisfied with your present situation!" he exclaimed. "Berel, do you want to begin to behave like a rebbe — to *be* a rebbe? In that case, give me your hand."

There at the foot of the ladder, Berel extended his hand. R' Meyer'l clasped it.

In later years, R' Berel — the future Rebbe of Radoshitz — would say, "Rebbe Meyer'l gave me one hand, but I grabbed with two hands."

At that moment, Berel sensed himself changing. He felt as though a Divine light was radiating over him. A fountain of high spiritual aspiration began to spout in his soul. His whole perspective of the world suddenly changed. A wall was no longer a structure of mortar and bricks, but a reservoir of Hashem's holy essence. Above each blade of grass he saw an angel hovering, tapping the grass and ordering it to grow. He saw the powers of evil wafting past. He was moved and frightened.

The love and fear of Hashem that he had known until then took on an entirely new meaning. Berel felt an endless and undying love for his Creator, together with a mortal terror that he had never experienced before. When he looked at R' Meyer'l of Stavnitz, he did not see a flesh-and-blood man, but a soul blazing with holy fire.

R' Meyer'l smiled. "You took it well," he chuckled. "You've jumped too high, all at once."

Suddenly, Berel was gripped by a new panic, lest R' Meyer'l tell the Rebbe of Lublin that Berel, the foot soldier, had transformed himself into a general without the commander in chief's permission. "I beg of you, Rebbe Meyer'l," he pleaded. "Please don't say anything to the Rebbe. He will not be pleased with what I've done. He will say that levels are achieved only through one's labors. Skipping stages is not something he approves of."

R' Meyer'l shook his head. "I promise nothing."

Berel's heart froze. As he watched R' Meyer'l leave the house, he clung to a frail straw of hope. R' Meyer'l had not promised to keep the secret — but neither had he declared that he was going to tell the Rebbe. Perhaps he had merely wished to avoid committing himself to silence.

R' Meyer'l had no such idea. He firmly believed that the Rebbe should know everything about his flock. And so, he related to the Chozeh the whole scene that had taken place at his lodgings. He told how young Berel had wished to skip over the hard work necessary to achieve spiritual height, and how he, R' Meyer'l, had given him his hand and influenced him.

"I had no idea how far things would be taken," the Rebbe of Radoshitz would relate in his old age. "From that day on, I received the 'cold shoulder' from the Rebbe. Nothing I did changed the situation at all. I gladly forfeited all the spiritual levels I had been freely granted, but even that did not help. It was as though the Rebbe had closed off the spiritual pipeline between him and me. He no longer wanted to know me. I spent much time looking for ways to be near him, but the Rebbe avoided me."

One day, young Berel was walking in the courtyard of the Rebbe's house when he saw the Rebbe's carriage approaching. "The Rebbe is going to Tomashov," the driver called out cheerfully. "Want to join us?"

Forlorn, Berel wished that he could.

The Chozeh emerged from the house and made his way to the carriage. As he walked, his keen eyes swept the courtyard. He saw Berel standing with bowed head, and called out to him.

"Berel, would you like to travel to Tomashov with us?"

Berel's head jerked up. The Rebbe was speaking to him!

At first, he found it impossible to utter a syllable. When the Rebbe asked him a second time, Berel managed to choke out, "Of course I want to come."

The Rebbe peered at him. "Can you take it upon yourself not to eat anything until I order you to eat?"

No sacrifice was too great in Berel's eyes, desperate as he was to find a way back into the Rebbe's favor. Enthusiastically, he undertook the Rebbe's command, and climbed into the coach.

The journey to Tomashov lasted several days. They drove at a leisurely pace, stopping from time to time at various towns where there were Jewish communities so that they might pray, eat, and rest: Berel served the Rebbe at every meal, handing him food and drink and anything else he might require. And after each meal, the Rebbe would inquire in the compassionate voice of an anxious, loving father, "Berel, have you eaten anything?"

And Berel would reply, "I have not eaten anything yet."

He waited for the command: "In that case, go eat." But it never came. One day passed, and then a second, and still Berel fasted. He did not taste so much as a crumb of bread or a drop of water for two full days and nights. His knees were beginning to buckle and his whole body trembled with weakness. He knew that the Rebbe was putting him through a severe test, and he prayed that he would not fail.

On the third day, the Rebbe's coach came to a town where throngs of *chassidim* were waiting eagerly to greet him. The feast they had prepared in the Chozeh's honor lasted an entire day. And all that day, Berel stood behind the Rebbe and served him. He sprang to fulfill every request and strained to hear every syllable the Rebbe spoke. Gradually, he felt his hunger grow overwhelming. The aroma of the tasty dishes made his head spin. People all around him were enjoying their meals with a hearty appetite, while he watched them, starving. He tried to avert his eyes, but he knew he must be alert for the Rebbe's needs.

As the sun moved westward across the sky and the afternoon waned, Berel felt the last of his strength desert him. At times, he was certain that the end had come and he would drop right there, on the spot. Mustering every last reserve, he whispered to himself that soon, surely, the Rebbe would tell him to eat.

But the longed-for order did not come. The Rebbe and his *chassidim* sang songs of devotion, after which the Rebbe spoke on Torah topics. For the others, it was a welcome and uplifting break in the daily routine. Under different circumstances, Berel would have gladly joined his fellow *chassidim* in their spiritual arousal. Now, however, he could focus on nothing but his hunger. Black spots swam before his eyes. He was near the point of collapse.

Bitter thoughts seized him. The Rebbe was so immersed in his devotions that he had forgotten Berel entirely. Soon, Berel's soul would leave his body, right there behind the Rebbe's back. *Go eat something*, screamed every cell in his body, *before you die!*

Still, Berel resisted the temptation. Then a new thought intruded. *You're standing behind the Rebbe*, a voice urged. *Just a little whisper in his ear should do the trick. 'Rebbe, I'm on the verge of collapse!' Then the Rebbe will immediately tell you to eat."*

But Berel resisted this temptation, too. *Whatever happens, I will obey the Rebbe's order*.

At long last, the feast ended. The men recited the Grace after Meals, danced around the table for a few minutes, and dispersed.

Berel had fasted for three complete days.

Back on the high road, the Chozeh looked over at a pale Berel.

"Berel, did you eat anything today?"

"I have not yet eaten anything," Berel answered with difficulty.

In astonished tones, the Rebbe said, "Why not? We just had a rich feast. They served the best foods."

Mustering his strength, Berel answered, "The Rebbe ordered me not to eat anything until he commands me to do so. The Rebbe has not yet commanded me to eat."

The Rebbe continued to look astonished, as though the matter had slipped his mind. He reached into his pocket and handed Berel three coins. "We are not yet far from town. Run to the bakery quickly and buy yourself a loaf of bread."

Berel ran like a deer. It was hunger itself that lent his weakened body the energy to run. A little later he returned to the carriage, a warm loaf fresh from the oven tucked under his arm. The aroma was intoxicating. Nobody who has not fasted three consecutive days can know the enchanting aroma of a warm, fresh loaf of bread.

Berel was a clever man. He knew that the Rebbe had not yet ordered him to eat. He sat holding the warm bread, waiting for the Rebbe to speak.

But the Chozeh was once again sunk in his devotions. Berel sat beside him, the smell of that bread hitting him like blows from a hammer. He was close to expiring on the spot, with a warm loaf in his hand.

He waited for half an hour. Berel dared not even cough to rouse the Rebbe from his devotions.

Suddenly, the Chozeh stirred. "Berel, have you eaten the bread yet?"

"No."

"Why not?"

"Because the Rebbe did not order me to eat. He only ordered me to buy the bread!"

The Chozeh gazed at him with his holy eyes. "Berel, go at once and wash your hands."

Berel ran to the bucket of water that was in the coach. He picked up the ladle and poured water over his hands.

But he did not recite the *Hamotzi* blessing and eat. He merely dried his hands, sat back in the coach, held the fragrant loaf, and waited.

The Rebbe was again sunk in his own holy thoughts. Once again, Berel sat perfectly silent. He could not speak, because he had washed his hands. He might have made some sound to attract the Rebbe's attention, but he chose silence instead.

Berel was a *chassid*. He would remain silent and devoted to the bitter end!

But his body had its own insistent nature. It knew that not eating meant not living. At this point, he was not only thinking about food because he felt hungry. The situation had gone far beyond that. If he did not eat now, he would simply die.

The Rebbe sat with closed eyes. But his spiritual eyes were wide open.

"Eat, quickly," he commanded. He did not even wait to precede the order with the word, "Berel." He knew that a single instant could spell the difference between life and death.

62 / TALES FOR THE SOUL

Berel tore a chunk off the loaf and ate. At the very last second, the Rebbe had saved his life. He had brought Berel to the brink, but had not let him pass over the edge!

"He calculated the precise timing with an exactitude that is unparalleled," the Rebbe of Radoshitz later recalled. "Had he made me wait even one more minute, there would no longer have been a Berel in the world. But it was all worthwhile, because it removed the last of the Rebbe's disapproval from me. The 'cold shoulder' was gone."

The holy Rebbe R' Chaim Meyer Yechiel of Mogalnitza, grandson of the Maggid of Koznitz, heard this story from the Rebbe of Radoshitz himself. He added, "May Hashem protect us from the predicament of a *chassid* who gets the 'cold shoulder' from his Rebbe. It is worth doing anything to appease him, to restore harmony between the rebbe and the disciple."

# Four Missions in One Night

THE CITY OF CHERNOBYL, IN THE UKRAINE, IS KNOWN AS one of the most famous centers of *chassidus*. It is the home of the Chernobyl dynasty of *rebbeim*. With the passage of time, the name of the city became virtually synonymous with *chassidus*, until it was all but forgotten that the city had once been a *misnagged* stronghold. That was before the arrival of the dynasty's founder, R' Menachem Nachum.

When R' Nachum came to Chernobyl, the opposition was fierce. Word spread that he was a student of the holy Ba'al Shem Tov and R'

Dov Ber of Mezrich. This information alone was enough to strew thorns in the new *Maggid's* path. From the first moment, he was greeted with suspicion and hostility, for fear he would try to recruit new souls for the chassidic "cult."

At the head of the opposition in the city stood Ziskind Kutcher, a former wagon driver turned prosperous businessman. Ziskind Kutcher's antagonism to the new *Maggid* lent the *misnagdim* confidence: R' Nachum would find himself bested before long, and would be forced to leave town in humiliation.

Ziskind Kutcher was a powerful man who brooked no resistance to his will. One of the area's wealthiest figures, his home was a palace fit for princes, boasting a central tower surrounded by four buildings in which his family and an army of servants lived. Exaggerated tales of his wealth were rife in Chernobyl. Some said that a herd of 100 horses lived in his stables; others said no less than 70 mezuzahs were affixed to the doors of his rooms. Here was not a man to be trifled with. Ziskind Kutcher always got his way. Anyone who dared oppose him would soon find himself brushed aside like a pile of refuse.

His very appearance inspired fear: He was a tall man, taller than most of the city's residents, and broad shouldered. His thick black beard was threaded with silver, his cheeks shone with ruddy good health, and his eyes were keen and piercing, seeking out pockets of resistance to his will so that he might crush them.

Ziskind's opinion was generally accepted without question in Chernobyl. No one dared voice an opposing view, even if Ziskind's view was not particularly sound. No one was interested in clashing horns with him. From such a clash, the people knew, Ziskind himself would emerge unscathed, while his opponent would stagger away, pulverized.

It was this community leader, then, who set out to wage war against the new *Maggid*, who had dared settle in Chernobyl without Ziskind's approval.

He threw his full weight against R' Nachum and the *chassidim* that R' Nachum had brought along with him. He disrupted all their activities and threw obstacles into their paths at every turn. If the *chassidim* announced that the *Maggid* would be speaking in shul at a certain hour, Ziskind would be in the front yard at the appointed time, drawing himself to his full height and booming, "He is from the cult. It is forbidden to listen to his sermon!"

He hounded the *Maggid* in every way, making R' Nachum's life a misery. His goal was to draw R' Nachum into a big controversy, from which he, Ziskind, would emerge victorious. But R' Nachum was made of steel. "For a controversy, you need two people," he would state. "And I refuse to be one of them!"

Determined not to quarrel, R' Nachum made no reply to Ziskind's curses and accusations, or to the regular disturbances during his sermons. He paid no attention to the insults and accepted his suffering with love. Gradually, the people came to admire him. Little by little, Ziskind became isolated in his corner, until he was nearly alone in his battle. All of his friends and supporters had moved over to the great Rebbe's camp.

Ziskind was undaunted. Soon, he vowed, he would launch a fresh attack against the *Maggid*. "And everyone in town will fight alongside me, shoulder to shoulder, until we've chased the *Maggid* away."

Winter passed, and the aroma of baking matzos wafted on the Chernobyl air. It was the night of *bedikas chametz*. After checking his home for *chametz* by candlelight, R' Nachum secluded himself in his room. A short time later, he emerged again, his expression shadowed. "Chaim Leib," he said to his helper, "I'd like to send you on a mitzvah mission."

Chaim Leib had been resting on a bench at the moment, catching his breath after the day's arduous labor. The cleaning was behind him, and he would shortly be going into the kitchen to begin the holiday-cooking marathon. At the Rebbe's words, however, he leaped up like a lion, every nerve quivering with expectancy. "Where do I go?" he asked.

"To Ziskind's house," R' Nachum replied calmly, as though the man were his dear old friend.

Chaim Leib cleared his throat nervously. "The Rebbe is doubtless aware that Ziskind —"

"I know," R' Nachum broke in. "Go and tell him that, though he has checked his home well, some *chametz* still remains in his home!"

Fearfully, Chaim Leib said, "I am afraid that I will not leave that man's house alive. He is a very powerful person. He'll crush me! Maybe I can pass the Rebbe's words on to Ziskind's servants and then run away?"

R' Nachum placed an affectionate hand on his helper's shoulder. "No! I want you to give my message to the great man himself. Go in peace. Do not be afraid. Those who act as messengers for a mitzvah are not harmed."

Chaim Leib's teeth chattered with terror all the way to the community leader's house. "I am taking my life into my hands," he thought bitterly. "Ziskind is the Rebbe's sworn enemy, and has been for a long time now. When he hears what I have to say, he will be certain that I've come to start a libel against him, in revenge for the trouble he's caused the Rebbe."

Had it been possible to do so, he would have fled the city. But an order from the holy Rebbe was even stronger than Ziskind's most powerful punch. Ziskind, after all, could only hurt him in this world, but a holy man's curse follows a man into the next one.

With knocking knees, he walked into Ziskind's courtyard. There were five buildings altogether: two on each side of the central courtyard, and in the center the magnificent tower building. Heavy metal bars greeted him at the central building's door. Behind them stood the guard. "What do you want?" he asked suspiciously.

Chaim Leib explained that his master had given him a message that he was to pass on only to Ziskind in person. He intentionally omitted to mention his master's name; R' Nachum was not likely to have many fans in this place.

After a few more questions, the guard permitted Chaim Leib to climb up to the second floor. Other servants stopped him there, each demanding to know his business. To each one, he repeated what he had told the guard. He walked down ornate corridors, treading on plush rugs. Sparkling mirrors winked down at him from the walls, and a golden chandelier dangled from the high ceiling. But Chaim Leib could not enjoy any of it — not when each passing second was bringing him closer to a face-to-face meeting with Ziskind.

"The seven levels of *Gehinnom*," he muttered as he was passed from servant to servant and room to room. At long last, he was permitted to enter the personal study of the master of the house.

Ziskind was seated at a large desk, perusing a Haggadah with commentary. He looked peaceful, a state of mind that Chaim Leib sorely envied at the moment. He longed to be standing in his kitchen, in the nonthreatening company of his onions and potatoes. He yearned to be anywhere but in Ziskind's study.

Ziskind lifted his eyes from the Haggadah. "Who are you?" he asked.

"Chaim Leib, R' Menachem Nachum's helper."

Ziskind's face grew purple with rage. "What brings you to my house?"

"The Rebbe sent me with an urgent message." Chaim Leib's heart hammered with fear. "He asked me to tell you that there is *chametz* in your house, and that you must seek it out and burn it."

"*What?*" Ziskind shrieked. He stood up, fists clenched. "Your Rebbe wants to make a fool of me, does he? *Chametz* — in *my* house? Do you have any idea how many servants have been cleaning this house for the past week? Not so much as a speck of dust is to be found anywhere on the premises. And you come to tell me that there is *chametz*?!"

Chaim Leib did not hear the last words. He was already running for his life, terrified that Ziskind would let loose his wrath in the form of a shower of blows. Chaim Leib raced through the halls, leaped swift as a deer down the broad staircase, and passed through the front door like a storm wind.

From the study window, Ziskind stood watching. "The nerve of that fellow!" he fumed. Then a look of uncertainty crossed his face. "Could the Rebbe be right, after all?" His expression hardened. "Nonsense. Impossible!"

"Did you tell Ziskind that there is *chametz* in his house?" R' Nachum greeted Chaim Leib, who stood panting and breathless before him.

"I told him."

"And what was his response?"

Chaim Leib faithfully transmitted Ziskind's contemptuous answer, word for word.

The Rebbe listened, then turned and walked back into his room, closing the door behind him.

Half an hour later, he emerged again and found Chaim Leib busily peeling potatoes.

"You haven't finished the job yet," he said. "Go to Ziskind and tell him that the *chametz* is to be found in the second building on the left, near the well. Let his servants conduct a careful search there, so that he may not enter Pesach with *chametz* on his property."

Chaim Leib turned as pale as the peeled potato in his hand. "I got out of there by the skin of my teeth. If I go back, he'll kill me on the spot!"

Calmly, R' Nachum said, "There is no need to be afraid. Go in my name and tell him what I said."

Sweat poured down Chaim Leib's face all the way to the rich man's house. Ziskind was bound to blow up like a pressure cooker, and those powerful hands would be given free rein to do as they wished.

Again, he knocked at the front door with a trembling hand. The guard met him with a guffaw. "You! You just bolted from here like a rabbit. Why did you come back?"

Through frozen lips, Chaim Leib managed to stammer that he must see the master without delay, for he had an urgent message to deliver.

To his surprise, both the guard and the servants after him — though clearly displeased — let him pass inside.

Chaim Leib found Ziskind still in his study, sipping a cup of hot tea. A spark of fury ignited in his eyes when they saw the Rebbe's helper. "What now?" he demanded disdainfully. "No, I know — you don't have to say a thing. Your Rebbe sent you to apologize for your blunder before."

"No," Chaim Leib managed to muster the courage to answer. "On the contrary, the Rebbe says to tell you that there is *chametz* in the second building on the left, near the well."

As he had the first time, the rich man reacted with scornful anger. He heaped his wrath on poor Chaim Leib's head, who cowered like a gnat before a giant. "Are you trying to test my patience?" roared Ziskind. "I warn you, your end will be bitter if you do!"

Chaim Leib turned tail and fled.

Upstairs, the master of the house was still raging. In the midst of his tirade, however, he had a sudden, uneasy thought — a slight doubt. *Could there be anything to it? Could some crumb have possibly been overlooked?*

At once, he dismissed the possibility with his usual firmness. *Chametz in my house? With my staff of servants? Impossible!*

"Did you do as I asked?" the *Maggid* asked Chaim Leib on his return. Chaim Leib's face was crimson from the exertion of running all the way home.

"I told him," he gasped.

"And what did he answer?"

Chaim Leib relayed Ziskind's response. The Rebbe sat lost in thought for some moments. Then he rose and returned to his room.

Hardly half an hour had elapsed when R' Nachum came seeking Chaim Leib once more among his pots and pans.

"Hurry over to Ziskind's again," he said. "You must save him from the prohibition of *chametz* on Pesach! Run and tell him that the *chametz* is in such and such a room (he described it), in the left-hand building near the well."

Chaim Leib felt every inch of his skin crawl with terror. Ziskind had reacted even more forcefully at his second visit than he had at the first. Who knew what he would do if he saw Chaim Leib again?

But he went.

This time, the guard refused to wave him through to the upper floor. He himself, he said, would deliver the Rebbe's message to his master.

FOUR MISSIONS IN ONE NIGHT / 69

The guard's entrance interrupted Ziskind in the middle of a pleasant talk with one of his sons. As he delivered the Rebbe's message, Ziskind nearly exploded with fury. He thundered, "He's still telling me I have *chametz* in my house? Does the '*Maggid*' have nothing better to do than play his silly tricks three times in a row?"

Frightened, the guard hurried to take his leave. Just before he left the room, he heard his master mutter to himself, "Maybe I should order my servants to search that room. The Rebbe was quite specific —"

Then he shook his head. "It is not possible. The *Maggid* is not going to dictate to me what to do in my own house!"

The guard did not know what to make of his master's words, but he faithfully relayed them to Chaim Leib, waiting below. Chaim Leib eagerly committed every word to memory.

The Rebbe's mind was eased to a degree after he heard this. For the fourth time that night, he secluded himself in his room. It was already after midnight, when he emerged once more, to find Chaim Leib cooking in the kitchen. R' Nachum's face was exalted.

"Go to Ziskind's house and tell him that I know exactly where the *chametz* is located. He must remove it from the bottom desk drawer in the room I told him about. It is in the left-hand corner of the drawer."

For the fourth time that night, Chaim Leib made the trek to Ziskind's house. He greeted the tired guard and asked for permission to see the master.

"This is unbelievable!" sputtered the guard. "Your Rebbe is sitting in his house on the other side of town, and sees what's going on in this house?"

The guard raced up to Ziskind's bedroom and knocked forcefully on the door. Some minutes later, a drowsy Ziskind stepped outside, wearing his bathrobe and rubbing the sleep from his eyes. "I hope you have a good reason for what you just did," he growled ominously.

Steeling himself against his master's anger, the guard passed on the Rebbe's message.

"This is the end!" Ziskind fumed. "Doesn't the Rebbe have anything better to do than to bother me four times in one night? I will spread this tale all over town!"

The guard stepped hurriedly back. As he made for the door, Ziskind muttered, "Now that I'm up anyway, bring me a candle. If all I have to do is open the bottom desk drawer, why don't I do it?"

By the time Chaim Leib left the rich man's courtyard, he knew that Ziskind had felt around in the bottom desk drawer in the room that the Rebbe had specified — and found a small loaf of bread that had been hidden in the recesses of the drawer.

⟆⟑

The next morning, after burning his *chametz*, Ziskind came to R' Nachum's house. His air of animosity had deserted him. He stood humbly in the Rebbe's room and pleaded for forgiveness. The holy Rebbe forgave him for embittering his life, and calmed the agitated community leader.

"But I am puzzled," Ziskind said. "Why did the Rebbe send his helper to me four times? If the Rebbe was able to 'see' with his inner eye, why didn't he tell me at once: 'There is *chametz* in your house, in such and such a building, in such and such a room, in the bottom desk drawer'?"

R' Nachum fixed him with his shining eyes, and explained.

"It is true that when people are close to me, when they are connected to me with their spirits and their souls, I can see what is going on in their homes without any trouble. There is no shadow separating us. But you have not been attached to me —

"After *bedikas chametz*, my inner eye raked the city that is under my care, and I saw that your home contained *chametz*. More than that I could not see. I sent Chaim Leib to you, and you opposed his message. But you did experience a moment's softening, when you wondered if I was right. At that moment, the connection between us was strengthened, so that I was able to see which building the *chametz* was in. By the third time I sent him, I was able to see the exact room, and by the fourth visit, when you wondered aloud whether I might be right, I was able to see the loaf of bread sitting in the bottom drawer!"

Ziskind trembled with reverence. From that day on, he became a new man, and one of the most fervent followers and admirers of R' Menachem Nachum of Chernobyl.

# He Who Succors the Poor

THE WAYS OF THE KOTZKER *CHASSIDIM* WERE DEEP AND incomprehensible to many people. R' Mendel of Kotzk led his congregation with fiery devotion and a passion for truth.

Kotzker *chassidim* cared little what others thought of them. They pursued absolute truth, whatever the price. They eschewed comfort and honor for themselves, and disparaged any falsehood and the pursuit of acclaim by others.

It was not for naught that Polish Jews said of them: "Kotzker *chassidim* do mitzvos secretly and *aveiros* openly. Others do *aveiros* secretly and only their mitzvos in public."

It is not suprising, therefore, to find that feelings ran high against the Kotzker *chassidim* in many places.

When the Rebbe arrived in Kotzk for the first time to make his home there, along with his household and an entourage of *chassidim,* antagonists gathered to pelt the group with stones.

The Kotzker was unmoved by the attack. With his usual depth of meaning, he stated, "If they are throwing stones at us, it is a sign that there are men of truth and ideals here."

In a certain town where anti-Kotzk feelings ran high, the local *shochet* was a Kotzker *chassid.* When disputes raged regarding the Kotzkers, the *shochet* found himself on one side of the fence while the majority of the people in his town stood on the other.

72 / TALES FOR THE SOUL

Day by day, the opposition grew — and all, of course, in the name of piety and fear of Heaven. Soon a new mantra was heard: "The *shochet's shechitah* is disqualified!" After all, how was it possible to rely on the *shechitah* of a Kotzker *chassid*?

One mother, complaining that her usually sharp-witted son had grown unable to absorb his Torah studies, refused to look for the true reasons for the change. Instead, she leaped to an instant conclusion: the Kotzker *shochet*! His *shechitah*, she decided, must certainly be unkosher. The townspeople were eating unclean meats. Was that not enough to close a child's mind to the Torah he was taught?

Within twenty-four hours, the *shochet* was evicted from the town in disgrace, and together with him went his wife and young children. They climbed onto the wagon, and the driver was ordered to take them anywhere he wished — as long as he left them far from their town.

The *shochet* did not allow the driver to go too far. In a nearby town, he and his family got off the wagon. The *shochet* put up his family in the communal guesthouse, which accommodated the poor who had no home, and he ran to see the local rabbi. He demanded that the people of his former town be summoned to a *din Torah* for removing him from his source of livelihood without proper procedure and investigation, thereby turning him into a pauper.

The rabbi was not eager to involve himself in the dispute. He sent the *shochet* on to a third town, where the local rabbi sang the same song. In this way, the unfortunate *shochet* went from town to town until at last he reached the capital city of Warsaw and the *beis din* of the *gaon*, R' Shlomo Zalman, author of *Chemdas Shlomo*, who agreed to deal with the matter.

When the Kotzker Rebbe heard that the Chemdas Shlomo had involved himself in the case, he turned at once to his student, R' Yitzchak Meir, author of *Chiddushei HaRim*, and asked him to travel at once to Warsaw to plead the *shochet's* case before R' Shlomo Zalman.

Upon R' Yitzchak Meir's arrival, the Chemdas Shlomo sat bolt upright in astonishment. "R' Itzche Meir the *ilui* (genius) has troubled himself to travel all the way to Warsaw to involve himself in a *din Torah* of a small-town *shochet*? This does not do honor to the Torah!"

The Chiddushei HaRim gazed into the great *rav's* eyes and said pleasantly, "If you'll give me permission, I'd like to tell you a story. Then all of your questions will be answered."

Zelig was a simple villager. He was a pious man who had never aspired to more than his humble place. He asked only that Hashem give him a bit of bread to eat and clothing to wear.

Most of the year, on snowy or rainy days, Zelig sat peacefully in the village shul, reciting *Tehillim* in the quiet tones of a man satisfied with little. His place was behind the stove, where it was warm. When the warm weather returned, Zelig would awaken from his winter freeze and go out into the fields, where he would gaze with satisfaction at the budding wheat. The crop was coming in nicely. He would earn his living this year.

With the wheat standing in the field, its kernels ripe and fat, Zelig would bring his scythe and begin to cut down the waving stalks. These golden bundles were the source of his livelihood. The grain he sold to the wheat merchants in nearby Lublin nicely supported him and his wife and children.

Zelig kept a tutor in his home, to teach his young children Torah. He supported this tutor as well. Often, the thought crossed his mind that his success in selling his wheat was all in the merit of the *melamed* who ate at his table, and engaged in his holy service in Zelig's home.

Zelig's laden wagon rolled into Lublin at high noon. It was filled to the brim with stalks of wheat, golden and tempting enough to entice even the most seasoned of wheat merchants. That day, the bargaining lasted late into the night. Zelig was asking a higher price than usual for his fine crop, and the merchants were resisting.

With an enormous yawn, one of them said at last, "It's very late. We have to get up early in the morning to say *selichos* before dawn."

"Where do you say *selichos*?" Zelig asked.

The merchant stared at him, then rolled his eyes in mock disbelief. "Is it possible to say *selichos* anywhere else but in the *beis midrash* of the holy Chozeh of Lublin?"

"I want to say *selichos* with the Rebbe, too," Zelig suddenly decided.

The merchants were glad to let him accompany them. "Listen," they said. "We'd like to continue negotiating the price, but we're too tired to go on now. Let us continue right after *Shacharis* tomorrow. Until then, you must, of course, keep your wheat piled on your wagon. If you find other customers who agree to your price, the choice is yours."

"That's fine," Zelig said confidently. They parted in friendship. Zelig found an inn in which to rest for a few hours before his new friends came to wake him before sunrise. To say *selichos* and pray with the Chozeh of Lublin was not something that happened every day.

The *selichos* carried Zelig to spiritual heights he had never visited before. He was flooded with holy feeling, and his sole yearning during those minutes was to identify completely with Dovid *HaMelech's* plea: "Let me dwell in the house of Hashem all the days of my life."

During *Shacharis*, however, Zelig began to return from the heights. He suddenly remembered his horse, standing in the shul courtyard and harnessed to a wagonload of precious wheat. From time to time, Zelig dashed outside to check on the wagon and the horse.

The *Shemoneh Esrei* lasted a longer time than usual. As the throng of worshipers prayed fervently, Zelig's mind was not fully concentrating. Could he possibly approach the King with his head full of horses and wagons?

No sooner had he taken three steps back and ended the *Amidah*, however, than he sprinted outside again. A shriek rose up in his throat and flew from his mouth. The horse and wagon were gone!

His frantic cries drew several men out of the shul. They joined Zelig at once in his search for his property. Running across the courtyard, they gazed in all four directions. But there was no sign at all of either horse or wagon.

Zelig cried bitterly to the Chozeh's disciples, "I'm left with nothing! A full year's income — lost in a single moment. As far as I am concerned, let my poverty be an atonement. My wife and children — well, they are being punished for my sins. But what about the *melamed* who lives in my home? His work is completely holy, and he is a part of my household. Now he will be forced to go hungry along with me during the holidays. And how am I to support him all year long?"

The *chassidim* were sympathetic. They decided to try to get him to the Rebbe without delay.

A short time later, Zelig was standing before the Chozeh, weeping bitter tears from the depths of his heart. "My horse and wagon have been stolen. My world has turned dark. That wheat provides me with a livelihood for an entire year."

At the simple villager's story, the holy Chozeh rose from his chair. He walked to the window overlooking the courtyard, pulled aside the curtain, and stood gazing out for a long moment. Then he turned.

"Do not cry," he said. "With Heaven's help, the stolen goods have been found. In the next village, not far from here, the thief is standing beside your wagon, selling wheat to the farmers surrounding him. Hurry and summon the police to stop him. You have already lost two sacks of wheat so far!"

Zelig was electrified. He had heard tales of the Chozeh of Lublin's wondrous "sight," but he had never witnessed it before. He ran to the police station, related his story of the theft, and added that he knew where the thief was to be found.

So confident was he in his assertion that the police wasted no time in following his instructions. They galloped at once to the village he'd spoken of, with Zelig following behind on a horse they lent him.

They found everything exactly as the Chozeh had described it.

In the market square stood the thief, vigorously bargaining with several farmers over the sacks of wheat. The policemen took him completely by surprise. Caught off guard, the man made no attempt to deny his guilt. He threw himself on the ground, screaming, "Have

76 / TALES FOR THE SOUL

mercy on me! My children are hungry. And besides, I did not manage to sell more than two sacks of wheat!"

⌒◡⌒

The police inspector — like police officers the world over — had not been hired for his soft heart. In a twinkling, the thief's hands were manacled with iron cuffs and he was thrown onto the same horse that Zelig had ridden on.

As the criminal and his victim sat astride the same horse, the thief used the short ride to Lublin to plead with Zelig for his life. "A merciful Jewish heart beats in that chest of yours. Can you find it in your heart to be hard and cruel toward a fellow Jew — your own brother? I beg of you, please tell the inspector that you choose not to press charges against me!"

He was not wrong in his assessment of Zelig. Zelig was a compassionate, forgiving man. "The moment we get to Lublin, I'll drop the complaint against you," he promised.

The thief's eyes glinted craftily. "By the way," he asked curiously, "how you were able to pinpoint my location so perfectly for the police? Are you some sort of magician or wizard?"

"Heaven forbid!" Zelig said. "Those are impure arts. No, I was working from a sacred source. I went to see the Chozeh of Lublin. He walked over to the window, looked out, and saw you standing beside my wagon of wheat. He even told me that you had already sold two sacks. All lies open before those pure eyes."

The thief nearly fell off the horse. "Such a great rabbi! I would like to meet him."

On their arrival in Lublin, Zelig tried to drop the charge against the thief, but the police inspector wouldn't hear of it. At length, however, he did agree to the extraordinary measure of permitting the man, under heavy guard, to pay a short visit to the Chozeh.

Shortly afterward, there was a large crowd gathered in the Rebbe's room. The Chozeh and his disciples were joined by Zelig and the thief, along with a considerable number of police guards, watching carefully lest the criminal attempt to escape.

Everyone expected the thief to fall at the Chozeh's feet and implore him to save his life. Perhaps the Rebbe could succeed in softening the police toward him, where a simple villager had failed.

Instead, to their astonishment, the thief shrieked angrily, "Rebbe, I don't understand! You have *ruach hakodesh* and nothing better to do with it than to track the activities of thieves? Why not use your all-seeing eyes for better things!"

The Chozeh of Lublin did not generally scold his fellow Jews, but this man needed to be put in his place. Sternly, he said, "Listen to a thief's *chutzpah!* What could be better than saving a poor Jew's income? Shall I not use the *ruach hakodesh* with which my Creator has endowed me, to save an oppressed Jew from his oppressor?

"Not only that," added the Chozeh, "but the life of a *melamed* who engages in teaching Torah and who has not tasted sin — his fortunes, too, are dependent on those of this villager."

The author of *Chiddushei HaRim* ended his story. To R' Shlomo Zalman he said, "Do you understand now why I hastened to Warsaw to involve myself in this *din Torah*? The holy Rebbe, R' Yaakov Yitzchak of Lublin, taught us that we must do everything in our power to rescue the oppressed from his oppressor. In our present case, the lives of a pious *shochet* and his family dangle on the outcome of this *din Torah*, which revolves around a libel with no foundation. Shall I not do everything I can to save this poor man from those more powerful than he?"

# Unnecessary Questions

THE BIRDS, AS THEY DID EVERY MORNING, TWITTERED merrily to greet the day. After nearly a week of heavy cloud cover, the sky welcomed back the sun. People walked through the bright streets that springlike day with smiles on their faces. A number of them waved to Yerucham in friendly fashion as they passed, but Yerucham saw no one. In his heart, the sun was not shining. A dark bank of clouds shadowed his eyes. This day had delivered a stunning — and totally unexpected — blow. He was still reeling from the shock.

Yerucham had held down the same job for several years now. His business was transporting goods for the Russian government, by means of scores of energetic horses.

The expression "by the sweat of his brow shall he bring forth his bread" described Yerucham well. Apart from all the hard work, he had the added insecurity of needing to renew his government license each year. Though he had managed, time and again, to have the precious license renewed, it did not come easily. At first, before he learned the secret, he set in motion an entire network of connections, pressures, and pleadings in his effort to obtain the contract. Then he discovered what really greased the wheels of the Russian government (among others in the world): filling the pockets of those bureaucrats whose help he needed.

Every few months or so, he would pay a visit to each of these bureaucrats. Setting a pile of rubles on the table before them, he would remark, almost casually, "In another two weeks, my license to transport government goods is up for renewal. I'm sure that your honor will remember my name on that day."

"Their honors," the corrupt bureaucrats, did remember his name. Yerucham had made certain of that.

For some years, Yerucham followed this procedure and prospered. Then he made a mistake. He believed that he had laid the necessary groundwork and could relax now. The machinery, he believed, would continue to spin on its own. There was no longer any need, he thought, to continue greasing the wheels so regularly. But he had calculated without taking into account the insatiable appetite of those greedy government clerks. When the time came for his usual visit to the clerks in question, he remained at home. The senior bureaucrat waited in vain for the Jew with the fat purse to come around.

"The license is in my pocket," Yerucham thought complacently, whenever he remembered the matter. "Who would compete with me now? Everyone knows that Yerucham is the government carrier. There's no cause for worry."

His error was driven home to him in a most distressing way. At the end of a long day's work, he was stunned to see a contingent of police officers waiting outside his house.

"But what have I done? What's this all about?" he protested in shock, as handcuffs were slapped onto his wrists.

"You'll hear everything down at the station," the policemen assured him gleefully.

And, a very short time later, he did. The local inspector demanded an explanation for various unpaid customs charges on goods that appeared in Yerucham's account books. Yerucham was speechless.

The accusation was well founded. Yerucham did not report a good portion of his income to the government's customs authorities. This was a carefully guarded secret, known to very few. His present predicament hinted at the presence of an informer. It was only later that Yerucham learned the identity of that informer: It was none other than the senior bureaucrat who had not received his accustomed bribe that year.

To win his freedom, Yerucham was forced to pay many times that amount in fresh bribes. He managed to extricate himself from prison by the skin of his teeth. The police inspector and his officers accompanied him to his home, and soon left with bulging pockets. After that, they suddenly "discovered" that the Jew's file had mysteriously disappeared.

Yerucham was a smart fellow. Even more, he was a *chassid* with a fervent belief in the wisdom of *chachamim*. He knew that his troubles were not over. Though grateful that he had managed to avoid a lengthy jail sentence, the problem of his livelihood still remained. His precious carrier license had already been taken from him. If he didn't do something — and soon — his family would go hungry.

He traveled at once to see his Rebbe, R' Dovid of Tolna. He wept bitterly, "Rebbe, save me, for the waters have climbed over my head!"

He explained how his livelihood had been taken from him, and that he had nearly ended up in prison.

R' Dovid's brow creased as he pondered the situation. At last, he said, "You must seek among your deeds."

Yerucham grew pale. "Does the Rebbe suspect that I am a sinner, Heaven forbid?"

The Rebbe chose to answer in the words of R' Yehudah to R' Huna, when four hundred barrels of R' Huna's wine went sour: "Do you suspect *Hakadosh Baruch Hu* of making a judgment without justice?

"If you have been so severely punished," the Rebbe continued, "it is a sign that your actions have not been kosher. You must search through your deeds and investigate the crevices of your conscience. If you recall a wrongdoing and repent wholeheartedly, I promise you that your former position will be restored to you."

Yerucham was silent. The Rebbe's words had penetrated to his very core. Lowering his gaze, he began to mentally review everything he had done lately. He was a good man and a pious one who feared Heaven, was scrupulous with both "large" and "small" mitzvos, and set aside regular times for Torah study. He was not a sinner; so it was no great sin that the Rebbe was asking him to find. No desecration of the holy Shabbos, Heaven forbid, or the consumption of non kosher food. On the principle that there is no man on earth who never sins, the Rebbe wanted him to search among his deeds for some wrongdoing that might not be so obvious to the eye.

Suddenly, Yerucham looked up. "I found it!" he cried. "I've found the sin. Now I know why this misfortune has happened to me."

"What did you do?" the Rebbe asked. "Please tell me about it."

UNNECESSARY QUESTIONS / 81

"I was busy with my work that day. A government official came to see me at home about a big deal we were to finalize. As we sat in my study, immersed in all the many details of our transaction, I heard voices in the front hall. Someone was shouting at my son, who shouted back. I tried to ignore the quarrel, but the voices only got louder. Finally, I went out to see what was going on.

"In the front hall stood a tattered beggar. His face was red as he shouted with all his might. While I'd been closeted with the government official, the beggar had knocked on the door of my home, requesting a donation. My son gave him a small coin. But the beggar, knowing that I generally gave him much more, had demanded to see me in person. My son explained that he could not disturb me, as an honored official was meeting with me in my study. The beggar insisted that I come out. When my son refused, the beggar became furious and started shouting at him. My son gave back as good as he'd gotten — whereupon the beggar began to hurl even more abuse at him. At that moment, I came out of my study. Seeing me, the beggar added me, for good measure, as a target of his abuse.

"I could not believe my ears. I, an intimate of high government officials, honored and respected by them all, and actually hosting one of them that very minute — to be so insulted in my own home? Enraged, I lifted my hand and slapped the beggar's face.

"A moment later, my anger subsided and I regretted what I had done. I apologized at once and did not let him leave my home until I had given him a nice donation."

R' Dovid of Tolna shook his head. "That was not the deed I meant. You apologized to the beggar and gave him a donation. It was not because of that act that you find yourself in your present trouble. Search further, and see if you can remember anything else."

Once again, Yerucham sank into thought. He strained his mind, sifting through his actions to find the one to which the Rebbe was referring.

He who searches shall find. The memory rose to the front of his consciousness, as clear and whole as if it had happened that very day.

Midnight had come and gone. After a hard day's work, Yerucham finally lay down to sleep. He had scarcely finished reciting the bedtime *Keri'as Shema* when his eyes closed of their own accord. Sweet slumber overtook him.

He was suddenly rudely roused from his deep sleep by a pounding at the door. Yerucham blinked in the dark, certain at first that the pounding was part of his dream. When it persisted, however, he woke fully — and angrily.

"Who's there?" he shouted at the door.

"In Heaven's name, open up!" an unfamiliar voice pleaded.

Throwing on a light robe and thrusting his feet into slippers, Yerucham hurried to the door.

A tall, sturdy young man stood on the doorstep. "Please give me a piece of bread," he supplicated. "I am very hungry."

"Isn't a healthy young man like yourself ashamed to go begging?" Yerucham demanded. He cast a measuring glance over the stranger. "If a weak, hunched-over pauper came asking for my money, I'd understand. But a great, hulking fellow like you? Go out and get yourself a job! Don't come around here trying to take my hard-earned money."

Shamed and humiliated, the young beggar left Yerucham's house and did not return.

"That's it," the Rebbe said, nodding. "That was your sin. Are *you* not ashamed of yourself? If a beggar comes to you in the middle of the night, that is a sign that he is in desperate straits indeed. He was apparently very hungry. Your job was to feed him, not to criticize and shame him because he was supporting himself by collecting money."

On the spot, Yerucham did complete *teshuvah* for his transgression. In the future, he resolved, should any poor man ask for his help, he would get it. Yerucham would give, and without checking the man's credentials first. Even if the beggar was healthy and strong, even if he were as tall as Og and twice as broad shouldered as Shimshon *Hagibor*, he would receive his donation at Yerucham's home.

Witnessing his *chassid's* humility and true repentance, the Rebbe grew radiant. Yerucham was making no excuses. He was not trying to defend himself. The Rebbe began to speak. This is the story he told.

The rich man stood at his tower window and gazed out over the flowering orchards spread below. The golden fields, the busy flour mill, the flocks of placidly grazing sheep, even the stream winding its way across the picturesque scene — all these belonged to him. He was an extremely wealthy man, the owner of numerous factories and businesses. At his disposal stood an entire fleet of ships and an army of clerks and laborers.

But, for all his wealth, he was not calm. The words that we recite in our *tefillah* — "He lowers the proud to the ground" — worried him immensely. Was it possible that he would lose his money someday, and become poor? The possibility was troubling. What's more, he couldn't see how such a catastrophe could come about. He felt completely secure of his possessions. If the beautiful mansion in which he lived should burn to the ground, he had other homes, no less beautiful. Should those, too, be lost, he had merely to sell off some of his tremendous assets and buy a new house.

Should all the trees in his orchards be cut down, he'd still have his fleet of ships. And if he lost everything else, he would still have his land. The land alone was a very valuable asset. In short, he concluded, it was not possible for him to become a pauper. Half his fortune might be lost, or even two-thirds, but the third that remained would be capable of supporting him in comfort — and his children and grandchildren as well — for the rest of their lives.

Still, the possibility that he *might* one day be poor, faint as that was, continued to disturb his tranquility. He simply could not rid his mind of these thoughts.

The rich man was very charitable, giving generously to the poor. When they came to his door he would chat with them a while, always ending with the same question: "Do you think it's possible that I, the richest man in the country, could ever become poor?"

And, one and all, the beggars would shake their heads "no." With their mouths full of his food, they would assure him that he would never be so dashed to the ground. He would always remain fabulously wealthy.

These remarks aroused a great prosecution against the rich man in Heaven. Hashem is the One Who makes people rich or poor. All wealth comes from Him, and if a wealthy man refuses to recognize this, then all will be taken from him so that he may witness, with his own eyes, how the rich and mighty can become the most destitute of paupers.

The Ba'al Shem Tov, aware of what was being said against the wealthy man up above, spoke in his defense. He asked that the man's fortune not be taken from him. Because of the Ba'al Shem Tov's prayer, it was decided that the rich man would have one more chance to pass the test.

Should he fail again, he would lose everything.

A few days later, a traveler came to the rich man's door. It was the Ba'al Shem Tov's disciple, R' Dovid of Mikoliov. Like all the others, he was treated generously and with warm hospitality. As he sat eating, his host asked him whether it was possible that he, such a wealthy individual, could ever become destitute.

"Of course!" answered R' Dovid promptly, to the rich man's surprise. "In a moment, your luck could change so that you do not even own the shirt on your back."

His host began to argue with him, describing the vast extent of his fortune and property. Finally, R' Dovid pointed at the darkened window. "Look, it's already very late. Let us rest now, and in the morning we can continue our discussion."

The rich man agreed. Off he went to his room for his night's sleep.

Sometime in the night, a wild knocking sounded at his door. Waking in confusion, he found his personal servant standing there in a state of great excitement. "His Majesty, the kaiser, has come to see you!" he gasped.

"Now?" the rich man asked, stupefied. "The kaiser? The king of all Prussia has come here, in person?"

His servant acknowledged that this was, indeed, the case.

In a very short time, the rich man was seated with the kaiser in his beautiful living room, surrounded by the kaiser's entourage. The fireplace blazed cozily as they all tasted the dainty cakes that the host had ordered served, and sipped hot tea from porcelain teacups. The rich man was not surprised at the kaiser's visit, since he was an intimate of the palace. What astonished him was the fact that the visit was taking place in the dead of night, as though the kaiser wished to ensure that no one would know he was there.

The kaiser had just taken a large sip of tea when his face suddenly turned ashen. A strangled sound came from his throat. The cup fell from his hand. An instant later, the kaiser slipped unconscious from his chair, to sprawl beside the cup on the rug.

The room was electrified with shock. "The kaiser is dead!" screamed one servant.

"How did it happen?" two royal officials cried, rushing to kneel at the kaiser's side.

The kaiser's personal physician was already there. After a brief examination, he looked up gravely and pronounced, "The kaiser has been poisoned to death."

Every eye turned to fix itself on the host. The cup of tea he had served the kaiser had been laced with poison!

In a twinkling, the rich man was seized by the kaiser's servants, who held him in a steely grip. They stood ready to gallop with him to the capital city, where he would be hung before dawn.

Just as the group was preparing to leave the mansion, a fire broke out in one of its towers. The rooms began to blaze furiously, tongues of flame blocking the exit. The rich man took advantage of the turmoil and confusion to escape his captors and slip out of the house through a secret exit. Outside, in the courtyard, he did not waste a second looking over his shoulder. He ran away as fast as his legs could carry him.

He ran for hours, mortal fear impelling every step. At long last, he reached a small town where he found lodging in a fellow Jew's home.

The next morning, even before he got out of bed, the man overheard his host telling his wife the news: That very morning, the palace had announced that a Jew had poisoned the kaiser to death! The news included a description of the poisoner. It also offered a large reward to anyone who would hand the Jew over to the authorities. To the rich man's trepidation, he heard his host describe him perfectly.

"Master of the Universe!" he whispered desperately. "Last night, he didn't see me clearly. Now, in the light of day, he will identify me and hand me over to the police before I have a chance to explain that it was all a frame-up. I must run!"

At once, he slipped secretly out of the house. To avoid detection, he clung to the fields and empty lanes.

Overnight — literally — the rich man was hurled down from his lofty position. He was now a hunted criminal. He slept by day and wandered the fields by night, lonely and afraid. His expensive clothes became torn and tattered. The coins in his pocket were spent, one by one, until he suffered from unrelenting hunger and thirst. He reached the point where he began to think that even death was preferable to the life he was leading.

But even as that thought crossed his mind, he realized that he still yearned for life. In the distance, he spied a troop of soldiers marching in his direction. Any second now, they would see him and carry him back in chains. Was there anyone in all the kingdom who would not recognize him by now?

In desperation, he threw himself into the gutter that ran alongside the road and dunked himself, head and all, in the dirty water that rushed through it. *Baruch Hashem* the gutter was there!

As he lay in the filthy water, waiting for the sound of the soldiers' boots to pass him and then recede into the distance, a sudden thought flashed through the once-wealthy man's mind.

*Open your eyes, and see how Heaven has proven that it is Hashem Who makes people rich or poor. Not only has He taken all my wealth away, He has also made my life worthless. I am being hunted like an animal, and thank Hashem for providing me a gutter to hide in when I need it.*

The thought grew and strengthened, filling his mind and heart until his spirit was humbled to the ground.

And, at that moment, the rich man woke up.

It had all been a dream. There had been no kaiser, no poison, no fire. Just one long, vivid dream. A dream that had been sent to show him the tremendous error of his ways.

In the morning, his guest, R' Dovid of Mikoliov, turned to him and asked, "Are you still interested in hearing an answer to your question about how Hashem makes people rich or poor?"

"I don't need it anymore," his host answered, from the depths of his heart. "Last night, I learned that all my wealth is just a gift that Hashem has chosen to leave with me for the time being. If He chooses, He can turn me in an instant into a destitute man, running for his life."

"And now," said R' Dovid of Tolna to his *chassid*, Yerucham. "Take a lesson from this story — a lesson about a rich man who asked too many questions. Take the story with you, and carry it deep in your heart. Learn to respect every Jew, to give charity to every poor man, and not to distress anyone. If a man as strong as Shimshom *HaGibor* should rouse you in the middle of the night, asking for food and water, feed him. And don't ask any unnecessary questions."

# Three Wondrous Coins

IT HAPPENED ABOUT 150 YEARS AGO.

The second Lelover Rebbe, the *tzaddik* R' Moshe, son of the dynasty's founder, R' Dovid of Lelov, decided to leave his native country of Poland and move to Eretz Yisrael.

This was no hasty decision. The strong desire to live in his beloved Eretz Yisrael had possessed him for years, filling his days and nights with longing.

"Three years before he left this world, R' Moshe of Lelov had already divested himself of everything he had. He couldn't bear the atmosphere outside of Eretz Yisrael," the Sanzer Rebbe confided to R' Yosele of Neustadt. Those close to the Rebbe realized this about him even before he understood it himself. One had only to glance into his face to see that he felt that his life would be unfulfilled until he reached the Holy Land.

R' Moshe of Lelov did not long for Eretz Yisrael's beauty, for its luscious fruits, or its lovely panoramas. Only one desire burned brightly in him: to help restore the *Shechinah* and bring the Redemption closer. And this, he felt, was something that he could do only in Eretz Yisrael.

"When I arrive in Eretz Yisrael," he said again and again, "I will go to the *Kosel Hama'aravi* and lift up my voice like a shofar, until *Mashiach* comes!"

Finally, the Rebbe set out. With him went his two holy sons, R' Yitzchak Dovid and R' Elazar Menachem Mendel — who would later succeed his father — and a few select disciples. They traveled through Poland, taking leave of various rebbes on their way to Eretz Yisrael. The Lelover Rebbe visited the Sar Shalom of Belz and the holy R' Yisrael of Rizhin. The Sar Shalom begged R' Moshe of Lelov to remain in Poland, saying, "You mustn't go to Eretz Yisrael. Every Jew in Poland needs you!" But R' Moshe paid no heed. He was fixed and determined on his path, and nothing could make him swerve from it — not even when the Rizhiner Rebbe pleaded, "Wait for me, and the two of us will travel up to Eretz Yisrael together to bring the Redeemer."

Still R' Moshe declined. Touching his snowy beard, he said, "My white beard will not let me wait any longer!"

When R' Moshe had departed, the Rizhiner Rebbe said to his sons, "The Polish people are foolish. They have such a light in their midst, and they are letting him leave them." And he went on to paraphrase the Gemara: "Poland is not [worthy] of the light of the candle" (*Shabbos* 12).

It was in the month of Elul 5610 (1850) that the Rebbe departed the city of Sadigur. Before he left, he wrote a letter to his *chassidim* in

Poland, who were deeply grieved over having to part with their beloved Rebbe. In the letter he wrote: "I have left my land and my birthplace and the home of my holy fathers, though parting from you all was exceedingly difficult. However, for love of our Holy Land and for other, hidden reasons, I girded myself with the courage to throw everything off. May Hashem guide me in the true path and let me achieve my goals and desires in peace."

The words speak for themselves.

In the month of Tishrei 5611 (1851), the Rebbe landed at the port of Akko. Upon setting foot there, he said cryptically, "A day for a year, a day for a year." From there he went directly to Tzefas, where he spent one Shabbos — a Shabbos that remained etched in the memories of the Jews of Tzefas for years to come.

On *motza'ei Shabbos*, the Rebbe took his leave of Tzefas, whose Jews had bonded to him with a fierce love. After a brief stay in Teveryah, city of the *Tanna'im* and the disciples of the Ba'al Shem Tov, the Rebbe's entourage — his sons and disciples — continued on to Jerusalem. To his family's urging that he first rest a few days, the Rebbe paid no heed at all. He was afire with the desire to proceed with his journey, as though he knew that his days were numbered. His one and only wish was to reach the *Kosel Hama'aravi* with all possible speed.

Still, the long and difficult journey had left its mark on the elderly Rebbe. Weak and fatigued, he rode on the back of a mule until they reached the hills surrounding Jerusalem. Then fresh blood suddenly seemed to course through his veins. He sat regally, urging his mule, and his own weakened body, forward. Joy shone from his face as he prepared to enter the holy city. With uncontrolled impatience he awaited his meeting with the remnant of the *Beis Hamikdash*, from which the *Shechinah* has never departed. As he rode along, he secretly fingered the *Kiddish* cup that the Chozeh of Lublin had given him, and which he had brought with him from Poland. He was careful to protect this cup from all damage on the road, hoping that, through its holiness, wondrous things would occur.

Several times, he whispered to his sons, "Soon — Soon — We are getting close to the gates of Jerusalem. I will go to the *Kosel* at once, with the cup in my hand and the shofar ready — With Hashem's help,

I will hasten the Redemption. I will blow a great shofar blast, and all Jews will come running."

But just before they entered Jerusalem's gates, something awful happened. The cup fell to the ground, where it shattered into pieces. The Rebbe paled; his heart foretold grim tidings.

The Rebbe wanted to visit the *Kosel* that very day, but his exhausted body would not permit him. Reluctantly, he decided to rest for a few days, and to realize his dream when his strength had returned. Unfortunately, Heaven decreed otherwise. On the very day of his arrival in Jerusalem, the Rebbe was beset by a serious illness, and became bedridden.

Imagine the Rebbe's pain when he saw that Heaven was preventing him from achieving his goal! He knew that his time was short. After a few days had passed and his illness only increased its hold on him, the Rebbe ordered his sons to pick him up, bed and all, and carry him to the *Kosel*.

The two men lifted their father's bed onto their shoulders and bore it out of the house that they had first entered only a few days earlier. The house was very close to the holy Western Wall. Slowly they stepped along, careful not to jostle their ailing father.

They had not gone far when a large crowd of Arabs appeared and blocked their way. The Arabs began to pelt the Rebbe with stones. It was clear that a mighty struggle was taking place — a war between the forces of evil and of holiness. The evil side was unleashing all its fury in order to prevent the full *tikkun* of all Creation, the day when Hashem would be "King of all the world."

For a few minutes the brothers hesitated, wondering whether to push on to the *Kosel* at any price. Their father urged them to ignore the Arabs, but the pelting grew stronger and gravely endangered the Rebbe's life. With no choice, the brothers turned and retraced their steps, while their father cried bitterly. He had lost his chance to visit the *Kosel Hama'aravi*.

And on that same bitter day, the Rebbe's hour of departure arrived. His deep grief over being prevented from helping to raise the *Shechinah* from the dust was added to the rigors of the long journey he had just undergone. R' Moshe bid farewell to his sons and disciples, promising them that he would always be at their side to help. He also promised that, should there ever be a drought, if they waited until his *yahrzeit*, plentiful rains of blessing would surely fall.

When he finished speaking, his holy soul left his body. It was the thirteenth day of Teves 5611 (1851), more than 150 years ago. Seventy-four days had passed from his arrival on the shores of Eretz Yisrael — corresponding to the seventy-four years of the Rebbe's life. Only then did the others understand the enigmatic words he had spoken when he set foot on the ground at Akko harbor: "A day for a year, a day for a year."

After his death, his sorrowful sons and disciples began to relate tales of his wonders to the people of Jerusalem.

Let us tell one now.

R' Avner looked depressed. There was no need for his friends and acquaintances to ask him what was wrong; the reason was well known. R' Avner had no children. When ten years of marriage had passed without any offspring, he decided to fulfill the words of the Gemara and divorce his wife. Perhaps it was her bad *mazal* that was causing this unhappy situation? R' Avner went to the town's *rav* to request that the *beis din* prepare him a *get*, so that he might establish a new home and try his luck a second time.

The rabbi stared at him. "You're concerned about that Gemara? Have you tried another of *Chazal's* suggestions, 'Go to a *chacham* and beg for mercy'?"

"No," answered R' Avner.

"In that case, go at once to the holy rebbe, R' Moshe of Lelov. His powers are great and his prayers pierce the very heavens. Ask him to bless you with children."

R' Avner wasted no time in taking the *rav's* advice. He traveled to Lelov and brokenheartedly poured out his woe before the Rebbe.

The Rebbe immediately gave him an enthusiastic blessing, promising faithfully that, in one year's time, his wife would be embracing her infant son.

R' Avner began to weep, shedding great tears of joy. Seizing the Rebbe's hand, he tried to shower kisses on it. The Rebbe snatched his hand away and hastily left the room. A moment later, he returned carrying a small leather purse.

"In here are three coins," the Rebbe told R' Avner. "When your son is born, hang this purse around his neck. It will help him all his life!"

Sure enough, exactly one year later R' Avner's wife gave birth to a baby boy. The moment he was permitted into the birthing room, R' Avner went over to the baby and dangled the leather purse from his neck, just as the Rebbe had instructed. Eight days later, the child was circumcised, and given the name Shaul.

When the child grew a little older, he tried to remove the bothersome purse hanging from his neck. Stopping him, his father explained that he must wear this purse all his life. Due to his tender age, the boy did not understand the significance of his father's words. But he did know one thing: He must not remove the purse. When he was older still, he was told that three coins lay inside.

One day, his curiosity overpowered him. Shaul opened the purse and reached inside to extract its contents.

In the palm of his hand lay three shining coins made of pure silver.

Pulse racing, the boy returned the coins to the purse. His heart whispered that there was some great secret hidden within those coins, and he decided that it was best not to touch them. As time went on, he grew accustomed to the feel of the purse hanging constantly around his neck, until the time came when he didn't even feel it anymore.

The years passed.

R' Avner died suddenly in the prime of life, leaving behind his widow and only son. Immersed in her grief, the mother neglected her child's education. With no one to supervise him, Shaul began to stray from the proper path and fell into bad company. He spent night after night carousing with his new friends. Soon he was spending entire nights playing cards and gambling with dice.

To her distress, the widow witnessed how her precious son was casting off the yoke of Torah and turning to ways that were empty and corrupt. In vain she tried to speak to him. It was like talking to a brick wall. There was only one small ray of consolation: Shaul promised that he was working hard for his living and was not wasting his time.

There was a degree of truth in this statement, as Shaul had become a shoemaker's assistant in order to earn a little money. What he did not mention was that he was spending all his nights drinking, carousing, and playing cards with his friends. With his nimble fingers, Shaul was a wizard with cards, and soon picked up all the game's secrets. In the circles in which he moved, his star was on the rise. He won game after game and was soon considered a veteran card-player.

His reputation began to circulate in the area, until it reached the ears of a man named Maximilian, who was known as one of Poland's greatest card sharks. When this gentile heard that the young Jew's reputation was beginning to eclipse his own, he became inflamed with envy.

"Impossible!" he stated flatly. "That Jew is going to learn that no one beats Maximilian."

He promptly traveled to Shaul's hometown, taking along a group of companions. These hangers-on were always around to cheer Maximilian on as he played.

Sometime in the night, Maximilian and his friends burst into the gaming-parlor where Shaul and his own companions were absorbed in a prolonged game of cards. It was clear that Shaul, as usual, stood to win the pot.

Maximilian approached, taunting, "Who's this kid? Let's have one game, and I'll demolish him."

Silence fell over the room. Shaul sat up straight and cried, "Who dares to challenge me?"

"I do!" Maximilian shot back. "Want to play?"

"Sure!"

A new deck of cards was broken out at once. A great deal of money was placed in the pot, and a new game began between the two card-playing greats.

Within minutes, the game ended with the triumph of the challenger: Maximilian.

94 / TALES FOR THE SOUL

Shaul paid no attention to the money he had lost. He was completely wrapped up in his anger over the humiliating defeat. "Another game!" he snapped.

"You want another game?" Maximilian's eyes danced. "You'll just lose more money."

"Let's see about that!"

Once again, Shaul placed his money in the pot. A new game began. To Shaul's dismay, the newcomer defeated him again, soundly and quickly. He lost both his money and his honor in one fell swoop.

*This is impossible,* he growled to himself in frustration. *This man is either a cheater or a magician. I know all the tricks and I prevented him from playing any of them. How did he fool me?*

He turned to Maximilian. "A new game!" he called.

"Please," Maximilian scoffed. "You'll soon be left with nothing but the shirt on your back."

"I don't care."

Like a man possessed, Shaul threw himself into the game. He was determined to thrash his opponent, or at least learn his methods. Perhaps the fellow was playing with a deck of marked cards — Shaul played again and again, until he had lost his last penny.

His blood boiled with the desire to beat his rival, but there was not a single coin left in his pocket. Suddenly, he remembered the purse hanging from his neck. Three silver coins of great value were right within reach!

*You mustn't touch them!* screamed a hidden voice in his soul. But Shaul was not strong enough to withstand the temptation. With a single, hurried motion he snatched up the purse and clasped it in his hand.

To his astonishment, his fingers did not feel the coins inside. He opened the purse and turned it upside down. There was nothing there.

Maximilian and his cohorts were watching his every move. They taunted him with mocking questions. Finally, unable to bear their scorn, Shaul got up and fled.

On his arrival home, Shaul flung himself onto his bed and wept bitterly. He had been humiliated and cast down. The pain was enormous. Alone in his room, he cried and cried. A troubled sleep came at last to stop the flow of tears.

When morning came, Shaul found that he felt too ill to get out of bed. He lay like a log all that day, trembling from head to toe. Alarmed, his mother summoned a doctor. The doctor examined him, then said gravely to the mother, "Your son is very sick. He needs to go to the hospital at once."

It was a double blow: Shaul's illness, and the loss of his three special coins. Both mother and son, deep in their hearts, feared that the two were inextricably linked.

Shaul's illness worsened by the day. The doctors threw up their hands in despair. "There is nothing left to be done. His condition is critical."

"There *is* something to be done," his mother declared. "We must pray!"

By this time, R' Moshe of Lelov, whose blessing had led to Shaul's birth, had passed on to the Next World. The widow sent a frantic telegram to her brother, who lived in Jerusalem. She begged him to go to the Rebbe's grave, which lay beside that of Zechariah *Hanavi* on the slopes of the Mount of Olives (until it, and hundreds of others, were uprooted by Arabs in the year 5725 [1965]), and pray for her son's recovery.

Shaul's uncle hurried to do his sister's bidding. He went at once to the Rebbe's grave, sprawled over it, and prayed from the depths of his heart.

He was still lying there when he suddenly fell into a deep sleep. In his dream, R' Moshe of Lelov was standing before him. "Why are you crying? If your nephew, Shaul, will correct his deeds and repent completely, his health will be speedily restored. But if he returns to his card dens and his crooked paths, he will have no more life!"

"I promise on his behalf," the uncle mumbled in his dream. He awoke.

He left the gravesite in a turmoil. With all his heart, he sensed that the dream was true. He dashed off an urgent letter to his sister, relating the dream in every detail, and telling her of the promise he had made in her sick son's name.

And, in distant Poland, on one fine day at the height of his illness, the patient suddenly began to take a turn for the better. Day by day his condition improved, until he was restored to full health.

When the widow received her brother's letter, she began to tremble. Looking at the date at the top, she saw, without a shadow of a doubt, that the day her brother had dreamed his dream at the Rebbe's grave was the day her son had begun to recover.

Shaul repented of his corrupt ways, and lived an upright life for the rest of his days. He never forgot how his condition had begun to improve in a single moment — the moment when, touching the leather purse around his neck, he had suddenly felt the three coins that had, in some wondrous way, returned to their pouch.

# The Curse of Money

ISAAC NUDEL, A WEALTHY LUMBER MERCHANT, WAS PLANNING his yearly trip to the large forests in his area. Each year, when the snows melted, he would visit these forests and negotiate with the counts and lords who owned them. Settling on a price, he would buy a huge quantity of trees. Scores of lumbermen would cut down the trees and send the logs, lying in long rows, floating downriver. Later, in his big factories, more workers would saw those logs into boards to be fashioned into furniture and other wood products.

Isaac's business enterprises stretched far and wide. He was known as one of the country's biggest lumber merchants and also as a generous philanthropist whose hand was always open to those in need.

From time to time, when he succeeded in winding up his business affairs in good time, he would visit his Rebbe, the holy R' Yaakov (son of the holy R' Avraham Landau of Tchechenov, and a foremost disciple of the Kotzker Rebbe). Upon the passing of his older brother, R'

Ze'ev of Strikov, R' Yaakov settled in the town of Yazov, near Lodz, where he became famous. He departed this world in the year 5656 (1796). Our story takes place during the period when he was living in the home of his father-in-law, the prosperous R' Aharon in Biala. There, Isaac would dispense his tithes. "Since the *Beis Hamikdash* was destroyed and we can no longer bring gifts to the *Kohanim*, all we have are the *tzaddikim*, who are the *Kohanim* of our own time. And who do I have that is a greater *Kohen Gadol* than the Rebbe?" he explained more than once to R' Yaakov, when the latter tried to rebuke him for the size of his donation.

This was Isaac's yearly routine. It seemed to him that the sun would shine on him forever. Then, one year, his business affairs began to founder. One client died, and his son refused to deal with Isaac. A second client suddenly made contact — for the first time in many years — with a competitor of Isaac's. A third *poritz* complained that a raging fire had swept through his forest that summer, destroying thousands of trees.

In short, Isaac's luck turned. Once he began to fall, he fell long and hard. An experienced businessman, he had naturally tried to protect himself against a dry spell. To prepare for a time when he would not be in a position to buy the trees he needed, he had built giant warehouses and stockpiled thousands of tree trunks inside — his insurance for a rainy day.

"To the warehouses!" he instructed his workers.

The men went off at once — only to return with downcast faces.

"What happened?" Isaac asked in alarm. In his blackest nightmares, he could not have anticipated the answer: "The trees have rotted!"

"All of them?"

"Every single one. The rot ate the trunks from the inside and left all of them hollowed trunks —"

Isaac's mind raced. "Swear to me that you will not tell a soul about this," he ordered. "If word of this catastrophe spreads, my creditors will come swarming out to demand what I owe them. You men will suffer as much as I will. Let's keep our lips sealed and get through this hard time together. With G-d's help, I will rise again and you will be able to continue earning your living with me."

The workers agreed to keep the secret. No one else knew about the merchant's downfall. But despair filled Isaac's heart, especially when he was forced to turn away those charity-collectors who had been accustomed to receiving generous donations from him. By dint of evasive excuses, he managed to put them off for a later date while avoiding explanations. In shul and in the street, he kept his expression impassive. But how long would he be able to keep his secret? His family, accustomed to a pampered life, began for the first time to put aside food to save for the next day. Even money for bread was scarce. How long could he keep up the pretense before everyone discovered the truth?

Isaac went about like a shadow of his former self. His conscience pained him. *It is about you,* he told himself, *that it says 'mashpil gei'im' ['He humbles the haughty']. You were proud of wealth that was not yours, of money that had been granted to you by Heaven. Now the Creator has taken the money back and turned your good fortune to failure."*

These reflections continued to torment him, gnawing away at his very bones.

A visit by Mr. Raskas, a veteran forest agent, sprinkled salt on Isaac's wounds.

Raskas had come to propose an excellent business deal: The *poritz* who owned the nearby town, and with whom Isaac had never yet dealt in business, had sent the agent to suggest that he sell his forest to Isaac. The deal was expected to reap a very nice profit for the lumber merchant.

"And how much does he want for his forest?" Isaac asked with feigned indifference. Inwardly, his heart was beating fast.

"It's a real bargain — 2,000 rubles in cash. But not a kopek less! The *poritz* is determined about that: either he gets the 2,000 in cash, or no deal. If he hadn't been so strapped for cash at the moment, he would never had made the price so low."

Earlier that very day, Isaac had conducted an inventory of his remaining assets. His eyes had darkened with sadness at the realization that, of all his former property, only a dismal 200 rubles were left. This was only a tenth of the *poritz's* asking price for the forest. This unexpected deal, which had come knocking at his door at just this moment, seemed Heaven sent — a last chance to save himself.

"Come back tomorrow," Isaac requested. "We are not speaking of an insignificant sum, after all. I need a little time to get the money together."

When Raskas was gone, Isaac lifted his eyes to the sky. In the ordinary scheme of things, there had been no purpose to his putting off the agent. He was grasping at straws, but straws were all he had. Only Hashem could help now. His heart overflowed with a plea for Heaven's mercy.

He was still sitting there, lost in thought, when a good friend came to visit. The other man was a prosperous merchant, as Isaac himself had been, and they had embarked on several business deals together.

Isaac turned to him with a proposal. "Invest 1800 rubles with me, toward the purchase of a big forest," he suggested. "We'll be equal partners in the profits. Fifty-fifty."

His friend hesitated a moment, weighing the matter. He was being asked to put up a small fortune as an investment. On the other hand, there was every prospect of huge profits. Isaac was as vigorous as ever, and was not the type to speculate in risky ventures.

The friend nodded his head and shook Isaac's hand on the deal. Then he sent to his home at once for the money.

Isaac drew a deep breath. He now had the 2,000 rubles he needed — 200 of his own, and the rest that his friend had invested. A powerful urge swept over him, to race over to the neighboring town and give the money to the *poritz* before the nobleman regretted his offer. But he was a loyal *chassid* who would not take such a big step without asking his Rebbe's advice. This was his last chance. Should he fail, Heaven forbid, he would be reduced to begging in the streets!

Isaac went to his Rebbe, R' Yaakov, and submitted a *kvittel* asking for a blessing for success in a big business venture. Along with the note he included a donation of a single ruble.

*The Rebbe will doubtless be surprised*, Isaac thought. *He will wonder why his former generous chassid is suddenly so stingy. But, lacking any other choice, I won't be ashamed to give just one ruble!*

The Rebbe read the *kvittel*, then picked up the donation with an expression of dissatisfaction. "This donation is not fitting for such a large enterprise. We are talking about a business deal worth thousands of rubles." He handed the ruble back to Isaac.

Taken aback, Isaac opened his purse and took out a three-ruble coin that he had prepared for his journey to the *poritz*. With all his heart, he hoped the Rebbe would be satisfied.

But the Rebbe was not satisfied. "This is not what I meant," he said firmly. "Show me your purse."

If Isaac was surprised, he showed no sign of it. With an impassive face he placed his purse, with the 2,000 rubles inside, on the table.

The Rebbe took out the bundles of bills. He set aside the larger bundle of 1,800 rubles, and took the small one, containing 200.

Isaac felt as though he was burning up. He could not wait another moment before setting the Rebbe straight. "Rebbe, there is a mistake here!" he cried. "I am no longer Isaac the prosperous merchant, whose money was as plentiful as the sand by the sea, who was the first to donate to every mitzvah and eager to give to anyone in need, even before he was asked! I must reveal my secret. My luck has turned. I am now destitute. Should my fortune not turn around for the better, I will be reduced to begging for handouts. This deal is my last chance. If I succeed, perhaps I will return to what I was before. And if I fail? May Hashem have mercy on me!"

He ended his revelation with hanging head. "And so, though I understand that the Rebbe needs this money for some worthy mitzvah, this time I cannot give a large donation as I used to do. I must satisfy myself with a very small donation, so that I can hand over the entire sum of 2,000 rubles to the *poritz*. 1,800 of them are not even my own."

The emotional outburst seemed to make no impression at all on the Rebbe. "Isaac, don't be so foolish. The *poritz* will give you time to pay him the entire sum. Even if you give him only 1,800 rubles now, you will not lose the deal. Ask him for an extension of time to pay the remaining

200. Explain that if your business succeeds, you will be able to do so in the near future."

Steadfast in his faith in the Rebbe's wisdom, Isaac traveled to the nearby town. The *poritz* was familiar with the lumber merchant's sterling reputation, and knew that he could rely absolutely on Isaac's integrity. He agreed to sell his forest for the 1,800, and to wait a while for the rest.

Isaac's wheel of fortune, which had reached rock bottom, began to inch upward again. He sold the trees at a good price, and even after he divided the profits with his partner he was left with 1,000 rubles in cash. He had witnessed the fulfillment of the words "*mashpil gei'im,* He humbles the haughty"; now he was seeing the next words come true: "*magbiah shefalim,* He raises the downtrodden."

Isaac lifted his eyes in gratitude. "Thank You," he whispered to his Creator. "After You cast me into the pit, You have raised my soul from the grave!"

He traveled at once to the *poritz* and paid his debt of 200 rubles. Then he returned to the Rebbe — this time with a donation of 500 rubles.

R' Yaakov accepted the fat bundle of bills, took out a single ruble, and returned the rest to Isaac.

"Wh-what is this?" Isaac stammered in confusion. "I gave the money with a full heart."

The Rebbe smiled. "I know, my son. But you once wanted to give only one ruble. I am taking it now —" He paused, then continued. "Did you think that your Rebbe had turned money-hungry? That I could not be satisfied with less than 200 rubles, and had sealed my ears to poor Isaac's pleas?

"Know this," the Rebbe said, and now his face glowed. "When you came to me that day, I saw that your fortune was about to sink even lower than you thought. A curse had entered your money, and it had been decreed that you would not prosper. Had you give the *poritz* the 200 rubles, you would not have seen any sign of blessing for the rest of your life!

"That's why I took everything you had. The only cash you actually gave the *poritz* was money that was not your own. That's why you were able to succeed."

The Rebbe added a final word. "Had you entered on this business venture without such a powerful and stubborn *emunas chachamim* (faith in your spiritual leaders), you would not have prospered. Your own faith opened the gates of success to you — much more than anything I did on your behalf. And now, riches will not leave you or your descendants for many, many generations!"

# I Will Speak to Him in a Dream

PESACH WAS AN AVERAGE YOUNG MAN WHO WORKED HARD to support his wife and two children: his firstborn son, Shimi, and his daughter Shaindel, just 8 years old. Hashem had granted him only these two children, but supporting even them was difficult. Pesach would awaken very early each morning, *davening* with the sunrise. Immediately after *Shacharis*, he would not return home but would go directly to the tannery where he worked, in the Polish town of Zigurzh. There, he engaged in backbreaking labor from morning to night, preparing leather hides for use in shoes, clothing, suitcases, and the like.

He would hurry off to work each day with a piece of bread and a bit of vegetable in a lunchbag dangling from one hand; in the other he held the *sefer Chok L'Yisrael*. In his moments of spare time he would look into the *sefer*, eager to feed his hungry soul with a bit of spirituality the way the bread fed his hungry body.

Then, one day, tragedy struck; without warning he suddenly died while at work in the tannery.

The young widow Baila mourned her dear husband, who had left her so abruptly in the prime of his life.

All of Zigurzh grieved with her. They mourned the good friend who had died so suddenly. Several communal activists began collecting money at once for the widow and her children. Even before the funeral, they handed her a large sum. At the time, she was too distracted by her grief to comprehend the extent of the *chesed* her neighbors had done for her. However, after a month or two, having money to provide her children with bread and other necessities proved to be of some comfort to her in her bereavement.

The days slipped quickly away — and with them, her dwindling supply of cash. The harshness of reality left the young widow with no choice: She began to search for work. At first, she moved from job to job. She did not balk at anything. However difficult the work, she did everything in her power to provide for herself and her two children.

Eventually, Baila found a steady job. She worked hard in a local printing house, earning a meager salary in return for long hours of exhausting labor. But hardly had she recovered from the initial, anguished grief over her husband's tragic death, when another blow to felled her.

Her son, Shimi, had been devastated by his father's death. In its wake, he was left without a prop and support — and without a guide. His mother, busy from morning to night with her work, could not adequately supervise the boy. He wandered through the house like a wounded animal, beside himself with pain. Whole months passed in this way, with Shimi neglecting his studies. He drifted through the streets of Zigurzh, getting into trouble. More than once, a neighbor brought the matter to his mother's attention, and she spoke earnestly to the boy about changing his ways. But Shimi continued as before, wasting his life in emptiness.

Baila flexed her tired legs after a hard day on the job. Her fingers were swollen from the difficult work, and her eyes were reddened with exhaustion. Lately, in her anxiety over her son, sleep had been eluding her.

Entering the house, she called out, "Good evening!" in a deliberately cheerful voice, as she did every night. But instead of two children running to greet her, there was only Shaindel. The girl was crying.

"Shaindel, what's the matter?" Baila asked in alarm.

"Shimi never came home today. I was so afraid of being all alone," Shaindel wept.

Without an instant's delay, the tired widow went out in search of her son. Shimi was not in any of his former yeshivah friends' homes. She raked Zigurzh from top to bottom, calling out her son's name in a hoarse voice, to no avail. Finally, near dawn, she returned home, her heart paining her. Shimi was nowhere to be found.

In the following days, she continued to search — in vain. At last, however, she found a few reliable witnesses who claimed to have seen him leaving town, carrying a small bundle in his hand.

Baila raised her eyes heavenward and cried, "Master of the Universe, You have taken my husband. Please, do not take my only son as well. Return him to me!"

Her prayer bore fruit.

Several months after Shimi's disappearance, the mailman brought a letter to Baila's home. As she opened it, a gasp escaped her. She recognized her son's handwriting.

*My dear mother,* Shimi had written, *Please forgive me for running away without saying good-bye. I was afraid that you would keep me from going. Our tiny town was choking me. I have gone to America, where I've found work in a big city called Detroit. I am doing well in my job. To prove it, I'm sending you ten dollars for your expenses. From now on, you won't have to work so hard. I will support you and my sister, Shaindel.*"

Baila counted the green bills over and over, hardly believing her eyes. The next day, she changed a small number of the dollars into Polish currency. To her joy, she found that each dollar bill was worth a small fortune in Polish zlotys.

A month later, she received a second letter from Shimi, along with more dollars. Shimi had stood by his word. He continued to send her

I WILL SPEAK TO HIM IN A DREAM / 105

money faithfully each month. Baila was finally able to straighten her poor aching back and work only half-days. Though she missed her son, he had found a way to lighten her load, and for that she was immensely grateful.

Six months passed in this way. Then, without any explanation, the letters stopped. For Baila, this was a terrible blow. She didn't know which to cry about first: her son's inexplicable, worrisome silence, or the need to go out again and work from dawn to dusk.

At first, she tried to console herself with the reflection that the absence of letters did not necessarily mean bad news. The letters would surely start up again soon. But a month passed, and then another, with no word.

Baila was beside herself with anxiety. A simple woman, she had no idea how to go about ascertaining her son's fate in faraway America. That land might have been a million miles away for what she knew of it. Then a friend offered a piece of sound advice: "Go to the United States Consulate in Warsaw. Ask them to find out what happened to your son."

She made the trip to Warsaw. The American consul jotted down Baila's request and promised to look into the matter with all possible speed. Baila went home and waited. She waited two months: one month was the time it took for letters to travel from Poland to America, and another month for an answer to return from Detroit to Warsaw. Finally, her patience was at an end. She traveled back to Poland's capital city and hurried to the consulate.

The consul was at his desk when she walked in. He saw the hopeful light in the woman's eyes, and wished he had good news to tell her. Sadly, the news was anything but good.

"I'm very sorry," he said quietly. "Your son is dead."

Baila let out a piercing scream. "That's impossible!" she shrieked. "He's so young — not yet 20! Could there be a mistake?"

The consul found it hard to look into Baila's brokenhearted face. The information he had been given was accurate enough. The missing young man, who answered in every detail to the description provided by his mother, had died and been buried in Detroit's Jewish cemetery. There was nothing more to be done.

Meilech (Elimelech) Weiss was Pesach's brother-in-law, and an enthusiastic Alexander *chassid*. Periodically, he would leave his home in Zigurzh to travel to his Rebbe, the Yismach Yisrael of Alexander.

Meilech had been more than a relative of the departed Pesach; they'd been good friends as well. When Pesach had suddenly passed away, Meilich had been plunged into inconsolable grief for a long period. The distraught widow came to him now with an urgent request. She was at the end of her rope. She has lost her husband once, and her son, Shimi, twice!

"Next time you go see your Rebbe, I beg of you to take me along," she pleaded. "I want to ask him for a blessing, and pour out my heart to him."

For his sister-in-law's sake, Meilich made the effort to push up the date of his upcoming visit. It was the least he could do to help mend her broken heart. They were ready to leave just two weeks later.

The journey was an arduous one, along difficult roads, and it lasted several days. At last, they reached the home of the Yismach Yisrael. Meilich instructed his sister-in-law in the proper way to write her *kvittel*, then accompanied her to the *tzaddik's* room.

The Rebbe took the *kvittel* and read it briefly. His reaction was completely unexpected.

A shout rose to the Rebbe's lips. "Lies, lies! Who is the wicked one who has had the audacity to tell such a lie?"

"Wh-what lie?" wondered Meilich.

"Who said that Shimi, your sister-in-law's son, is dead? I see him clearly. He is in America — alive and well! Who has perpetrated such a lie?"

The widow stared at the holy Rebbe with confusion-filled eyes. She could hardly believe what she was hearing.

"Hear what I say," the Rebbe told her, pouring balm on her aching heart. "Your son, Shimi, works hard from morning to night. In the evenings, he goes out carousing with his friends, and so he has forgotten about his widowed mother and young sister. He will soon remember you, and you will receive a sign that I am not lying, Heaven forbid. In one month's time, you will receive a letter from your son — a letter containing a great deal of money."

Baila was thunderstruck. "But — but the American consul in Warsaw said that my son is dead!"

The Rebbe paid no heed to her remark. "Good news is coming," he promised.

Meilich understood that the interview was over. He hurried his sister-in-law out of the room.

The Rebbe's prediction proved correct in every way. A month after their meeting, Baila received a letter from Detroit. In it, Shimi apologized for his long silence. He announced that he was thinking of coming back to Zigurzh for the festival of Pesach, and was sending a much larger sum of money than usual for his mother's holiday expenses.

Overjoyed, Baila hurried to buy everything she would need for the festival. She left her work at the printing establishment and spent her days scrubbing and cleaning the house in honor of the upcoming holiday — and her very important guest.

He arrived a week before Pesach. The meeting of the mother and her long-lost son was an emotional and tear-filled one. For Baila, the sight of Shimi was bittersweet. While she was ecstatic to have him near her again, she was grieved to see that her dear son had shaved his beard and was now wearing modern, American clothing. She suspected his hold on *Yiddishkeit* was tenuous, at best.

Secretly, she concocted a plan together with her brother-in-law. After the holiday, Meilich would take Shimi along on a visit to the Alexander Rebbe. The sight of that holy face, she hoped, would move her son to mend his ways and grow closer to his Creator. It was up to the uncle to see to it that the young man agree to come.

Meilich conducted the matter with great tact. In a casual, non-demanding way, he dropped a word here and there, to pave the way for the stubborn lad to agree to accompany him to Alexander after Pesach.

He did his work well. Shimi agreed to go.

Along with the *kvittel* that he prepared for his meeting with the Rebbe, Shimi included a generous donation. Together, he and his uncle went in to see the Rebbe.

But what happened next was something that neither of them could have foreseen.

No sooner had Shimi set foot over the threshold and glimpsed the Yismach Yisrael's face, than his own went completely white. His body began to tremble all over.

"Do not be afraid," the Rebbe called. "Admit how wicked you were, to be so callously cruel to your poor, widowed mother during her difficult time. Why did you spill her blood? I pulled you back here by the hairs of your head."

Shimi burst into racking sobs. He could not speak. He cried bitterly for a long time, tears that flowed from a deep and genuine remorse.

"If you will undertake to support your mother and sister, I guarantee that you will never lack for money for the rest of your life," the Rebbe promised, adding, "on the condition that you choose a good path and never, Heaven forbid, abandon your *Yiddishkeit*."

"Rebbe!" Shimi finally managed to choke out. "I have brought my mother a large sum of money — enough to support herself and Shaindel for a long time, and to marry my sister off respectably. And I promise to live as a kosher Jew always!"

"In that case," the Rebbe said, "you will surely have a good life." And with a radiant smile, he dismissed the young man.

When they had left Alexander behind, Meilich was unable to contain his curiosity. "Why were you so shocked back there, when you first saw the Rebbe?"

Shimi glanced at his uncle. "Some time ago," he said, "I began to have a recurring dream. It was a very strange dream. In it, an old man would shout at me, asking me why I had abandoned my widowed mother, and telling me that it was a mitzvah to send money to support her right away. He would also urge me to go visit her soon. I have been filled with fear, because I sensed that it was a genuine dream. I sent the letter and the money, and made plans to travel back to Poland.

"When I saw the Rebbe, I recognized him immediately as the man in my dream." Shimi shuddered. "I'd been afraid of him in Detroit — and I am seven times more afraid of him today, after I've seen the way he sits here in Poland and sees exactly what I'm doing in America."

# A Public Outcry

THE DARK WINTER CLOUDS THAT COVERED THE SKY OVER Sokolivka, in the Ukraine, perfectly reflected the mood of the town's Jewish population.

For two months now, not a smile had been seen in Sokolivka. Even the children, with their specially honed instincts, sensed their elders' black mood, and they, too, hardly laughed or played these days. Here and there, a child still too young to sense the atmosphere would toss pebbles into one of the flocks of chickens roaming the lanes, and burst into delighted laughter at the sight of the hens flapping and scolding. At once, his mother would shush him: "Quiet, my child. This is no time for laughter."

The Jews of Vohlin, Podolia, Reisin, and other portions of White Russia were troubled and afraid. The area's farmers had organized themselves under the banner of a former high-ranking Polish army officer by the name of Bogdan Chmielnicki. These men were forming regiments from which to stage an uprising against the Polish government (which, in those days, ruled the Ukraine and many other territories). The farmers were angry and bitter. The accumulated rage of many years had gathered in their hearts, driving them on to war.

Ukraine's landowners were mostly Catholic, unlike the farmers who worked their land, and who belonged to the Pravoslav faith.

110 / TALES FOR THE SOUL

Working conditions were extremely difficult, and salaries were too meager to make ends meet. More than once, a leader among the farmers would go to the landowners and plead, "Please consider our plight. Lighten our load a little, and raise our salaries."

The haughty landowners would stare at the farmer as if he were no more than a piece of livestock. All pleas were met with scorn, or were not answered at all. There were even incidents where the master's servants were dispatched to give the outspoken farmer a sound thrashing.

The farmers, humiliated and oppressed, grew angrier and angrier. Secretly, they began to organize themselves into groups to oppose their masters. But until they had a leader to unite them, all their efforts to rebel were useless.

Bogdan Chmielnicki had been educated in Poland and served as an officer in the Polish army in Poland's war against the Turks. At that time, he was still loyal to Poland and the thought of rising up against the ruling party had never crossed his mind. Later, however, on his return to Russia, he became embroiled in a quarrel with one of the Polish landowners there. Furious, he decided not to confine his revenge to that landowner alone. He turned his personal war into a general one against the entire Polish government.

He was well aware of how the farmers suffered under the landowners' rule, and understood their simmering rage. Chmielnicki harnessed these farmers to his war chariot. Traveling from place to place, he spoke against the landowners; he would ride into town on his mighty horse, heading immediately for the market square, which was always full of people. Standing on a barrel or high wooden platform, he would call out in his thunderous voice and ignite a flame in his listeners' hearts:

"Hear me, my brothers! The wicked Poles have used us. They have taken advantage of us, stolen from us, and sucked our blood. No more! We will rise up against them and throw their yoke off our necks. Rebellion against the Polish government! Revolution!"

The farmers greeted his words with deafening cheers and whistles. Inflamed with the desire for revenge, they surrounded their new leader with terrifying enthusiasm.

Chmielnicki, a fine demagogue, managed to turn the farmers' just outrage to suit his own purposes. He soon had a gigantic army at his back, numbering in the tens of thousands. This formidable force called themselves "Cossacks."

The Polish landowners scoffed at first, believing that the attempted rebellion would come to nothing. Then they began to tremble when they realized that they were hearing the genuine trumpets of war. The national fury that had been building up for years was now a mighty reservoir of military strength — and was nothing to scoff at any longer.

A varied collection of soldiers flocked to Chmielnicki: oppressed farmers, shopkeepers tired of paying heavy taxes, and Pravoslav priests who hated the Polish Catholics. The charismatic leader used his military expertise to build his army, piece by piece. He appointed officers to head each group of soldiers and divided them into troops, platoons, regiments. When he was satisfied that his war machine was ready, he launched his great uprising against the Polish rulers.

His surprise attack was phenomenally successful. Like wheat before a scythe, scores of cities and towns fell to the Cossacks. After only a few days, the city of Kiev fell to the rebels. In the year 1648, Chmielnicki entered Poland at the head of a tremendous force, and immediately conquered the city of Levov (Lemberg). The Polish troops defending the ruling landowners in Russia and the Ukraine were small and ineffective, and they fell like flies before the rampaging Cossacks.

Within a short time, the tide of war was decisively turned in the Cossacks' favor. Jan Kazimir, king of Poland, was fearful of losing all of Poland to Chmielnicki. He quickly agreed to sign a peace treaty in which the Cossacks were granted near-autonomy in their conquered territories.

Had the Cossacks been content with this victory, Jews throughout the area would not have been so downcast and afraid. But the wicked Chmielnicki, like Haman in his day, was an enemy of the Jews. As a youth, he had been educated at a Jesuit institution in Levov, whose priests taught and nurtured a virulent anti-Semitism. His Cossack soldiers likewise hated the Jews — first, because hating the Jews was a natural fact of life, like the sun rising in the east; and secondly, because many of the overseers of the properties on which these farmers had worked were Jews. Chmielnicki fanned the flames of this hatred until they burned high and strong. The Cossacks turned their rage against the Jews even more furiously than against their true oppressors, the Polish landlords.

Like a swarm of locusts, the Cossacks spread over the country, and everywhere they went they left devastation behind. They burned homes, plundered property, and massacred souls. If a Jewish town or village happened to fall into their hands, they were determined to leave no one alive: man, woman, child, young and old fell to their swords. They were all swept away in a river of blood, murdered in terrible cruelty. The Jews lived in mortal fear of Chmielnicki, and called him "Chmiel the Wicked."

The news of the Cossacks' destructive sweep had reached Sokolivka, where we began our story. A few wounded survivors had somehow managed to escape the Cossacks' swords and make their way to the town, filling horrified ears with tales of the Cossacks' large-scale spilling of Jewish blood. A heavy cloud of fear and depression settled over the town. From the start of the uprising until now, two uneventful months had passed in Sokolivka. Despair had the town in its grip. The people felt weak, helpless — virtually paralyzed.

But not all of them. On the night after the news of Chmielnicki's pogroms reached Sokolivka, ten of its residents fled the town. Little did they know that they were leaping from the frying pan straight into the fire. A large troop of Cossacks were camped not far away. The ten men ran directly into their waiting arms. Eight were slaughtered; two managed to escape and retrace their steps to Sokolivka.

"There's no use trying to run," they told their friends. "There is no place to go."

If the people had been afraid before, they were panic stricken now. They walked around as though they had lost their wits, shades of their former selves. Then they locked themselves into their houses, afraid to stick even a toe outside — as though mere wooden walls could protect them from the furious onslaught.

The Cossacks continued to move closer, ready to make an example of Sokolivka's Jews as they had in so many towns before. Dread hung over the city like a gray pall. That night, community leaders met in urgent session, to decide what was to be done.

"Send them a bribe," said the meeting's chairman.

His suggestion met with bitter laughter. "Our money will be theirs in any case, the moment they start killing us," the chief *gabbai* retorted.

"Well, what do *you* suggest?"

"Let us hide until the danger passes," the *gabbai* said feebly.

The town *shochet* was the one to laugh now. "So why haven't you hidden until now? Go ahead, burrow under the haystack in your barn, and hope that the Cossacks are too stupid to think of that. A brilliant plan!"

"And what does the *shochet* suggest?" countered the *gabbai*.

The *shochet* cast his eyes down. "I thought we might escape — just run to a safer place."

"And just where might that safer place be?" asked the *gabbai*, relishing his revenge. "They've surrounded the town and swarmed over the whole land. To where can we run?"

"Then let us climb up to our rooftops and cast ourselves down, to die *al kiddush Hashem* (in the sanctification of G-d's Name)!" cried the elderly *dayan*, trembling violently.

"There is no need for that," protested the town rabbi. "The Cossacks will do that for us — and make a far better job of it, too. I've heard that they don't bother asking anyone whether they wish to convert. They just kill. Better to die at their hands, and not to stand before the Heavenly Court on the charge of taking our own lives."

A shudder seemed to pass through the group. Hopelessness was stamped on every face. There was no solution. They were trapped in a burning house, with no way out. They were lost! In the depths of his fear and despair, the *shochet* lost hold of his wits and had to be led home, babbling incoherently. His family put him to bed at once, and kept his madness a secret to spare him shame.

That night was a wakeful one in the town. No one managed to close his eyes. When sleep overtook a person, he would doze off for a few seconds and then jar himself awake, moving from a bad dream into the worse one of reality.

Early in the morning, the Cossack soldiers circled the town and cut it off on all sides. There was no escaping now. Like lions, they roared: "Death to the Jews!" "Death to the killers of our Messiah!"

Nimble children climbed trees in order to see who was doing the shouting. Hundreds of armed soldiers, swords gleaming, were camped nearby. All that stood between the killers and the town was a narrow stream that would not deter anyone. The Cossacks were in no hurry; no one was about to get away from them. They began to collect firewood and build a number of sturdy blazes on which to cook their breakfast. From time to time, raucous laughter rang out in the still air. A few of the sharper-eyed soldiers, noticing the Jewish children peering at them from the trees, waved their swords threateningly, the shining blades catching the sunlight. The gathering storm cast an even deeper terror on the townsfolk. The Angel of Death was encamped nearby, and there was no one to stop him.

The Cossacks soon finished their meal, clearing their throats menacingly like beasts of prey. Actually, they were far worse than beasts, who hunt for survival and, once sated, leave weaker animals alone. These murderers were going about massacring people without reason or goal, caught up in a madness of bloodletting that knew no satisfaction. The more the streets ran with Jewish blood, the more they longed to kill.

A stranger slipped into town. He was tall, his face shone like the sun, and he wore a leather belt slung around his hips. Wandering through the market square, he found it empty. The shops were all shuttered and even the shul was closed. All the Jews were cowering inside their homes.

"Jews, where are you?" he thundered. "Have you all gone to sleep? Get up and cry out to your Creator. Come to the square and cry out in a mighty voice to Hashem."

The man began to go from house to house, pounding on the doors and shouting his message. As they listened, the despairing Jews began to take new heart. They suddenly remembered their G-d, the Source of all life. In a short time, some 700 Jews had gathered in the market square. Trembling men, women, and children stood facing the stranger. He rebuked them energetically.

"What's the matter; have you forgotten to pray? Have you thought of everything except your Creator? Is it possible for Jews to abandon the faith of their fathers? Our ancestors in Egypt were in no less danger, and what does the verse say about them? 'And *Bnei Yisrael* cried out to their L-rd and their anguish rose up to the L-rd.' King David promised us, in his *Tehillim*, 'They cried out to You and escaped; they trusted in You and were not defeated.' Do you not believe that Hashem can save you? He wants your prayers, and brings upon you the fear of death so that you will fear Him and draw closer to Him!"

Hardly had the words left his mouth than the Jews of Sokolivka began to wail and cry in prayer from the depths of their hearts. Their ancient faith was rekindled in that hour. Like a coal lying among the ashes whose inner fire has not yet been extinguished, all they needed was a puff of air — a reminder — and they burst into flame.

Through the market square rang verses of *Tehillim*, well soaked with tears. There was no man, woman, or child present who was not completely immersed in thoughts of repentance. Their fervor would have melted a heart of stone.

The Cossacks continued to advance. Their force was licking the edges of the town like wildfire, and their warlike cries carried clearly on the air. The Jews prepared to give up their lives for the sanctification of G-d's Name.

And then —

Two speedy messengers, riding on light-footed horses and exhausted from their ride, reached the Cossack commander. They carried bitter news: Another Cossack division, attacking a nearby city, had suddenly been overtaken by the far weaker Polish forces. "If you don't come to our aid, our downfall will be your responsibility, and Chmielnicki will hold you accountable," the messengers cried, in their commander's name.

The Cossack leader rapidly weighed the situation. Here, in town, were helpless Jews, waiting to be murdered whenever he chose. There, on the adjoining battlefield, stood a Cossack division about to go under — unless he rode to their aid at once.

He passed word along to his troops: The decision was made to turn around and leave Sokolivka behind. They would deal with the town at some later date.

Chmielnicki's Cossacks destroyed some 300 Jewish communities in Poland and Russia during the pogroms of 1648-9. Great cities such as Tulchin and Nemirov were razed to the ground. One hundred thousand Jews were massacred by sword or other atrocities. R' Shabsai Sheftil Horowitz eulogized these souls in a haunting poem, comparing the destruction to the ruin of the two Holy Temples. Many other *kinnos* (lamentations) were written over the ensuing generations, commemorating those terrible times.

Sokolivka and some of the other towns who poured out their hearts in public prayer were saved from the destruction. Those Jews saw with their own eyes how Divine Providence, in its mercy, spared them from the enemy's sword.

# A First-Class Ticket

YEKUSIEL PEPPER'S GROCERY STORE WAS FULL OF CUSTOMERS that morning, as always. His was the only such store in the small Hungarian town of Zembar. Though he did not have to worry about competitors, Yekusiel nevertheless tried to do his best for his customers. He ordered the freshest loaves of bread, straight from the bakery, and tasty milk, cheese, and butter from the local dairy. Zembar was primarily a Christian town. The Jewish Pepper family lived alone, in peace, among some 300 Christian families.

Then came the year 5680 (1920). Anti-Semitism began to sprout in Hungary in that year, and several cities and towns had already experienced small pogroms. Little Zembar was far from the center of things, and it seemed as if the wave of anti-Jewish sentiment had skipped over the town without touching it. But that morning, in his grocery, Yekusiel Pepper discovered that anti-Semitism was alive and well in Zembar.

The incident began when Yanush, the local schoolteacher, went over to the eggcrate to choose the best and largest eggs. Suddenly, he straightened up and spat in disgust, "These eggs are rotten. The Jew is trying to poison us all!"

Yekusiel squirmed uncomfortably. Yanush had exaggerated; the eggs were not rotten, though in truth they were not quite fresh. These last weeks, he had not been able to move old stock as quickly as usual, and had hidden a few of the older eggs at the bottom of the pile. Yosuf, the priest, cried from the other end of the store, "The Jew is growing rich at our expense. He is not ashamed to sell us spoiled goods!"

The two had planned these remarks ahead of time, only pretending that they were spontaneous. They created a tense atmosphere in the shop. All at once, other customers discovered that the goods they were inspecting were inferior. The priest repeated his accusation several more times, loudly, and managed to drag several of the more susceptible customers out of the store with him. They stood in the doorway shouting, "Here is Yekusiel, the Jew, who's grown rich at our expense and who sells us spoiled goods!"

Yekusiel Pepper grew pale. Such a thing had never happened to him before. It was true that his shop earned him a nice profit, and true that his customers were almost all Christian. But he had always tried to sell fine, fresh products and had made his money honestly. What was happening today — and why?

He did not understand that the storm of anti-Semitism that had been enveloping Hungary had now descended in all its fury upon the quiet town of Zembar.

If Yekusiel thought that the unpleasant winds would die down by the next day, he was mistaken. On the contrary: The small tempest that had swept through his shop was only a prelude of what was to come. All that day, people walked through the village streets repeating what the priest and the schoolteacher had said. The Jew had grown rich on Christian money, and was trying to poison them all with rotten eggs and moldy cheeses. If no one remembered ever buying a moldy cheese from Yekusiel, that was beside the point. Like a flock of sheep, they followed the leaders. No one dared raise an opposing voice.

The priest and the teacher were not satisfied with merely inciting the townspeople. That was only the beginning. The two were only softening up the town, to prepare it for the unveiling of their true plan. They had decided to finish off the grocer using the old, rusty weapon that had never failed the Christian world: the infamous blood libel.

One day soon afterward, while the townsfolk were busy in their fields and the children were in school, the teacher sent one of his pupils, Gustav, home, claiming that the boy had been disrupting his class. As the child walked innocently home, he was waylaid by a figure in black. Within minutes, the blood libel was set. The boy lay lifeless, and twenty small bottles were filled with his blood. Gustav's anxious parents searched for him everywhere, to no avail.

That night, Gustav's body was placed inside a large wicker basket and set beside Yekusiel's front door. The bottles of blood were hidden in Yekusiel's cellar.

In the morning, as he prepared to leave for his grocery, Yekusiel was alarmed to see police officers striding purposefully toward his house. Their grave faces left no doubt as to their intention. He noticed a crowd gathering in front of his door, their attention fixed on a large clothes hamper standing there. The people were waving their arms in agitation. Curious, Yekusiel began to weigh the option of stepping outside to see what the commotion was all about — but the policemen arrived first.

The priest and the teacher had been diligent that morning. Early as it was, they had already visited the local police station to announce that the boy, Gustav, son of Thaddeus, a quiet, peaceful man, had disappeared the day before — and was now lying dead in the Jewish shopkeeper's front yard.

Panicking, Yekusiel fled through the back door. By the time the policemen broke in through the front door, after prolonged pounding and shouting without receiving an answer, Yekusiel was far away from the scene. The police officers searched the house. When they discovered the bottles of blood in the cellar, they took Yekusiel's wife and children into custody. Terrified, the family was dragged off to the police station and placed under heavy guard.

Yekusiel hid all that day like a frightened rabbit, crouched behind some large boulders in the open fields some distance from the village. Every noise made him startle, and even the swoop of a bird passing overhead made him jump. He wondered what was happening back in the town. Only after nightfall did he leave his hiding place and drag himself back to the village.

Partush, a Christian who was Yekusiel's good friend, had a house at the very edge of town. Yekusiel knew that he was in grave danger — a danger whose source he did not yet understand. He believed that Partush could help him.

"Yekusiel, how did you get here?" Partush exclaimed, drawing him quickly inside. "I'd heard that you were gone. Where did you disappear to?"

Breathless, Yekusiel gasped, "Partush, you have to tell me what happened. Why did policemen come to my house early this morning?"

Partush told him everything. Yekusiel nearly broke down in tears when he heard that his wife and children had been arrested. The police were searching for him assiduously.

"You must not show yourself anywhere," Partush warned. "All the village knows that you murdered Gustav and filled twenty bottles with his blood."

"But that is a bald-faced lie! I'm not the sort to harm a fly. Why would I want to kill a sweet young boy? Gustav used to come to my store every morning. I liked him. He was such a nice-looking child, and had such good manners." His throat closed as he spoke, and his eyes glistened with tears.

Partush laid a hand on his shoulder. "Yekusiel, you don't have to convince me. I know you well, and I believe in your innocence. You can stay here without fear."

For two nights and a day, Yekusiel remained hidden in his friend's home. Fear disturbed his peace during the day and banished sleep at night. On the second morning, Partush approached him, his expression sober.

"Yekusiel, you must leave my house," he said without preamble. "The village is boiling like a teapot. The police are searching for you everywhere. If they find you here — they will kill us both!"

Yekusiel put up no argument. He thanked Partush for giving him temporary refuge in a dark hour, and left the house. His heart hammered within him as his eyes scurried to and fro. No one must see him!

Where was he to go? This was the question he asked himself ceaselessly. He felt like Cain, wandering the world with the bitter knowledge that death awaited him if he were found.

Then he remembered. Not far from the village, in the town of Kerestir, lived the holy R' Yeshayala Steiner, the Rebbe of Kerestir. The Rebbe enjoyed a reputation for bringing about wonders and succoring countless Jews in their times of trouble. All that day, Yekusiel concealed himself behind the boulders, biding his time until darkness fell. When the sky grew black, he slipped out and made his way to Kerestir through fields and orchards. He was very careful not to go near the high road. It was midnight by the time Yekusiel reached the Rebbe's house, shivering and exhausted.

He entered the Rebbe's room crying in great agitation, "Help me!" Presently, when he had calmed down a bit, he told the Rebbe about his predicament.

R' Yeshayala gazed at him and asked, "When did you last eat?"

Yekusiel could not remember when, but he suddenly felt a tremendous hunger. R' Yeshayala said quietly, "Eat first, and then we will talk."

This was R' Yeshayala of Kerestir's way. His first concern was his fellow Jews' physical well-being. He would say, "There are rebbes who speak of Torah matters that are wrapped in secrecy. There are those who delve even deeper, speaking of the most hidden secrets of all. But

I, Yeshayala, say, 'Eat, and do not be hungry.' " The Rebbe would not say another word until Yekusiel had eaten and drunk his fill.

"Listen," the Rebbe said then, "at this moment, I have no advice to offer you. But you are not in a hurry to go anywhere. Stay here for a few days. Rest a little, and perhaps Hashem will grant me a good idea for you."

For four days, Yekusiel stayed in Kerestir. He was restless and nervous. Every carriage that entered the Rebbe's courtyard made him jump. He was certain that the police were hot on his trail. More than once, Yekusiel entered the Rebbe's room at the end of his patience, and begged the Rebbe to spare him his suffering. But, each time, the Rebbe put him off. "Not yet, Yekusiel. Not yet."

Then, one night, the Rebbe sent his *gabbai* urgently for Yekusiel.

"Go home at once, in peace and health," R' Yeshayala said. "Hashem will help you and preserve you from all harm."

Yekusiel was dumbfounded. He tried to ask a question, but the Rebbe interrupted with a command. "Take the express train, which passes through here in half an hour. Make sure you buy yourself a first-class ticket."

Yekusiel burst into tears. "Rebbe, it makes no difference where I sit. My fate is clear to me. I shall be taken out and executed in the end. I am crying for my family. I do not wish them to come to harm."

"What do you intend to do when you return to Zembar?" asked the Rebbe.

"To walk up to the police station and give myself up," Yekusiel sobbed. "I am tired of living like a hunted animal. I want to end this!"

The Rebbe hid a smile in his white beard. "*Nu, nu,* when you return to Zembar you will surely go to the police station." He extended a hand to speed Yekusiel on his way. Suddenly, Yekusiel remembered something. "But, Rebbe, the express train doesn't stop in Zembar. My village is too small."

"Go in peace!" the Rebbe said vigorously. "The train will stop in Zembar. Do not delay any longer, or you'll miss your train!"

Yekusiel ran swiftly, but his heart was still heavy with worry. It was only his faith in his spiritual mentor that propped him up in that black hour.

He went to the train station. Purchasing a first-class ticket, he told the clerk that he wished to leave the train at Zembar. To his astonishment, the clerk did not correct his mistake. Yekusiel stepped aboard the train onto a first-class compartment and seated himself on a broad, comfortable seat. It came as no surprise to him that the compartment held just one other passenger. With the price of tickets so steep, who would waste his money on first-class travel?

The other traveler was dressed in expensive clothing and looked like an important person. But this did not interest Yekusiel very much. His troubles preoccupied him to the exclusion of all else. He hung his head and brooded darkly over his plight.

The train barreled along at a rapid clip, the scenery slipping past like the blink of an eye. Yekusiel thought of the hanging tree that awaited him at the journey's end, and pictured his family bitterly mourning his death. A sudden, irrepressible sob rose up in him. As the train sped through the night, Yekusiel wept long and hard, not caring who heard him. In fact, he had completely forgotten that he was not alone in the compartment.

The well-dressed passenger looked at him curiously. "Why are you crying?" he asked with compassion.

"And how shall I not cry?" countered Yekusiel, through his tears. "Wouldn't you cry if you knew that each minute of this journey was bringing you closer to certain death?"

"What are you talking about?" the man asked in astonishment. "Can you explain yourself, sir?"

Yekusiel was only too glad to explain everything. He began with the morning when the priest and the schoolteacher had suddenly turned on him, and ended with the blood libel in which he now found himself starring.

At that moment, the train shuddered to a halt. Someone cried out, "Zembar!"

Yekusiel stood up to leave the train — and was surprised to see his fellow passenger do the same. The man's clothes were of the expensive kind that belonged only to high officers and government officials. All at once, Yekusiel understood that the train had made this unusual stop at Zembar not out of deference to him, but to the other man.

A FIRST-CLASS TICKET / 123

On the walk from the station into town, the two struck up a conversation. The man begged Yekusiel to tell him the whole truth. He revealed that he was here on the very same matter. He had been sent over from the high court in the city of Pest to look into the matter of the murdered boy, Gustav.

Yekusiel stood firm. "Every word I've told you is the honest truth. This is a despicable blood libel, plain and simple. I have never harmed another person, and I certainly would not have hurt that poor boy in any way."

The emotional outburst left its mark. It was obvious that Yekusiel spoke the truth. The high court official was silent for a time, and then continued walking. He broke the silence at last with a string of questions. "Where will you sleep tonight? And what do you intend to do tomorrow? You are, after all, a wanted man."

In all innocence, Yekusiel replied, "I am going directly to the police station to give myself up. That's one answer to two of your questions."

The official considered this. He shook his head. "No!" he said emphatically. "Don't go to the police now. Find some lodgings for the remainder of the night, and present yourself at the police station only at noon tomorrow. In the meantime, I will try to clarify matters. If I learn that you had no part in the murder, I will make certain that the truth is brought to light."

Yekusiel could hardly believe what he was hearing. Fervently, he pressed his companion's hand and thanked him for his trust. But the official was not yet finished. He added, "Tell me, please, where can I find a place to rest tonight?"

"Go straight on until you reach the 'Deer's Horn.' They serve good beer there, and they'll also give you a decent bed for the night."

They parted ways. Yekusiel found refuge at the edge of town, in Partush's house. To his relief, Partush was willing to let him in.

The man from Pest continued on to the inn.

The 'Deer's Horn' was filled with merrymakers. Men were drinking and dancing with raucous abandon. The official from Pest sat down and watched the revelers with a thoughtful eye. He opened his leather briefcase and took out a small notebook. The impression he gave was that of a traveling salesman — which was exactly the impression he wished to make.

Slowly, he inched closer to the drinking men, sighing as though all the world's cares rested on his own weary shoulders. Turning to a boisterously laughing pair, he groaned, "What are you two laughing about? I wish I could be as happy as you."

They paused to stare at him. "Why can't you be as happy as us?" one of them asked.

"I'm over my head in troubles," he said, banging his fist down on his accounts book. "And what are *you* so happy about, if I may ask?"

"We're about to get rid of Yekusiel, the Jewish grocer who's grown rich at our expense," they crowed. "In just a few days they're going to hang him from a tree, and his money will be divided among all the villagers."

The "salesman" sighed. "That's exactly why I can't be happy. In my own village, too, there's a thieving Jewish tavern-keeper who has grown fat and rich at the expense of good, honest Christians. But we can't get rid of him."

"Oh, no? Just do what we did," the two said gleefully. "Then you, too, will be able to dance the night away."

Without further ado, they dragged the investigator out of his chair and into the circle of dancers. As soon as he could extricate himself, the official resumed his seat.

"No, I can't dance with you," he sighed. "You are smart fellows. You knew how to fix that Jew of yours. As for me, I don't have a clue about what to do with mine." He groaned again, seemingly from the depths of his soul. His eyes were pleading. "Give me a good idea. I also want to see 'my' Jew hanging from a tree!"

The two men vaguely sensed a trap, but the alcohol they had consumed had addled their wits and loosened their tongues. In a hoarse whisper, they told the man from Pest about the blood libel they had staged against Yekusiel Pepper. The investigator listened attentively, allowing them to prattle on unhindered. Their confidences were punctuated by frequent drunken hiccoughs.

When they'd finished their tale, the party began to break up. The two men and their cronies left the tavern to stagger for home. Above, the sky was fading and the stars were growing pale. Each of the carousers eventually found his way to his own bed, where he collapsed, completely drunk.

Only the investigator from Pest stayed behind. He sat at the tavern table and wrote assiduously in his notebook for a long time after the others had gone.

In the morning, the investigator made his way to the local police station. He introduced himself to the police inspector with his full name and title, and asked for assistance. The inspector promised his help in every way. While most of the village still lay lost in slumber, a contingent of police officers fanned out to visit several homes. They returned a short time later, dragging the priest, Yosuf, and the teacher, Yanush, handcuffed behind them.

The two were not alone. Another two men had been arrested as well: the two who had babbled to the investigator at the inn the night before.

Yekusiel knew nothing of these developments. He passed what was left of the night in Partush's house, then *davened Shacharis* with deep fervor. Partush, hearing the commotion at the police station, went out to see what had occurred.

It wasn't long before he was rushing home again. He pounding jubilantly on Yekusiel's shoulder as the Jew was winding up his *tefillin*. "Yekusiel, you prayed well! I believed in your innocence from the first. But now, everyone will see justice done!"

"What do you mean?" asked the bewildered Jew.

"The priest and the schoolteacher have confessed that they were the ones who killed poor Gustav, then poured his blood into little bottles in order to frame you and get rid of you once and for all. They had no intention of confessing, but two witnesses testified against them — witnesses whose names were written down in a notebook belonging to the investigator from Pest. And what's most amazing of all, the two witnesses themselves have no idea how the investigator managed to find out what they knew. They themselves have no memory of ever talking to him."

"The investigator from Pest?" Yekusiel shouted eagerly. "Where did he find those witnesses?"

"I've heard that he sat in the tavern at the 'Deer's Horn' last night and struck up a conversation with those two. The fools thought that he was some sort of traveling salesman, and spilled the whole story. The police are looking for you everywhere — in order to tell you that you're a free man. Your wife and children have been released!"

"The investigator!" Yekusiel cried again. "And I sent him to the 'Deer's Horn' without even thinking." He shook his head in wonder. "How wonderful are a *tzaddik's* ways. The Rebbe sent me on an express train in the middle of the night — in a first-class compartment, no less — and look at the outcome!"

He burst into joyous laughter. "Now I understand why the Rebbe smiled at me as he said that I would surely present myself at the police station. The holy ones see everything. Everything!"

# Rashi's Learning Partner

IT WAS SUMMER'S END OF THE YEAR 5723 (1963). THE SUN'S rays beat down mercilessly, keeping most people indoors. Those who did have to go outside tried to hurry to attend to their tasks and quickly return home to avoid the worst of the heat.

The *beis midrash* in the yeshivah was also very hot. Air-conditioning was non-existent in those days. The boys dripped with perspiration as they pored over their *Gemaras*. But they were preoccupied with a matter far more serious than the heat. Rosh Hashanah, the New Year, was fast approaching. In just a few days, everyone would be trembling before the Throne of Judgment.

The students at Yeshivas Shevet-Sofer (Pressburg) in Jerusalem's Givat Shaul neighborhood were earnestly preparing for the great day. Their trepidation and awe were almost tangible. Each student learned with redoubled diligence, each tried to minimize idle talk, each strove to improve his *middos* — in short, each did his best to ready himself for his audience with the King of kings. In addition, the yeshivah students were preparing for a general test on the first *perek* of *Maseches Kiddushin*, scheduled to take place on Thursday, the 23rd of Elul.

The yeshivah administration decided that it would be a good idea for the students and faculty to travel to Meiron on Tuesday, to pray at the grave of the *Tanna* R' Shimon bar Yochai and to mark the *yahrzeit* of his son, R' Elazar, which would fall out a few days later on the Shabbos of *Parashas Nitzavim-Vayelech*, the 25th of Elul.

The students set out from Jerusalem early Tuesday morning, accompanied by the yeshivah's faculty: the *Rosh Yeshivah*, R' Zalman Weber; the *mashgiach*, R' Yehoshua Frankel; and the *maggidei shiurim*. This was no pleasant ride on a comfortable, air-conditioned bus. The Pressburg Yeshivah students and their *rebbei'im* sat crowded

128 / TALES FOR THE SOUL

together for several hours in an open truck called a lorry. The *Rosh Yeshivah* and *mashgiach* sat up front beside the driver, while the rest filled the space behind.

One of the *rebbei'im* was R' Shmuel Baruch Alizarov, author of *Devar Shmuel*, a commentary on *Maseches Pesachim* that has become universally accepted in the yeshivah world. A youth from the Givat Shaul neighborhood — a Vizhnitzer *chassid* by the name of Avraham Wasserman — had asked permission to join the group and take advantage of this extraordinary opportunity to travel to Meiron. (In those days, it certainly was a rare opportunity, as every trip was a journey of considerable undertaking).

There was a tarpaulin stretched over the top of the lorry to protect the travelers' heads from the relentless sun, but the heat penetrated their quarters along with clouds of dust. The truck moved slowly, making a great deal of noise, and the seats were small and cramped.

Despite the discomfort, the atmosphere in the lorry was positive. The yeshivah boys were not spoiled; they knew how to be satisfied with what they had. With solemn demeanor they kept their eyes fixed on the pages of the *sefarim* they had brought along: small *Gemaras*, *Chumashim*, *Mishnayos*, works of *mussar*, and *sifrei Tehillim*. It was afternoon when they arrived at Peki'in. There they recited several chapters of *Tehillim* and then continued on directly to Meiron. They reached Meiron with the sun's setting rays. Reverently, they entered the cave that held R' Shimon bar Yochai's tomb.

The yeshivah *davened Ma'ariv* and ate a simple meal. Then they spent the rest of the night in a Yom Kippurlike manner. Led by R' Zalman Weber, the group recited the entire *sefer Tehillim*. The *Rosh Yeshivah's* strong voice filled the cave as he slowly recited each verse aloud, word by word. The group was enveloped by a spirit of purity and holiness. When they finished *sefer Tehillim* late that night, they lay down to catch a bit of sleep. They awoke before dawn, immersed themselves in the nearby *mikveh*, and *davened Shacharis*. Some of the boys urged the driver, Chaim Berashi, to immerse in the *mikveh* as well, and he finally consented.

From Meiron, they prepared to descend to Tiberias.

The atmosphere in the lorry was exalted. The boys sang the first line of the *Shir Shel Yom*: "*Keil nekamos Hashem, Keil nekamos hofia*" ("Hashem is the G-d of vengeance; the G-d of vengeance has appeared"), and went on, without knowing why, to sing, "*Al tira mipachad pisom*" ("Do not fear a sudden danger"). One student, Yitzchak Nachum Neustadt, looked out at the swiftly passing scenery. It was passing *too* swiftly. "The driver is going too fast," he said fearfully, as the truck approached a curve in the mountain road.

Then it happened.

The lorry slipped sideways, lurching toward the edge of the road. The driver lost control of the overloaded vehicle. Before he could stabilize the truck, it overturned and fell heavily down the mountain slope. The truck rolled over a few times, to the horrifying sound of crunching metal, before finally coming to a stop.

Those boys who had not been seriously injured began to crawl, white faced and trembling, from under the overturned lorry. Deeply shaken, each checked himself to see if anything had been broken. As the minutes passed, the proportions of the catastrophe became clearer.

Several of the boys had been badly injured, some had received moderate injuries, and there were those with only light wounds. There were broken arms and legs, deep cuts and bruises, broken teeth.

But all this was insignificant compared to the real tragedy of that day. Four lives were lost in the accident. The driver, Chaim Berashi, had been thrown from the truck's cab and crushed beneath its heavy wheels. The other three casualties were yeshivah students.

Two of the boys died on the spot. The third, Yitzchak Nachum Neustadt, managed to crawl clear of the lorry's wheels, as though nothing had happened. He stood up and took a few steps, his face gray as he spat out some blood.

"Are you all right?" his friends asked, running over.

"I feel fine. Take care of the others who were hurt worse than me," Yitzchak Nachum said weakly.

He climbed to a higher elevation along with his friends, then suddenly sat down on a large rock at the roadside. His friends came closer to see what was wrong — and were frozen in shock. The youth had expired as he sat on the rock. A massive cerebral hemorrhage had taken his young life.

*✶*

A wave of hysteria swept over the boys, especially after they learned that the *Rosh Yeshivah*, R' Zalman Weber, had been seriously injured. He managed to ask that his *yarmulka* be placed on his head, and then he lapsed into unconsciousness, remaining so for several days. (During this period, he was often murmuring. Listening closely, those present were able to hear snatches of what he was saying. The *Rosh Yeshivah* was testing the students in the first *perek* of *Maseches Kiddushin*.)

All three of those who had been sitting up front in the lorry had been injured. Apart from the driver, who was killed, and the *Rosh Yeshivah*, seated in the middle, who was unconscious, the right-hand passenger, the *mashgiach*, R' Yehoshua Heschel Frankel, was also hurt. The truck's battery had broken free and crushed R' Yehoshua's ribs. (This, however, was the smaller of his troubles. A large quantity of gasoline from the engine had poured over his feet, burning through his socks and into his skin. For many long months afterwards, the *mashgiach* suffered agonizing pains.)

The hour revealed the *maggid shiur*, R' Shmuel Baruch Alizarov, in all his greatness. Until that day, the boys had recognized him as a great *talmid chacham*, but he had always behaved with quiet humility. Now they saw another side of his personality. As the students stumbled around, confused and frightened, R' Alizarov took up the mantle of leadership. He supervised the evacuation and treatment of the injured with almost superhuman ability.

The first thing he did was visually scan the area. At once, he spotted an injured boy in imminent danger. It was their guest, the *chassid* Avraham Wasserman, who had received a powerful blow to the head and whose face was masked in blood. Without wasting a moment, R' Alizarov took off his shirt, tore it into long strips, and bound up the injured youth's head. In this way, he stopped the flow of blood from the head and saved the youth's life.

Afterwards, R' Alizarov raced down to the Mesivta D'Rabbeinu Yochanan in Tiberias to summon help. He personally supervised the transfer of all the wounded to the Poriah Hospital, and did not rest until everyone had been attended to.

The funeral took place on Thursday, the 23rd of Elul, attended by an enormous crowd. An hour before it was slated to begin, R' Shmulevitz, *Rosh Yeshivah* of the Mirrer Yeshivah, entered the Pressburg Yeshivah. For a long time he stood weeping uncontrollably. When someone asked him whether he had known the boys who had died, he replied, "No, I didn't. But when I heard that three outstanding yeshivah boys had been killed, I felt as though I'd lost three of my own students. The Torah world has lost three good boys. What difference does it make which yeshivah they learned in?"

All of Eretz Yisrael was shaken by the tragedy. Traffic accidents were not as common in those times as they are today, and the incident was horrifying. The three boys who had lost their lives had been among the yeshivah's finest: Mordechai Falk, Yitzchak Nachum Neustadt, and Avraham Binyamin Friedman, may their memories be a blessing.

Mordechai Falk, apart from being an outstanding *masmid* and an original thinker, was also extremely pious in his behavior. He excelled in all three of the pillars that uphold the world: in Torah, in *tefillah*, and in acts of *chesed*. A modest boy, only a few of his friends knew of his custom to write in a small notebook every day, filling the pages with the day's activities. At night, before going to bed, he would read over the pages and inspect everything he had done that day, to see if he had sinned, Heaven forbid, either knowingly or unknowingly, and to see whether there was a need for him to rectify any error, small or large. This was something that had been practiced by great men in previous generations, and Mordechai sought to reach their lofty levels. His tragic death cast all of his acquaintances into deep mourning.

Later, it came to light that Mordechai's father, R' Sholom Falk, a fine man who taught in a Talmud Torah in Petach Tikvah, had received a Divine hint about his son's death. He was standing in his classroom that day, teaching his students, when his watch suddenly

132 / TALES FOR THE SOUL

stopped working. The hands remained frozen at the exact moment that his son was killed in the accident!

Mordechai Falk had a good friend, Ze'ev HaLevi P., who for various reasons had not joined the rest of the yeshivah on the trip to Meiron. The terrible news about the accident reached him as he sat in the yeshivah's *beis midrash,* and he was heart broken. Three of his friends had taken a trip to pray at the graves of *tzaddikim,* to elevate themselves and prepare for the Day of Judgment. And all three would never come back.

He was most pained by the death of his close friend, Mordechai Falk. While he believed fervently that Hashem is just in all His ways, he could not help asking himself the troubling question: Why? Why had this harsh fate been decreed on three wonderful yeshivah students who had devoted their lives to Torah?

One night, several weeks later, Ze'ev had a dream. In the dream, he saw his friend, Mordechai Falk. Mordechai's face was glowing.

"Mordechai, my friend!" Ze'ev exclaimed. "What happened to you?"

"Ze'ev, I've seen your great pain, and I've come to encourage you." Mordechai radiated joy. "Don't be sad over what happened to us. It only appears to be a tragedy — that's in the physical world. Here, everything looks very different. I am very happy.

"You should know this," Mordechai continued. "As soon as I came up here they let me enter *Gan Eden,* and they opened up the hall of the holy *Tanna,* R' Shimon bar Yochai. I immediately joined his *mesivta,* because we had merited to sacrifice our lives for the benefit of *Am Yisrael* on a trip that was wholly devoted to praying at his holy gravesite.

"Do you remember my regular custom of learning the *parashas hashavua* on *erev Shabbos* each week, *shnayim mikra v'echad targum,* with Rashi? Do you know what my reward was for that? I have merited learning together with the holy Rashi himself, and I cling close to his presence. Isn't that wonderful? Why cry over my fate?"

RASHI'S LEARNING PARTNER / 133

At these revelations, Zevie's hair stood on end. Still, he did not lose his composure. He asked his departed friend:

"I have two questions for you. First, how did you come to enter *Gan Eden* without first undergoing judgment in the Heavenly Court? And, second, why did you and the others have to experience such a strange and difficult death at such a young age?"

Mordechai answered, "A year ago, on Rosh Hashanah of 5723 (1963), a very harsh and bitter decree was issued on the entire Jewish *yishuv* in Eretz Yisrael. A terrible tragedy was to befall the community, because of their sins. But Hashem in His Mercy had pity on His nation, and instead chose a public sacrifice to atone for the masses — four pure souls, including three yeshivah students from the holy city of Jerusalem. We, the four who died, were sacrificed on behalf of you all. There was a different accounting for the three of us, and for the lorry driver who was also killed.

"Now you can understand why more people were not killed in the terrible accident. The police officer who visited the scene was astounded. 'Who saved you? Only four casualties from a smashup like this?' Yes, only four. Only four sacrifices were decreed — no more!

"And not only that. Those who were seriously hurt in the accident also received their injuries according to a precise accounting. Every scratch, every scrape, every broken tooth was taken into account. For each, there was a specific reason. All was calculated by Heaven in accordance with His judgment.

"Now you will understand why we did not undergo judgment. A *korban olah* rises directly to *Gan Eden* and does not have to stand in judgment before the Heavenly Court."

The image of the departed youth suddenly vanished.

Ze'ev awoke trembling, his mind in turmoil. But it had all been a dream.

For the next few days, he walked around in a trance, oblivious to his surroundings. His spirit was troubled and his peace of mind gone. All day long he saw his friend Mordechai Falk's happy face before him. He could not forget the dream for a moment. For days on end, he reviewed everything that his friend had told him. Had it been a true dream, or merely his own heart's reflections carried back to him? How could he find out?

He decided to act. He would appeal to the Master of Dreams Himself to grant him the answer. But in order to do this, he must be on the proper level. To be worthy, he must sanctify himself.

Ze'ev began to practice all kinds of purifying tactics. He immersed himself in the *mikveh*, then fasted and prayed all day long, begging Hashem to enlighten him, to send his friend to tell him whether or not the prior dream had been real or just a product of his own imagination.

But Mordechai did not come, neither on the night following Ze'ev's fasting and praying, nor on the following nights.

After a long period of time elapsed, Ze'ev nearly despaired. He stopped thinking about the dream as much. But he kept on working to perfect his holiness and purity.

Eighteen months later, his friend suddenly appeared again in Ze'ev's dream. Mordechai said, "Heaven has been watching you and following your progress. Now you are worthy of receiving an answer to your question. That is why I have been sent to you.

"You are not certain whether or not your previous dream was a true dream, or just the product of your imagination. Of course it was a true dream! And, in order to remove any doubt from your heart, I will give you two signs.

"The first sign: Seven weeks from today, you will become engaged to your future wife, in a good and fortunate hour. Your bride's name is Devorah *bas* Shimon.

"The second sign: Three weeks after that, your *kallah's* uncle will suddenly show up — the uncle of whom all trace was lost in Europe during the Holocaust, and who has long ago been given up for dead."

When Ze'ev awoke in the morning, he immediately remembered the amazing dream of the previous night. Fresh doubts stole into his heart. Had *this* dream been real, or was it, too, mere wishful thinking?

He wrote down all the dream's particulars in his notebook.

A few days later, a *shidduch* was suggested to him. The proposed match was with a fine girl who had recently moved to Eretz Yisrael from Argentina. Her name: Devora *bas* Shimon.

The *shidduch* made slow progress. It was exactly seven weeks from the night of Ze'ev's dream that he celebrated his engagement to Devorah *bas* Shimon!

He had not forgotten the second sign.

"Do you have a brother who was lost during the Holocaust?" he asked his *kallah's* father after the engagement party.

"Yes. How did you know?" the father asked in surprise. "My dear brother was sent to a labor camp, where he disappeared. We have no knowledge of what happened to him. Apparently, he was one of the holy six million who were lost."

"He is alive. You will see him soon," Ze'ev said with a smile.

His future father-in-law gave him a strange look. His daughter, he thought, was betrothed to an odd young man — or a very imaginative one.

Three weeks later, to the day, an express telegram sent by Ze'ev's future father-in-law reached the yeshivah. It stated: *You were right! You were right! My brother has suddenly arrived. He lived through the war and fled to Russia, where he was sent to the labor camps. Miraculously, he has just been freed, and he came to Eretz Yisrael at once to find us.*

Then Ze'ev knew with absolute certainty: His dreams has been true ones, and in fact each of the four who had died was a public sacrifice — an *olah temimah*.

And he knew, too, that whoever makes the effort to learn the Torah portion each week, *shnayim mikra v'echad targum* with Rashi, will find his reward.

[Special thanks to R' Tzvi Wertheimer, a student of the Pressburg Yeshivah at the time of the incident, who supplied me with many of the details in this story.]

# The Keeper of Promises

IT WAS NIGHTTIME IN THE GREAT *BEIS MIDRASH.*

The *beis midrash* of Chevron Yeshivah, in the Geulah section of Jerusalem, looked different tonight. It was usually filled with hundreds of young men absorbed in Torah study: gesticulating with their hands, walking around in pairs, arguing, debating, holding heated discussions. "Night *seder*" at Chevron was a byword in the yeshivah world.

Not tonight.

People passing along Rechov Chagai stared in surprise at the yeshivah building, which was almost completely dark tonight. Only at the far left-end of the *beis midrash* did a few lights show. Listening, they could hear only a trickle of voices coming from the *beis midrash*: the learning of just three students.

*Is this possible?* they asked themselves. *Was this the Chevron Yeshivah that always bustled with life until late into the night, where the sounds of nighttime learning merged sweetly with the Torah of the early risers?*

What those passers-by did not know was what had occurred just hours earlier. A fleet of buses had parked in front of the yeshivah, and hundreds of Chevron boys had climbed aboard to attend the wedding, in another city, of one of the yeshivah's outstanding students. Only three boys were left behind in the yeshivah, so that the light of Torah should not be extinguished for even one night.

The three understood the weight of the responsibility that had been laid on their shoulders. As their friends danced before the *chasan* and *kallah*, these three drank the wine of Torah. They delved into their learning, delighting in each new kernel of understanding, each fresh and original thought.

The shrill ringing of a telephone shattered the quiet of the night.

The phones back then — some fifty years ago — were large, clumsy affairs, very different from our sleek modern ones with adjustable volume. The volume of the ring could not be controlled; it was made by a thin clapper placed between two metal caps, creating a clatter that could not be ignored.

The tranquility of the *beis midrash* had been pierced abruptly by the shrilling of the phone, but at first the students let it ring on and on, simply because the phone was located inside the locked yeshivah office. Apart from that, it was not their job to answer phones. They continued learning. Eventually, after dozens of rings, the racket subsided.

It started up again almost at once.

When the third round of ringing began, the boys realized that something had happened. The loud, persistent ringing sounded like an alarm. They debated what to do about it. Clearly, they must try to answer the phone. But how could they enter the locked office?

One of the students jumped up in excitement. "Wait a minute. Why are we hearing such loud ringing? The window must be open! I'll climb inside and pick up the phone."

He quickly jumped onto a chair and climbed nimbly through the window into the dark office. Heart pounding, he raced over to the blaring telephone and lifted the receiver.

"Is this the Chevron Yeshivah?" a woman's voice asked.

"Yes."

The caller breathed a sigh of relief. "We're calling from Sha'arei Tzedek Hospital. We are sorry to have to inform you that Mrs. Minna died here a short time ago. Arrangements must be made at once for the funeral."

Mrs. Minna was the yeshivah's cook. A childless widow, she hadn't any family left in the world, apart from some relatives by the name of Borowski who lived in the city of Chevron. She had poured all her soul into the food she cooked for the yeshivah boys, hoping and praying that it would please them and give them the strength to study diligently. In return, the boys showed her great appreciation and respect. Many of them felt as if they were her own sons.

From time to time, as she chopped and stirred in the yeshivah kitchen, Mrs. Minna would wipe her tearing eyes (whether the tears came from the onions she was chopping or her grief over her childlessness, no one ever knew) and tell the boys, "The *Rosh Yeshivah*, the *gaon* R'

138 / TALES FOR THE SOUL

Yechezkel Sarna, *shlita,* promised me something several times. When my day comes, he said, I will merit something that not many people merit."

"What will that be?" the boys asked curiously.

The cook would then lower her voice and answer emotionally, "He told me: 'Hundreds of *bnei Torah,* the students of Chevron Yeshivah, will follow you to your final resting place.' You have no idea how the *Rosh Yeshivah's* promise has comforted me! I know that my life has been harsh and bitter, but I comfort myself with the knowledge that hundreds of *talmidei chachamim* will pay me their last respects."

In his wisdom, R' Yechezkel Sarna had hit on the path to the widow's heart, and had thereby strengthened her downtrodden spirit. Though she had no one in the world to mourn her passing, when her time came she would merit a funeral "like a *Rosh Yeshivah's*"!

But now — everything was ruined. The cook had chosen to die on one of the extremely rare nights when the entire yeshivah was out of town!

"What terrible luck," the three students whispered to one other in distress. It was 9 o'clock. It would be at least three hours, maybe four, before the rest of the yeshivah returned from the wedding. Bodies are not left overnight in Jerusalem; it was impossible to postpone the funeral. Instead of a huge funeral, there would be a paltry procession, consisting of the *Chevrah Kadisha* and three Chevron Yeshivah students.

One of the boys cried, "We can't let this happen! The *Rosh Yeshivah* promised her. That promise meant everything to the cook. Let's go to the *rav* at once and ask his advice."

"Which *rav*? What are you talking about?" his friends asked in surprise.

The student was already halfway out the door. "Come with me!"

The chief rabbi of Jerusalem, the *gaon* R' Tzvi Pesach Frank, lived close to the Chevron Yeshivah. Within minutes, the three boys were standing in the rabbi's room, waiting respectfully for him to notice them.

THE KEEPER OF PROMISES / 139

The chief rabbi sat near his desk, black glasses slightly askew as he peered into the pages of the *Gemara* spread before him. His lips chanted a silent tune as he learned. A long time passed without his being aware that he had visitors. At last, they began to cough and shuffle their feet. Time was of the essence.

R' Frank lifted his head at once. "Please, what is your question?"

One of the three took the role of spokesperson. He related what had happened, and concluded, "We've come to ask if there is a way that the funeral can be postponed until tomorrow, so that we can fulfill the *Rosh Yeshivah's* promise and do a *chesed shel emes* for the childless cook by accompanying her to her resting place with honor. Or must we have the funeral at once, tonight?"

R' Frank shook his head vigorously from side to side. "No, *chas v'chalilah!* You must see to it that the funeral takes place at once, and as speedily as possible," he ordered them. "A promise is a big thing, but if the cook's *mazal* was to die on the particular night when the yeshivah boys are all away, there is no permissible way to delay the funeral. If you knew how much pain it causes a person's *neshamah* until the body is buried, you would make all haste and not entertain the idea of postponing the funeral for even a minute!

"Here in Yerushalayim," the rabbi added, "we have a saying: 'Better for a body to rest under the ground for a thousand years than to wait even one hour above ground without burial!'"

The three boys left the rabbi's house with clear instructions: "Have a funeral with a small *minyan* — tonight!"

"We'll have to make the arrangements quickly," one of the boys said. "We have to go to the *Chevrah Kadisha* to organize a gravesite, and take care of the body's *taharah* and the *levayah*. Let's run over to the hospital right away!"

"And what about the yeshivah?" inquired his friend. "The lights are burning, the *beis midrash* doors are wide open, and there's not a soul inside. We have to at least close up first."

"You're right," the other two agreed.

They returned to the yeshivah to douse the lights and lock the doors. But as they entered the building, they once again heard the shrill ringing of the phone.

140 / TALES FOR THE SOUL

The boys' eyes met in a mute question: *What had happened now?*

It was quick work to climb the chair a second time and slide down through the window into the office to answer the phone.

The cook's last days had been filled with suffering. As her illness rapidly weakened her body, her life was ebbing away like a candle. Using strength she hardly had, she scribbled a phone number on a piece of paper.

"Please," she told a nurse, handing her the paper. "Have pity on me. When I die, call this number and let the yeshivah know, so that my dear sons, the yeshivah students, can participate in my funeral."

The nurse could not avoid the look in Mrs. Minna's eyes whenever she pronounced the words "my sons." She promised.

Her final moments came as darkness was falling. Mrs. Minna's condition worsened dramatically. As her blood pressure fell almost to zero, the doctors came rushing into her room. They left with grave faces. "It will be soon," they said. "She is in a terminal state."

The yeshivah administration had made certain that the cook received the best care. The nurses did not budge from her bedside. When they heard certain noises emanating from her throat, they hurriedly summoned the doctors again.

"She is dying," the doctors said.

A moment later, she was gone.

The doctors determined the precise moment of death, the moment when a person ceases to exist physically and his soul soars heavenward. The nurse did not forget her patient's plea. She went to the hospital phone and dialed the number Mrs. Minna had given her. To her astonishment, no one bothered to answer the phone. She let it ring and ring, then hung up and tried again. It was only on the third try that someone finally picked up. She passed on the news, and her job was done. In a little while, the body would be transferred to the morgue adjoining the hospital. Chevron Yeshivah would see to the rest.

Suddenly, a hoarse scream pierced the old hospital building.

"She's not dead! She's alive — she's breathing! She's moving — she opened her eyes!"

Several nurses had suddenly noticed a strange movement from underneath the sheet that covered the cook's body. Coming closer, they were startled to see the "dead woman's" hand pulling the sheet down, to reveal a pair of wide-open eyes.

The hospital was in turmoil. The doctors were summoned posthaste. Their amazement was total. "But she was dead!" they whispered in shock. "This is impossible!"

The nurses ran about with their eyes popping out of their heads. "It's a miracle. It's *techiyas hameisim!*"

Indeed, it appeared to be an open miracle. The woman's death had been ascertained in the clearest possible way. There had been no heartbeat or breathing, and her blood pressure had plummeted to zero. And then, in a stunning reversal, she was suddenly alive again!

That was when the nurse remembered. "Oh, my goodness. I already informed the yeshivah!"

She raced back to the phone.

"This is Sha'arei Tzedek Hospital again. We spoke to you a little while ago."

The boy heard the nurse's voice, breathless and emotional. "Yes?"

"We wanted to let you know that there has been a mistake. Mrs. Minna has not died. That is, she died, but she seems to have come back to life — Or else it was a mistake, and she only died a clinical death."

"How is she now?" the student asked in astonishment.

"She is still in critical condition. Technically speaking, I'd say she is dying. But she is certainly not dead."

"Hey, fellows, listen to this!" The boy popped his head jubilantly through the office window. "All plans are changed. Mrs. Minna did not die!" And he related what he had just been told.

The sounds of Torah were soon echoing through the *beis midrash* again, as the three resumed their learning with renewed vigor. Late that night, hundreds of yeshivah students returned from the wedding, dressed in their best and completely oblivious to the drama that had been enacted while they were away.

The next morning, the yeshivah phone rang again. This time, it was the secretary who answered. He listened, then spread the news: "The cook has passed away."

At midday, hundreds of yeshivah boys followed the cook's modest coffin, paying their last respects. Heaven had delayed her passing for additional long hours, so that R' Yechezkel Sarna's promise might be fulfilled: "When your day comes, you will merit something that not many people merit. Hundreds of yeshivah boys will follow you to your final resting place."

Blessed is He Who keeps His promises!

# The Scales of Heaven

T HE "MAZEL TOV" PLATE WAS BROKEN AT 10 P.M. BY 1 a.m., Tuvia Fruchtman was checking his passport.

It had been a long road to this point for Tuvia and his family. His eldest daughter, Esther, was a precious diamond. Wonderful *middos*, a good heart, a noble spirit — he wished such a daughter on all his friends! The problem was, Esther was not an only daughter. Tuvia Fruchtman and his wife struggled hard to earn their living — and they had six daughters to marry off.

When it came to *shidduch* suggestions for Esther, the parents adhered to the highest standards. They wanted a boy who was great in Torah, diligence, *yiras Shamayim* and good *middos*. This was their bottom line. Privately, however, Tuvia was forced to admit that he placed a good deal of emphasis on another factor: how much the other side was prepared to give the young couple. To his distress, he was neither the first nor the last to discover a dismal fact of life: If you have a daughter, you are expected to give more. "You have to pay for a good boy!" his older friends explained when Tuvia's daughters were still small. They urged him to open savings accounts for each of the girls. "The years will fly past," they warned. "You'll suddenly find yourself getting ready to marry off all six girls, one after the other. Start saving now!"

Tuvia accepted the advice of those more experienced than he. He worked hard to earn more money, and his wife, too, worked full-time. But their plan was brought up short by reality. Their combined salaries were sufficient to allow them to live comfortably, and even to save a bit, but they could not bridge the gap between such a lifestyle and the ability to provide his daughter with an apartment — or even 80 percent of an apartment.

So Tuvia and his wife devised a plan: On the day that Esther, their eldest, became engaged, Tuvia would prepare to travel abroad on a fund-raising trip.

He prepared his passport as Esther's *shidduch* progressed. On the night of the engagement, after all the guests had left and the *kallah's* sisters were straightening up the house, Tuvia went to his drawer to check his new passport and make sure that all was in order. Tomorrow, with G-d's help, he would visit a travel agent and order a ticket for America. He smiled sadly when he recalled the saying: "The *chasan's* side obligates itself to pay 50 percent of the wedding expenses; the *kallah's* side obligates itself to pay the other 50 percent — and *Klal Yisrael* obligates itself to pay 100 percent."

Tuvia's case was different. He had accepted 99 percent of the responsibility (the *chasan's* father had promised only to outfit his son respectably!). It was up to him to travel abroad now, to collect the rest of the payment.

"Whoever has not been through this *Gehinnom* does not know what he is missing," warned his childhood friend, Shlomo Dvinsker, who had already traveled abroad twice for *hachnasas kallah*. Tuvia thought that

Shlomo was only speaking out of his own pessimistic nature. His old friend always tended to see the dark side of things. Apparently, someone in Manhattan had not smiled at him, or else one of the Jewish diamond traders had not treated him pleasantly enough.

Tuvia's first days in Boro Park were wonderful. To his good fortune, he had a sister who lived in that celebrated Jewish neighborhood, which saved him the unpleasant need to be the guest of various strangers. On the contrary, his sister, Mrs. Sarah Hoffman, and her husband, Mendel, went out of their way to show him every consideration. He believed that their attitude was helped along by the fact that he had never before imposed on their hospitality — but when he contemplated the future it was with a pang. His daughter was only the first of six. If he had to travel abroad six times, would his sister and her husband agree to host him every time? Perhaps they would begin putting him off with various excuses.

He did not know them as well as he should have — not his brother-in-law, and not even his sister. Had he asked them, they would have removed all his worries and anguish over the future.

They gave him two days to rest and recover from jet lag. At 8 p.m. each night, he became exhausted. By his biological clock, it was already 3 a.m., and his eyes began to close of their own accord.

After those initial two days, his brother-in-law urged him to rise early: "If you don't begin seriously today, you'll have wasted the price of your ticket."

Mendel woke Tuvia at 6 o'clock the next morning. They went to the *mikveh* together and *davened Shacharis* in shul. After a quick breakfast, the two set out on their first fund-raising journey. Tuvia was stunned that his brother-in-law planned to take off a full day's work on his behalf. "Why are you doing this?" he exclaimed.

Mendel chuckled. "So that you won't come back to us again in another month!"

Then, to make sure that Tuvia did not take his joking seriously, he quickly added, "Today I'll show you the ropes. Learn the rules. Then, tomorrow, you'll be able to manage on your own."

That day, they visited several big offices owned by wealthy Jews. When they returned home that evening, Tuvia was very happy. If every day was as successful as this one had been, he would be able to return to Israel in two weeks with all the money he needed!

Tuvia soon had to face the bitter truth: Mendel had paved the way for him that first day. They had visited only his brother-in-law's good friends, to whom Mendel had spoken beforehand. You might say that Mendel knew exactly how much money Tuvia would collect during the first day's venture.

Tuvia returned home happy on the second day, as well. Mendel had saved some of his friends for Tuvia to tackle alone on that day, and all Tuvia had to do was collect the money that they had already agreed to give. But he didn't know this. All the businessmen played along, as though they knew nothing. They all "listened to his story" and were "deeply moved by his difficult situation."

From the third day on, however, the picture changed completely. Mendel's list of friends dwindled to nothing, and Tuvia had to work on his own. He found that there were quite a few people who were not moved at all by the fact that his eldest daughter had become a *kallah*. For every Jew who gave, there were two who did not. The humiliation was great. Like a beggar, he had to tell and retell his story with each new visit. There were those who cut him off impatiently before he had even begun, throwing a 10-dollar bill at him. And there were others, more experienced, who heard him out to the end, but gave little. The common thread between the two was that both made Tuvia feel equally uncomfortable. They were doing him a favor.

At the end of the week, Tuvia seriously considered packing his bags and returning home. His first visit to the United States had left him disappointed and unsatisfied. He did not have half, nor even a third, of what he'd hoped for. With tears in his eyes, he went to the closet and began to pack.

His sister saw what was happening. "What are you doing?" she exclaimed in surprise. "Don't you like it here?"

"I like it very much," he told her with a heavy heart. "But I feel that I'm an imposition — and, besides, I've had my fill of humiliation.

For the sake of a few dollars, I have to pour out my lifeblood and abase myself countless times a day. Enough!"

Taken aback, his sister phoned her husband at work. "Mendel, you have to come home."

"What happened?"

She gave him a concise update of the situation. "I haven't done enough for my brother. He wants to leave." She saw that Tuvia was continuing with his packing.

"Tell him that I'll finish up here and come right home," Mendel said hastily. "Don't let him go. We'll put our heads together and come up with a plan."

The plan, it seemed, was about to come from Mendel's workplace.

A colleague of his, having heard his raised voice on the phone, asked curiously what had happened. Mendel told him of his brother-in-law's plight. His friend thought for a moment, then said, "Have you tried Shimon Shickman?"

Mendel looked askance at him. "What am I, a *rosh yeshivah* or rebbe?" Shimon Shickman was one of Brooklyn's richest men, worth tens or perhaps even hundreds of millions. To enter his ornate Manhattan office was not a privilege open to just anyone. To get to see the great man, you had to pass a gantlet of secretaries and aides, and your request had to be accompanied by illustrious Torah figures. And even then, you needed luck. Should you happen to find favor in Shickman's eyes, you might walk out with a sizable donation. There were persistent rumors that some had received checks for five-figure amounts, and even higher. This was impossible to prove; whoever did merit such a donation made sure to keep it quiet.

Mendel's colleague returned his gaze impassively. "I have some pull with Shimon Shickman's office. One of his assistants is a good friend of mine. Shall I talk to him?"

The cross look left Mendel's face instantly. He glowed. "Are you serious?"

"Is today Purim?" the other countered. He went on to promise Mendel that he would speak to the rich man's assistant that very afternoon.

Mendel went home filled with his news, only to find his obstinate brother-in-law on the point of leaving his home. His wife's entreaties had been to no avail. Tuvia was bitter and disillusioned. Mendel's news changed the picture a bit.

"Are you serious?" Tuvia asked.

"Is today Purim?" Mendel replied with a twinkle. "It's worth your while to wait and see. The situation could change from one extreme to the other in just one day — if Shimon Shickman agrees to see you."

While Tuvia did not hide his doubts, he was inclined to change his mind about going at once. Though he did not return his clothes to the closet, neither did he continue packing the items that still remained inside.

Mendel would not return to his office until Tuvia promised that he would not escape in his absence.

That afternoon, it indeed appeared as if Mendel's colleague had "connections." Shimon Shickman's assistant spoke with the "big boss," who agreed to a short meeting with Tuvia on the following day.

Mendel decided to accompany Tuvia on the visit.

Both Mendel and Tuvia spoke from the depths of their hearts. Tuvia, especially, was very emotional. His hands shook and his eyes welled up with tears. His words went directly from his own heart into that of Shimon Shickman's. It was clear that the rich man liked him. Shickman thought a few moments, then asked them to leave the room. On their return, a signed check was sitting on the desk.

Tuvia could not keep his eyes off the rectangle of paper. His hair stood on end and an almost electrical current swept through him as he saw the amount written on the check. It was a sum he had never dreamed of in his wildest imagination. He wanted to throw his arms around Shickman and kiss him soundly in gratitude, but the wealthy man motioned for him to remain seated. He did not enjoy thank-yous.

In the end, Tuvia left his sister's home only one day later than he had planned the morning before.

The taxi drove slowly, because a fierce winter storm was turning Brooklyn's streets into a windy snowscape that day. As they passed a corner, they saw a man standing in the snow, well muffled in a coat and scarf, waving wildly at the taxi. Tuvia motioned to the driver to stop. To his astonishment, he found that the snowy figure was none other than Shlomo Dvinsker, his old friend, who had made a trip to the States as well.

"I'm stuck on the street with my suitcase," he explained breathlessly. "I ordered a car service, but it never showed up." Tuvia was more than happy to invite him to share his cab.

On the way to the airport, the old friends chatted easily. Shlomo did most of the talking, painting a picture for Tuvia of an unbearable situation. With both a daughter and a son engaged back home, Shlomo was returning to Israel empty-handed. He had no devoted brother-in-law to sweep the fields clear of thorns and turn them into sweet-smelling rose beds. His trip had been a failure.

"How much did you collect, though?" Tuvia asked.

"Hardly a penny! I don't even have enough to pay back the loan I took out from a *gemach* to buy my plane ticket here." Suddenly, as though unable to bear the pain any longer, Shlomo burst into anguished tears.

Tuvia melted. With compassion-filled eyes he watched his friend weep brokenheartedly. All at once, an insane idea popped into his head, an idea that had no basis in logic or reason and which Tuvia did not stop to consider. He whipped out the check he had received from Shimon Shickman and pressed it on his friend.

*A moment of madness*, he described it to himself later. But he felt no regret at all, and stood firm against the tide of Shlomo's protests and pleadings that he take the money back.

"Impossible," Tuvia said staunchly. He had no idea where the strength came from.

Back home, his family and friends would think he was out of his mind. "The poor of your own city come first!" his wife would complain. "It also says, 'Do not hide from your flesh and blood.' "

THE SCALES OF HEAVEN / 149

That was all true. But Shlomo's situation was many times worse than his own. Tuvia had been driven to give him the money. There was no turning back now.

Upon their arrival at the airport, the two would-be travelers learned, to their dismay, that they would have to turn right around and return to the city. No planes were able to take off in the snowstorm.

Tuvia and Shlomo made the return trip to Boro Park. Tuvia was reluctant to reappear at his sister's home, lest he let slip what he had done. Instead, he went along with Shlomo to the home of a well-known *machnis orchim*, a host of outstanding hospitality to strangers in need. There he waited for two days with a heavy heart. He did not know whether he had done a great mitzvah or had behaved with irresponsible foolishness. He suspected the latter; but there was no way to change things now.

Kennedy Airport returned to normal functioning. Tuvia and Shlomo headed there for their return trip to Israel, where they parted ways. They would be flying on different airlines.

Tuvia was beside himself with pain and sadness. Though he did not wish to regret what he had done for his old friend, his heart troubled him constantly with the thought that he might have been kind to a stranger at the expense of his own family.

A kosher meal was served him, but Tuvia had no appetite. He could not eat even a morsel.

"Eat, it's good," his neighbor urged. Tuvia turned to see a smiling American seated beside him.

"Thank you," Tuvia murmured. Against his will, tears began to course down his cheeks. The tears sparkled for a moment in the sunlight, and then dripped dolefully down onto his untouched tray.

His gregarious neighbor was insistent on learning the reason for those tears. There was a story here! Tuvia was beseiged by pleas to tell his story. At last, he yielded. Within a matter of minutes, he had revealed the whole tale of his stay in New York, of the difficulty and disappointment, of the generous check he had received, and his impulsive decision to pass it on to his unfortunate friend.

The man appeared stunned by the depths of Tuvia's compassion. "I've never heard of such a thing!" he whispered. "You're right, you shouldn't have done it. You've hurt your family."

Tuvia bit his lip.

The man went on: "A few days ago, I concluded a large and successful deal in my line of business. I'm on my way to Eretz Yisrael now, to thank Hashem for His *chesed* to me, as I always do at such a time. It is my custom to go to one of the big yeshivos in Yerushalayim on each visit and give them my '*ma'aser* money.' But this time, I'm going to do something else."

Before Tuvia knew what was happening, the man had written out a check, payable to Tuvia Fruchtman. With disbelieving eyes, Tuvia looked at the amount. It was exactly the same figure as Shimon Shickman's check!

Heaven had righted the scales, down to the last dollar.

# The Rebbe in Vienna

AFTER SHAVUOS 5674 (1914), AS HIS HEALTH WORSENED, R' Yisrael of Chortkov traveled to Germany to consult with expert doctors there. His *chassidim,* watching him prepare for the trip, were surprised to see him do something he had never done before. The Rebbe equipped himself with articles of spiritual value, such as items of clothing that had belonged to his father before him, holy *sefarim* he had inherited, and the like.

On his journey to Germany, the Rebbe passed through many cities and towns. In each place, his *chassidim* would swarm out to the train station to greet their Rebbe. When he reached Cracow, in Galicia, his *chassidim* from that city accompanied him to the point near the Weichsal River that marked the border of the three powers of the day: Austria, Russia, and Germany.

After parting from his *chassidim,* the Rebbe lifted his eyes heavenward and declared, "Austria says, 'The world is mine!' Russia says, 'The world is mine!' Germany, also, says the same. And I say: '*LaHashem ha'aretz umelo'ah*' ('The world and all it contains belong to Hashem!')."

The *chassidim* were surprised. Then the Rebbe added a few more words that made no sense to them. "Some time before he passed from this world, my holy father told me: 'I saw a black glass in a dream.' He paused, then added, 'The day does not begin to give light until it is completely dark.'

"My father-in-law, *z"l*, said, 'Vienna is a royal city.' And I say that it is good to make *Kiddush* in Vienna."

The large crowd stood open mouthed at these mysterious utterings from the Rebbe who was known for his measured statements. Three months later (on Tishah B'Av 5674 [1914]), World War I broke out suddenly. Jewish lives were endangered, and the Rebbe and his family were forced to move to Vienna. Only then did his *chassidim* understand what he had been referring to earlier.

When the Rebbe arrived in Vienna, he set to work raising the standard of *Yiddishkeit,* which at that time was at a low level. Some 200,000 Jews lived in Vienna then, but only a small number of them observed Shabbos. R' Yisrael pleaded with every Jew who came to see him for advice or a blessing, "Promise me that you will keep the Shabbos." Hundreds of Viennese Jews promised.

The Rebbe remained in Austria's capital even after the thundering cannons were stilled and the war was over. His *chassidim* came from Galicia to ask him to return to them, but the Rebbe declined. "Hundreds of Jews have promised me to keep Shabbos. If I leave, who knows whether they will be able to keep it up."

The words that he had spoken before the war, "It is good to make *Kiddush* in Vienna," took on a second meaning. Not only did the rebbe make *Kiddush* on wine in Vienna, but he made many Jews holy (*kadosh*) there as well.

The Viennese fabric wholesaler, Leon Taub, was one of those people.

R' Leibel, a fabric merchant, hurried toward "the Strasse" ("the Street"), a roll of new cloth under his arm. The large fabric store on the corner was filled with customers, as usual. R' Leibel's brow furrowed as he gazed around in surprise. Salesclerks were politely helping customers and answering their questions. All was as usual, except for one thing: The store's owner, R' Leibel's good friend, seemed to be missing. Where was Leon?

R' Leibel approached the head clerk and asked where the owner was.

"L-leon?" The clerk seemed flustered. "Uh — uh, he's not here at the moment. I'll be happy to help you instead. What can I do for you?"

The crease in R' Leibel's brow deepened. In all the seven years that he had been doing business with Leon Taub, he had never come in to find the energetic Leon missing. And what about the strange look that suddenly crossed the head clerk's face, and his obvious fumbling for an answer?

R' Leibel turned as though prepared to leave. He walked toward the door until the clerk had stopped watching him. Then, abruptly, he turned back and slipped into the office.

"No one is to come in!" a familiar voice called out sternly. "Ah, is that you, R' Leibel? I didn't mean to shout at you."

"What's the matter, Leon? Don't you feel well?" Anxiously, R' Leibel studied his friend's drawn face.

"*Ach*, what do you care?" Leon answered boorishly.

R' Leibel was taken aback. What had happened to Leon's impeccable Austrian manners? But the Chortkov *chassid* was not one to take offense. He knew all too well that a cutting remark can disguise a cry for help.

"Why is today different from all other days?" he asked. "Why are you behaving like this?"

Leon shrugged hopelessly. "Suppose I were to tell you — how can you help?"

THE REBBE IN VIENNA / 153

" 'If a man has a worry in his heart, he should talk about it,' " R' Leibel quoted. "Tell me. Maybe I can help."

Leon sighed. "My family is undergoing a crisis. It's about my daughter." He pulled a folded handkerchief from his pocket and dabbed at his eyes. "M-my only daughter," he said, and was unable to continue because he was crying too hard.

"What happened to her?" R' Leibel asked fearfully. "Is she ill?"

"W-worse!"

The atmosphere seemed suddenly heavy and close. Leibel was afraid to hear the rest. He chose to remain silent and wait.

"She — she's gone ahead and gotten engaged to a *goy*! My only daughter is engaged to be married to a *goy*! To assimilate!"

Leon looked R' Leibel in the face, and continued brokenly, "You know me, R' Leibel. I am not a mitzvah-observant man. Still, I have a powerful desire to remain within the framework of the Jewish people at any price. I cannot bear this!" He leaped convulsively from his seat. "If this comes to pass, I will put an end to my life! Yes, I will commit suicide! I will kill myself!" He began pacing around the room like a madman, knocking over furniture and any other object that stood in his way. Despairing cries issued from his throat.

It took R' Leibel a great deal of time and effort to calm his friend's fevered spirit. "Leon, all is not yet lost. She can still be saved. But you have to listen to me."

"I'll do whatever you say, Leibel."

"Come with me now, to my Rebbe — the Rebbe of Chortkov."

The two walked at a very rapid clip through Vienna's broad streets. The beauty of the broad "Strasses" was lost on them as they traversed the distance to the Rebbe's house. Nothing could be greater than Leon's eagerness to arrive at their destination. R' Leibel was hard put to keep up.

Breathless and panting, they arrived at the Rebbe's house. Leon rapped on the door until R' Leibel stopped him, explaining that this was not the way to enter a rebbe's home. "Besides, you have to write a *kvittel*."

Quietly, reverently, R' Leibel entered into the Rebbe's presence, with Leon following hesitantly behind. Leon was clearly moved by the Rebbe's regal and holy demeanor. He had never seen anyone like this in all his life.

R' Yisrael read the *kvittel*, and then R' Leibel described the situation in his friend's home. Lifting his eyes, the Rebbe gazed piercingly into Leon's face.

"Will you take it upon yourself to observe the Shabbos?"

"Holy Rebbe, in order to save my daughter, I'm ready to do anything!"

"Do you promise?" the Rebbe pressed. Leon gave his word.

"In that case, I want you to bring your daughter here."

"That's impossible," Leon protested. "My daughter hates religious Jews. She will never agree to come."

R' Yisrael said simply, "Try!"

Leon would never forget his daughter's mocking expression. "Father, have you become a fanatic, like all those other long-beards?" she asked scornfully, in reply to his request that she accompany him to the Rebbe's. "You, Leon, the enlightened and progressive Jew, have started consorting with black-coated *chassidim*? If you'd decided to convert to a different religion, that's fine — But this!" She shrugged. "Well, if you want to wear a *shtreimel* seven days a week and eat pickled herring from morning to night, that's your concern. But me? My feet will not cross the Rebbe's threshold!"

In the end, however, after prolonged pleading and coaxing, her father got her to relent. She did not forget to point out that she was doing this only to make him happy, and also to prove that the Rebbe would have no influence at all over her. His words, she assured Leon, would make no impression on her whatsoever.

But when she came to the Rebbe's house and stood before his radiant countenance — a face utterly devoid of human baseness — she forgot all the promises she had made to herself. Like her father, she was mesmerized by the Rebbe's holiness, and entirely conquered by the force of his personality. She listened to him with great courtesy.

"Why do you want to marry a non-Jew?" the rebbe asked mildly. "You could take a Jewish boy of good family and live a pure Jewish life with him. What have your parents done to you, that you should so embitter their lives?"

The girl could not bear the Rebbe's rebuke. Slowly, she began to retreat toward the door. On the tip of her tongue trembled the words, *Rebbe, I regret my evil impulse.* At that moment, however, her imagination stepped in, painting a rosy picture of the life she would live with her gentile fiance.

"Rebbe, I cannot go back on my decision. I've already linked my lot with my fiance, and I can't undo that now."

"In that case —" R' Yisrael stood up, eyes blazing, "*he* will leave *you!*"

Two days passed. Leon and his family were seated at the breakfast table, sipping coffee, when a powerful knocking at the door shattered the morning peace.

"Who's that knocking so early in the morning?" Leon complained. He stood up and went to the door.

The gentile fiance burst inside, his face baleful. The bride's smile disappeared as she saw how angry he was. Without even a "hello," he said, "Our connection is severed from this day forward. I don't want to have anything to do with you!"

The door slammed behind him as he went.

Wide eyed, the girl stared at the door. The Rebbe's words echoed loudly through her head: "He will leave you!"

That very day, Leon hired a pious *talmid chacham* to begin teaching his family the rudiments of *Yiddishkeit*. In just a short time, the family had changed so much as to be unrecognizable. Leon — now Aryeh — joined the Chortkov *shteibel* in Vienna, and his daughter eventually married one of the finest young men in the city's Jewish community!

# Of Chicken Soup and Cholent

JERUSALEM, DURING THE JORDANIAN BOMBARDMENT OF 5708 (1948).

The city was under siege, surrounded by Arabs intent on destroying Jews just because they were Jews. Their bloodthirsty hands were eager to choke any Jewish throat. Because not every throat was accessible to them, they sent their messengers: mortar shells that spread ruin and mourning wherever they were dropped. The shriek of the warning siren that preceded each shelling was followed by wailing and tears, bereavement and pain.

Walking through their streets exposed the Jews to death and destruction, so most chose to cower at home, lips murmuring a prayer that their homes not become their graves. There was not much business being transacted these days; people sheltering fearfully at home did not do much buying or selling. The yeshivah students, too, remained inside the walls of their homes for fear of the dreaded Jordan Legionnaire shells.

But there were a few exceptions, a few brave individuals who took their lives into their hands and walked through the streets to their yeshivos. Ignoring the horrific dangers that awaited them each time they set foot outside, they immersed themselves in Torah with great devotion and self-sacrifice.

The besieged city suffered a harsh and hungry winter. There was little bread or water to be had. The yeshivah students pored over their *Gemaras* despite their hunger pangs, trying to focus only on the holy words of the *Tanna'im* and *Amora'im*. With their minds on the heights, they could put aside, for a while, the hollow feeling that came from not having enough to eat. In Heaven, as everyone knows, there is no hunger.

One of these students was R' Yehoshua Sharabani, a luminary of the Sephardic community. Apart from his brilliance in the revealed Torah, he was one of the foremost Kabbalists in Jerusalem, an expert in the hidden Torah. R' Yehoshua Sharabani would learn for 36-hour continuous stints in an Old City *beis midrash* (except for pauses for *davening*, of course). Alongside him learned other Torah scholars, who, like him, chose to ignore the war that was happening outside the *beis midrash* walls. One of these was the well-known *gaon*, R' Shimshon Aharon Polanski, known as the *rav* of Teplik, who lived in the Beit Yisrael neighborhood (near his good friend, R' Shlomke of Zhivil). He, too, paid no heed to the shells whistling past outside, as he sat near R' Yehoshua Sharabani and learned with devotion. A great friendship sprang up between the two scholars, and each highly respected and esteemed the other.

Inside the *beis midrash* walls, neither war nor hunger had a place. So what if destruction was raining down outside? So what if their stomachs were empty? They were learning the living Torah. They could forget all the rest.

From time to time, however, it was impossible to forget. When the Legionnaires aimed their cannons at the immediate neighborhood, the danger became very real indeed. When that happened, an old *mekubal* by the name of R' Efraim HaKohen, of the Kabbalistic yeshivah Porat Yosef, would run with all his might to the *beis midrash*, to urge those learning there to move to a safer place.

R' Yehoshua Sharabani had an outstanding son by the name of R' Yosef Chaim, who, like his father, never set foot outside the tent of Torah. He was the head of a young family, and every member of that family knew hunger very well. More than once, they had gone to bed with empty stomachs. Sometimes they were too hungry to sleep at all. Then, one day, great joy filled the house: A friend who had traveled out of the country had returned with a basket of apples for the hungry family. Their eyes lit up at the sight. You may be sure that those apples disappeared with the speed of lightning.

It is easy to understand, then, R' Yosef Chaim's happiness when he managed to secure an entire chicken in honor of the Shabbos! When was the last time his family had tasted a piece of chicken? No one could remember.

When he joyously brought the chicken home, the house filled with an air of celebration. "We have chicken!" the children crowed.

"We have chicken for Shabbos," their mother corrected them.

She took the chicken to the kitchen to *kasher* it. On a special wooden board, she inspected the fowl's innards — and soon saw something that cast doubt on the chicken's *kashrus*. The more she looked at it, the stronger her doubts grew. An expert opinion was needed here.

Whom should they ask?

The answer was clear to R' Yosef Chaim. Not far from his home lived the great *gaon*, R' Yaakov Chaim Sofer, author of *Kaf HaChaim*. The chicken would be brought to R' Yaakov Chaim, and his opinion would be binding.

Taking the wrapped chicken with him, R' Yosef Chaim walked to R' Yaakov Chaim's house. R' Yaakov Chaim took his time examining the suspect chicken, turning it from side to side, feeling it and scrutinizing it carefully. At last, he gave his ruling. "The chicken is *treif*. You must throw it away."

R' Yosef Chaim Sharabani was a pious man. If the Kaf HaChaim ruled that the chicken was unkosher, there was no room for doubt. Still, his heart was heavy. His family was so hungry, and had been so happy to see the chicken. In their imaginations, they had already seen themselves seated around the Shabbos table eating the delicacy. Now the trash can would be the receptacle of their dreams.

He walked through the streets, the bundle of chicken still under his arm and his head filled with these sad thoughts. He was about to toss away the chicken, but had not yet done so when he saw his father, R' Yehoshua Sharabani, approaching down the street. Seeing his son's downcast face, he asked at once, "What's wrong?"

R' Yosef Chaim showed his father the chicken bundled under his arm, and told him about the question with which he had gone to the Kaf HaChaim. His father exclaimed, "I am surprised at you, my son. What have you done? Do you bring such a serious question to the Kaf HaChaim? Did you really think he would rule any other way? He is extremely stringent, and tends to rule things unkosher that are far less serious than this!"

"Then what ought I to have done?"

"Go to the *rav* of Teplik, the *gaon* R' Shimshon Aharon Polanski. He, too, is extremely knowledgeable in halachah, but he is not as stringent as the Kaf HaChaim. If there is a way to halachically rule the chicken kosher, if there are legitimate authorities to rely on, he will find it."

R' Yosef Chaim immediately set out for the Beit Yisrael neighborhood and knocked on the door of the *rav* of Teplik.

The door opened. In the doorway stood the smiling figure of the *rav*, beaming at his visitor. "Welcome, R' Yosef Chaim, son of my dear friend, R' Yehoshua Sharabani! What can I do for you?"

R' Yosef Chaim showed him the chicken. Without telling him about the Kaf HaChaim's ruling, he asked the *rav's* opinion.

R' Shimshon Aharon took the chicken, studied its insides well, thought for a while, and then pronounced, "Kosher. It is undoubtedly kosher."

"There is no room for stringency?" R' Yosef Chaim asked in a trembling voice, as the echo of the Kaf HaChaim's firm tones rang in his ears.

"No, it is absolutely kosher. You have nothing to worry about," the *rav* reassured him.

R' Yosef Chaim's heart swelled with joy. Infinitely lighter in spirit than he had been upon his departure earlier, he returned home, placed the chicken in front of his wife, and declared happily, "It's fine. The chicken is completely kosher."

He did not say a word about the difference of opinion he had encountered among the two experts he'd consulted.

The rebbetzin soaked the chicken and salted it. When the *kashering* process was complete, she divided the chicken into two parts — one half for the Friday-night soup, and the other half for the Shabbos-lunch cholent. She cooked the soup at home, but prepared the cholent in a heavy pot to be baked in the large, very hot oven it required. On Thursday evening, she sent one of her children with the pot to the central oven in the next neighborhood. On the pot handle she tied a piece of numbered tin that would distinguish one pot from another in the large oven.

Many families picked up their cholent on Shabbos morning, but the Sharabani family was stringent about not carrying anything on

160 / TALES FOR THE SOUL

Shabbos, even inside the city's *eiruv*. Therefore, instead of waiting until Shabbos morning, they had their pot brought home to them on Friday afternoon. The cholent would continue to cook overnight at home.

The rebbetzin waited and waited, but the cholent did not arrive. The person who usually brought it to them did not appear. Shabbos was fast approaching. At last, her patience at an end, she sent her son to the oven to bring the cholent back.

As he took the pot from the oven, the boy nearly fainted from the delicious aroma it emitted. "What a meal we'll have on Shabbos morning!" he thought happily. It took an iron will and tremendous self-control not to taste a bit of it right on the spot.

The boy passed through the marketplace on his way home. He saw the wine shop. Suddenly, he remembered that his mother had given him money to buy a bottle of wine for Shabbos, as not a drop remained at home with which to make *Kiddush*. Entering the busy shop, the boy set the hot cholent pot down in a corner and took his place in the long line.

In those days, buying wine was nothing like it is today. There were a number of wines in Jerusalem, and a shop would contain several large wooden barrels filled with the various kinds. From a tap in the side of the barrel, the shopkeeper would pour wine into bottles according to the buyer's taste. If the customer wanted only one specific type of wine, he could get that — or he could mix wines from different barrels into his wine bottle. The boy waited with rising impatience as each customer chose the wine he wanted. At last, it was his turn. He asked for a simple bottle of wine, and quickly. It was time to get home for Shabbos. His worried eyes kept darting out to the street, where other shops were closing up as the sun dipped lower into the sky.

At last, the bottle of wine was in his hands. The red liquid sparkled and bubbled after its hasty pouring. Cradling the bottle in his arms, the boy began to race for home. His mother was probably waiting for him anxiously. No doubt she had already lit the Shabbos candles.

"Here's the wine!" he gasped, bursting inside.

"The wine? Very good — But where is the cholent?"

Like a bolt of lightning on a dark night, the recollection exploded on the boy. "Oh, no! I forgot the cholent in the wine shop!"

He ran as fast as his legs could carry him, all the way back to the wine shop — only to find it locked and shuttered. The pot was sitting, forgotten, in a corner. Even if he ran to fetch the shop's owner, there was not enough time to get the pot onto the stove at home before Shabbos.

⁓ও ৯

The cholent was gone, but the children were comforted by one thing: There was still the other half of the chicken in the soup for tonight. In good spirits they set off for shul, *davened*, and then returned home. They sang *Shalom Aleichem*, and the father made *Kiddush*.

The rebbetzin went to the stove to get the chicken soup. A moment later, the family heard her scream, "Fire! Help, help! Fire!"

The family leaped up and raced to the kitchen. There was no fire, only the scorched smell of food that had been burned beyond repair. Opening the soup pot, they were astounded to find nothing inside but the burnt, lumpy remains of what had once been chicken and vegetables. Not even a dog could eat what the pot now held. No one could venture to explain how it had happened. Nothing like this had ever occurred in their home before. How could soup, simmering on a low flame, burn away to the extent that the chicken inside turned to lumps of coal?

The young children were beside themselves with anguish. No cholent, and now no chicken soup, either. Of all that glorious chicken, they had not tasted a single bite.

But their father, R' Yosef Chaim Sharabani, was happy. He had no doubts about what had happened.

"Don't you understand?" he asked his hungry children gently. "This chicken falls into the category of a 'question that a *chacham* has ruled on.' The Kaf HaChaim said that the chicken was *treif* and ordered me to throw it away. I didn't want to, so Heaven prevented me and my family from eating it — and the chicken ended up tossed in the trash, just as R' Yaakov Chaim Sofer instructed!"

Nevertheless, R' Yosef Chaim was surprised at the turn of events. Hadn't the *rav* of Teplik pronounced the fowl absolutely kosher? The

162 / TALES FOR THE SOUL

*rav* was a *gaon* who knew the *Yoreh Deah* portion of the *Shulchan Aruch* as well as he knew the streets of his own neighborhood!

Yes, R' Yosef Chaim was surprised.

On *motza'ei Shabbos*, he went to see the Kaf HaChaim once again and related the whole story of the chicken. R' Yaakov Chaim smiled and said, "What else did you expect? It is clear that this was exactly what ought to have happened. You tried to outsmart the circumstances — but the chicken was *treif*! Heaven protected you from eating something that was not kosher."

But the *rav* of Teplik had declared the chicken kosher. Impatiently, R' Yosef Chaim waited for his chance to meet with the *rav*, and to ask him a burning question: "Are there two Torahs?"

"Heaven forbid!" exclaimed R' Shimshon Aharon, when R' Yosef Chaim finally saw him on the following Tuesday. "Listen, my young friend. The chicken was undoubtedly kosher, just as I told you, based on the great halachic authorities. But once you had asked the Kaf HaChaim, who forbade it, it was forbidden. Heaven guarded his honor and prevented you from eating the chicken."

[My thanks to R' Aviel Chori, who submitted this story, having heard it from the *gaon* R' Reuven Sharabani, son of the *Gaon Hatzaddik* R' Yosef Chaim Sharabani, and grandson of the *tzaddik* and *mekubal*, R' Yehoshua Sharabani.]

# A Long-Ago Intifada

THE *GAON* R' HILLEL MOSHE (MEISH'L) GLEIBSTEIN LEFT Bialystok for Jerusalem in the summer of 5629 (1869). All of Jerusalem hastened to show him respect, for despite his youth he was known as an outstanding scholar. His teacher and friend, the author of *Chiddushei HaRim,* said of him, "Had he not immersed himself in the study of Kabbalah, he would have reached the level of scholarship of the Sha'agas Aryeh!" This, from the Chiddushei HaRim, was more than just simple praise for R' Meish'l.

When he was no more than 15 or so, R' Meish'l was introduced by a *chassid* in his hometown, R' Elazar Bialystoker, to *chassidus* and the secrets that lay behind some of their unusual practices. Meish'l took to it at once, and over the next ten years became one of the Kotzker Rebbe's foremost disciples.

After R' Mendel of Kotzk passed on from this world, R' Meish'l traveled to Lubavitch to be with his second teacher, R' Menachem Mendel, author of *Tzemach Tzedek.*

Kotzk and Lubavitch — on the surface, there seem to be no two groups on more opposite extremes. Kotzk was characterized by a passionate search for truth, while a cold, penetrating logic, "the mind dominating the heart," was the byword of Lubavitch. But the combination worked well for R' Meish'l, who knew how to find the inner point of each approach and use it to build another rung in the ladder leading him ever upward.

It was after the Tzemach Tzedek's passing that R' Meish'l moved to Jerusalem. He was fortunate enough to lease the apartment that the holy *mekubal*, R' Shalom Sharabi, had once lived in. The apartment's windows faced the *Har HaBayis.* Every day, R' Meish'l was able to see and mourn anew the destruction of our Holy Temple.

Today, we have become so used to seeing the mosques on the *Har HaBayis* that the sight seems normal to us, as though they had always been there. Indeed, for the Jews living in the Old City at that time, they too became accustomed to the sight. They hardly even noticed it any longer. But for R' Meish'l, coming to Eretz Yisrael from a different country and viewing things with fresh eyes, this was something new and horrifying. He was so disturbed that he could not sleep at night.

How could he sleep, when before his very eyes was the site of the King's palace that had been razed to the ground, and in its place an impertinent servant had erected his own polluted dwelling place? R' Meish'l knew no peace.

When he had taken his leave of R' Yaakov Aryeh of Radzimin, the Rebbe had whispered in his ear, "Pray there that *Mashiach* should come." Now, R' Meish'l understood what the Rebbe had meant.

On his arrival in Jerusalem, R' Meish'l made contact with all of that city's great men of Torah: the *Maharil* Diskin, the *gaon* R' Shlomo Zalman of Lublin, author of *Toras Chesed*, and R' Eliyahu Dovid Teumim. He formed deep and lasting friendships with all three, who in their turn greatly admired and respected R' Meish'l.

R' Meish'l's soul aspired to great heights in the service of Hashem. But from the moment the Radziminer Rebbe whispered those words in his ears, and the moment R' Meish'l first looked out at the view from his windows, an all-consuming fire burned within him, destroying his peace. His imagination was inflamed with visions of hastening *Mashiach's* coming, visions that made his heart beat faster, night and day.

Every Jew is obligated to wait for *Mashiach* and to anticipate his arrival. But R' Meish'l took things further. He did not satisfy himself with prayer alone, but engaged in all sorts of practices, open and hidden, with the goal of helping to hasten *Mashiach's* long-awaited arrival.

Just a short time after his own arrival in the city, R' Meish'l had become a dominant figure in all areas of life there. His active mind was never at rest, as he came up with new and innovative ideas wherever he saw the need for change, action, correction, and improvement. He was especially eager, as we have said, to contribute to the hastening of the *geulah*. To this end, he established the *Mishmeres HaMikdash* program near the *Har HaBayis*. These were groups of *Kohanim*, *Levi'im* and *Yisraelim* who learned the laws of *korbanos* near the place where the *Beis HaMikdash* once stood. He also founded the *beis midrash* near the Western Wall, in which prayer services were held three times a day. Today this seems axiomatic, but 130 years ago there were no regular prayer services at the *Kosel*. This was an entirely new institution in that time, when the Western Wall stood bereft and neglected for the better part of each day.

And R' Meish'l set up a *ner tamid* (eternal flame) by the grave of the *Tanna*, Shimon *Hatzaddik*.

There were those, well versed in the hidden Torah, who believed that R' Meish'l's soul had its roots in that of the *Kohen Gadol*, Shimon *Hatzaddik*. This is the only way to make sense of R' Meish'l's tremendous self-sacrifice in the matter of the *ner tamid*. Once or twice each week, he would go to the cave where Shimon *Hatzaddik* is buried, carrying an earthenware jug full of olive oil. With this he would enter the dark cave to keep the *ner tamid* burning.

The *ner tamid* was made of a large, deep glass bowl, in the center of which sat a thick metal casing and wick. R' Meish'l would pour olive oil into the bowl and the light of the small flame would flicker through the cave. Apart from this, he organized public prayers three times a week beside the grave.

But even this was not enough. He showed great concern for the resting places of all the great men of Torah from previous generations, and urged his fellow residents to do the same. With tremendous energy and devotion, R' Meish'l had a kosher *mikveh* built near the graves of the Sanhedrin.

When R' Meish'l came up with the idea of establishing the *ner tamid* and public prayers at Shimon *Hatzaddik's* cave, he went around to Jerusalem's rabbis to elicit their consent to the plan. Not all of them, however, saw eye to eye with R' Meish'l regarding this scheme. This was a departure from previous custom, and there were those who were reluctant to adopt it.

Then two things happened in the cave — things that demonstrated to all doubters that the *Kohen Gadol* himself approved of R' Meish'l's plans.

First, there was "the Yom Kippur miracle."

On *erev* Yom Kippur, R' Meish'l visited the cave. He lit three wicks and poured in enough olive oil to allow them to burn for three days. During the days between Yom Kippur and Sukkos, he sent people to the cave, but the key to the iron gate broke and they were forced to turn back. Because of the holiday, no one was able to return to the cave until *erev* Hoshana Rabbah. On that day, he sent his representative. When the man arrived, distressed because the *ner tamid* must have stopped burning for several days, he was stunned to see the three wicks still lit! The bowl was empty of oil and the wicks themselves were dry, but at their tips burned tiny flames that whispered their own message. They had burned for days without oil!

The following year came "the miracle of the container of oil."

On *erev* Rosh Hashanah, R' Meish'l's messengers came to the cave bearing a full container of oil. The container held two *unkiyos*, ounces, of olive oil. R' Nachum went into the inner room, where the tomb was situated, and filled the bowls. When he was done, he passed the rest of the container to R' Yehoshua Yosef, in the outer room, to use what little oil was left to replenish the lights burning there.

R' Yehoshua did not know that the container was nearly empty, and began to pour oil lavishly into the bowls. To R' Nachum's shock, the oil poured out of the container in a thick stream, as though the container were full! In stunned silence, he watched R' Yehoshua pour an additional five *unkiyos* of oil into the glass bowls. Only when all the bowls were filled did the oil stop pouring.

These miracles threw all of Jerusalem into a turmoil. A panel was set up to take the three witnesses' testimony, and the facts were verified, as brought down in the introduction to R' Meish'l's work, *Mishkenos L'Avir Yaakov.*

R' Meish'l lived in Jerusalem for about forty years. A few days before his passing, on 24 Cheshvan, 5668 (1908), he left Jerusalem. He died in Chevron, city of our forefathers, which he had frequented over the years, and where he was laid to rest. There was great mourning in Jerusalem after his passing. An amazing story spread through the city: At the very moment that R' Meish'l's soul was leaving his body, several people were standing beside Shimon *Hatzaddik's* tomb. Suddenly, a powerful wind blew through the cave,

A LONG-AGO INTIFADA / 167

extinguishing the flame of the *ner tamid* — something that had never happened before.

With R' Meish'l's passing, his only son, a fine young man by the name of R' Mendel (named for R' Mendel of Kotzk), took upon himself his father's customs and practices. He, too, was careful to keep the *ner tamid* in Shimon *Hatzaddik's* cave lit at all times. He made sure that the container of oil was always full, and that the flame was never allowed to go out. (In fact, he was so dedicated to this mitzvah that during the winter of 5673 (1913), when he was still a young man, he went to the cave despite the frigid, rainy weather. He caught a cold that developed into pneumonia, which led to his death a few days later.)

Things went smoothly for several years. Then a new neighbor — a young Arab shepherd — moved in next door to Shimon *Hatzaddik's* cave. Seeing R' Mendel arrive devotedly at the cave so often, the Arab's curiosity was aroused. After R' Mendel left, he entered the cave to see for himself.

Times change, but the hatred that the Ishmaelite bears for the Jew remains strong. It passes from generation to generation, unconnected to social circumstance or political situation. The next time R' Mendel came to the cave, he was shaken to the core to see the *ner tamid* extinguished. The glass bowl was shattered and the oil was spilled everywhere. The container of olive oil resting on the floor had been overturned, and its contents poured out. Deeply disturbed, R' Mendel brought a new bowl the next day. It wasn't until he had restored the *ner tamid* to its usual state that he felt calmer.

Two days later, he returned to the cave — to find the same scene of wanton destruction. It was clear that the violence had been deliberate. R' Mendel trembled, beside himself with anguish.

Deeply downcast, he left the cave — and found himself under a hail of large stones. A group of Arab youths were waiting outside, along with their ringleader, the shepherd who lived next door. They pelted R' Mendel viciously, intending to kill him. Hastily, R' Mendel ran back into the cave and locked the metal gate. After a while, the group dispersed amid raucous laughter.

R' Mendel gathered his courage. He ran home — only to return at once with more oil and new bowls. In a short time, the *ner tamid* was lit once again.

He returned the next day. To his chagrin, the Arab had done it again. The fire was extinguished and the bowls shattered.

It was impossible for him to battle single-handedly against these people, R' Mendel realized. Leaving the cave, he ran directly to the home of his Rebbe, R' Dovid'l Biderman, the Lelover Rebbe in Jerusalem, who had also enjoyed a special relationship with R' Mendel's father, R' Meish'l.

The Rebbe was deeply distressed by R' Mendel's story. "They are ruining the *ner tamid* that your father established at the grave of the holy *Tanna*? Listen to my advice, R' Mendel. Go to your father's *kever*, and tell him what those Arabs are doing to his *ner tamid*. Come back to me tomorrow, and we'll see what happens."

The next day, at dusk, R' Dovid'l was sitting with his *chassidim* as usual, exchanging tales of *tzaddikim*. From one topic to another the discussion wandered, until it reached the *ner tamid* that R' Meish'l had established in Shimon *Hatzaddik's* cave. R' Dovid'l was lavish in his praise of R' Meish'l and the innovations he had made. As he spoke, he heaved a heavy sigh.

He was still talking when there came the sound of a shriek from the street nearby. Someone was screaming in Arabic, pleading to be allowed in to see the "holy Jewish wise man." Presently, an old Arab entered the *beis midrash*.

The Arab sprawled to his full length on the ground at the Rebbe's feet and began to wail bitterly. He said that he had a young son, an innocent shepherd, who lived near the cave of Shimon *Hatzaddik*. Yesterday, as he was bringing his cow home from the pasture, the ground opened up and the shepherd fell into a deep hole filled with water. Every effort to rescue him had failed. They had sent down a rope several times. The shepherd would grasp the rope and climb up to the surface. But each time he came level with the top of the hole, he would lose his hold on the rope and slip back inside. He was lying there now, bleeding and broken, with hardly the strength to reply to his father's anxious calls.

"And why have you come to me?" the Rebbe asked quietly.

The old Arab sighed. "Every time my son climbs up to the top, he falls again — as though someone were pushing him back down. It's not natural." Even the Arabs knew the address of *Nabi Daoud* in times of trouble. This old man had come to the right place.

"Your son is not as pure and innocent as you say he is," the Rebbe said sternly. "He is a wicked criminal, and he is receiving the punishment he deserves because he has impugned the honor of the *tzaddik* who lies in that cave!"

Hearing this, the Arab broke into fresh wailing. He swore by Mohammed's beard that he would make sure his son mended his ways. But R' Dovid'l was not satisfied with the father's promises.

"Go to the hole, and tell your son that if he vows never to harm another Jew, and not to touch the *ner tamid* in the cave but rather to do everything in his power to guard the cave — then he will be saved. Otherwise, that hole will be his grave!"

Together with a great crowd, Jews and non-Jews alike, the old Arab made his way back to the hole. Crouching there, he shouted the Rebbe's message down to his son. From the depths came the echoing cry: "I promise!"

The rope was tossed down again. Before the eyes of hundreds of witnesses, the injured youth climbed out, and was rescued.

It was an awesome instance of *kiddush Hashem*, when everyone saw that there is a G-d of Israel and that He speaks from the mouths of His devoted servants and *tzaddikim*.

A few hours later, a procession was seen making its way toward R' Dovid'l's house. On a stretcher lay the injured shepherd, who had come along with his entire family to thank the Rebbe for saving his life.

From that day forward, the *ner tamid* had a faithful guardian — the Arab shepherd, now recovered from his injuries. He checked the flame each day and made sure that it never lacked for oil. His entire family was known as good neighbors to the holy cave, and their peaceful relationship with the Jews lasted many long years.

# The Power of Shabbos Clothes

IT HAD BEEN A HARD YEAR FOR YESHIVAH YEINAH SHEL Torah, a yeshivah for special boys. The institution was beset by financial troubles. That summer, three out of four of its main supporters abroad had died, and the heirs inheriting their estates did not show the same enthusiasm for the yeshivah as their fathers had. Then, in the winter, the computer company owned by the yeshivah's fourth supporter suddenly went bankrupt and was swallowed up by a giant computer firm. The stream of donations dried to a trickle. By the time summer came around again, the yeshivah was subsisting on high-interest loans and sharply slashed budgets.

The administration held an emergency meeting. "If the situation continues this way, we will have no choice but to close down the yeshivah!" the *Rosh Yeshivah* exclaimed in anguish.

"One hundred forty students, each one of them with his special story — and only we know how painful some of those stories are — may find themselves back out on the street," the principal added gravely.

"If I may make a suggestion," requested the *mashgiach,* "I know that the philanthropist Shmuel Black, who died last summer, left

THE POWER OF SHABBOS CLOTHES / 171

behind an heir — a very successful young man, Robert, called Bob. He's a very wealthy man. They say he's doubled the inheritance he received from his father."

"We know all that," the *Rosh Yeshivah* said. "There's nothing new here. The son, though an Orthodox Jew, has no interest in contributing to our yeshivah. We sent someone to him during the winter, and what did Bob tell him?"

"What?" asked the *mashgiach*.

"That he already gave enough to museums and humanitarian organizations in the United States, such as the A.S.P.C.A. and the 'Let Animals Live' foundation. You understand: If we were a museum or took care of injured horses or orphaned puppies, then Bob would give happily. But an institution like ours, that represents the last chance for a group of borderline teenagers to live their lives as mitzvah-observant Jews — 'not interested'."

The *mashgiach* was undeterred. "The man we sent was not imaginative. We need to send someone with personal charisma — a daring, confident man who won't be afraid to open his mouth and really get this Bob fired up."

"Do you have someone in mind?" the principal asked.

The *mashgiach* never hesitated. "Yes. A young fellow who lives in the apartment opposite mine — a man with a lot of personal charisma and self-confidence. In the month of Tishrei he serves as head *chazan* in the big *Yaakov Avinu* shul in the United States, and during the rest of the year he earns his living as a fund-raiser. I think he could be our man."

"In that case," exclaimed the *Rosh Yeshivah*, "what are we waiting for?"

On *Motza'ei Shabbos,* R' Chizkiyah Kirshman boarded a plane, en route to the small Montana town of Mills City. Bob Black lived there, and the city was headquarters to the chain of large department stores that he owned throughout Montana and other states across the United States.

It had taken no small effort to get the fund-raiser to leave home at this time. R' Chizkiyah had just completed a fund-raising tour that had begun in Nisan and ended at the end of Sivan. "And when do I get to be home with my family?" he protested. "I just came back, and the children missed me terribly. I can't leave again now."

"You can't," agreed the *Rosh Yeshivah*. "But neither can my 140 students be tossed into the streets. They have no homes. They have no place else to go!"

R' Chizkiyah was not persuaded. He said he needed time to think it over. The next day, the *mashgiach* took him on a brief tour of the yeshivah, followed by another urgent conversation. With a sigh, R' Chizkiyah buckled under the pressure.

On all of his fund-raising trips to the United States, he had never yet had occasion to visit Montana. He had never even heard of Mills City. But his reputation as a man of courage was well deserved. Directly from the airport, he took a cab to Bob Black's beautiful mansion at the edge of town.

Mr. Black was in his office, occupied by a meeting with his assistants, when his phone rang. A secretary was on the line, calling from his home. "There's a religious Jew at the front gate, asking to see you. What do I do with him?"

"Give him $10 and send him on his way," Black said impatiently, and hung up the phone. "Yes, Mr. Bauman. Where were we?"

The telephone buzzed again. "The Jew says that he doesn't need money, he wants to talk to you."

"I have no time," Black said curtly, hanging up again. But his conscience troubled him, and he found it difficult to concentrate on the meeting. "What could that Jew have wanted?" he complained out loud at last, and sent one of his aides to phone his house.

"Is that fellow still there?" Black asked his secretary. When he heard that he was, he ordered, "Put him on."

"*Shalom aleichem!*" R' Chizkiyah greeted Mr. Black a moment later, in a voice that blended warmth and positive energy. "I'd like to introduce myself. My name is Chizkiyah Kirshman, and I am the *chazan* of *Yaakov Avinu* —"

His staff was astonished to hear their normally stern boss burst into sudden laughter, and say, "Wait for me at my house. I want to meet the *chazan* of *Yaakov Avinu!*"

Bob Black chuckled all the way home, and looked forward to meeting his interesting visitor. The moment he entered his house and laid eyes on the fellow, he said, "Can I see the letter from Yaakov *Avinu* authorizing you to be his official *chazan?*"

"Here it is," replied Kirshman, and broke into song. He sang, cantor-style, *"Hineni He'Ani Mima'as,"* a haunting portion of the Yom Kippur liturgy. By the time he was finished, Black's eyes glistened with tears.

"Wonderful! Let's hear more," Black said.

Kirshman sang, *"K'vakaras Ro'eh Edro."* Black melted.

Then the two enjoyed a lively conversation. R' Chizkiyah was a very personable, likable and friendly fellow. Black enjoyed this visitor, who brought life and warmth into his huge, cold house. He asked Kirshman to stay on as his guest, and Kirshman agreed.

He stayed for three days, without dropping so much as a hint about his purpose in coming. He and his host spent all of Black's free time together, and Bob Black laughed during those days as he had not laughed in a long time. He "played hooky" from the office, just for the sake of enjoying his guest's company.

At last, however, Black's curiosity got the better of him. Kirshman hadn't come to Mills City just to entertain him with snippets of *chazanus*, interesting Torah insights, and anecdotes, riddles, and jokes to make him laugh. On the third night, after dinner, he asked his guest bluntly, "Perhaps you'd like to tell me why you came here?"

The atmosphere between them was friendly and warm, and Kirshman decided to strike while the iron was hot. Besides, his children were waiting impatiently for him at home. It was now or never.

He began speaking in general terms at first, and then brought the talk around specifically to Yeshivah Yeinah Shel Torah.

Black's face darkened. "Aha!" he cried furiously. "I suspected as much! What a pity — I thought you were different from those others. But you are a *shnorrer* like all the other *shnorrers*, only a little more clever than they." He shook his head. "I'm not sorry I let you stay. I enjoyed every minute of your company. But I'm not going to donate a cent."

"And why not?" Kirshman said, his face falling. His trip had been in vain.

"I live by a rule: Each man to his own mitzvah. My father supported yeshivos in Eretz Yisrael, while I contribute to American society. I support the arts, museums and scientific endeavors, and humanitarian organizations such as the A.S.P.C.A."

R' Chizkiyah marshaled all his persuasive powers to try to convince his host that a donation to the yeshivah was also a form of removing suffering from living creatures. But his words fell on deaf ears. Bob Black was obstinate. "You're wasting your time. I'm not giving."

Sadly, Kirshman went up to his room and began to pack. His face was set in lines of unaccustomed bitterness. He was not used to disappointment on this scale.

There was a soft knock on his door. His host stood there.

"The yeshivah is one thing, our friendship is another. Please stay with us for Shabbos. You bring joy into my home."

R' Chizkiyah was stunned. "I have a family of my own in Jerusalem," he said. "They are prepared to sacrifice for the sake of a worthy goal. But when it's clear from the start that there is no purpose, why should my children suffer from my absence any longer than they have to?"

"You're right," Mr. Black said with a smile. "But what do you think about doing something simply for the sake of Heaven, without any thought of profit?"

"What 'sake of Heaven' is there in my staying? Is it a mitzvah to be a guest? No, the mitzvah is to host guests!"

Jokingly, Mr. Black responded, "You are making it possible for me to perform the mitzvah of hosting a guest. Without you, it would be impossible. In other words, you are the object of my mitzvah!"

"Very nice joke," R' Chizkiyah called after Mr. Black, who had already started back downstairs.

At the foot of the stairs, Black looked up and called back, "Rabbi Kirshman, if we enjoy your company over Shabbos, perhaps I'll donate something — in your honor."

R' Chizkiyah stayed.

On Friday night, R' Chizkiyah appeared dressed in his *shtreimel* and long frock coat. Bob Black gazed at him in silence. "This is what we wear in Yerushalayim," Kirshman explained with a broad smile.

Black said nothing. A strange look came into his eye. Without a word, he turned and left the ornate dining room with its beautifully set Shabbos table. He returned a few minutes later, bearing an old Yerushalmi frock coat of faded gold, and a threadbare *shtreimel* whose golden-brown fur was thin and very bedraggled.

"I also have Yerushalmi clothing," he said, with visible emotion.

"Did you get them from one of the museums you help support?" R' Chizkiyah asked, a deliberate sting in the question.

Bob Black recoiled. "Museum? What are you talking about?"

"I'm sorry," Kirshman said at once, with genuine regret. "I was just surprised. Where *did* you get those clothes?"

"If you like, I'll tell you where. After the meal."

"I'm too curious to wait that long!"

"Patience, patience!" Black wagged a finger at his guest. "The story is a long one."

Nachman Schwartz barely managed to escape from Jerusalem with his life.

The Turkish pasha's gendarmes had been hunting him for two weeks. Nachman was 18 years old and, according to Turkish law, he was ripe for the military draft. Every soldier was needed to help the Turks fight their share of World War I. Like many others, Nachman had chosen instead to hide from the authorities.

The Turkish army spared no effort in tracking down draft evaders. Those who were caught were sometimes hanged publicly from the

Jaffa Gate, as an example and a warning to others. Later, they began offering a reward to anyone who handed a draft evader over to the authorities. That was when the local Arabs began to inform on their Jewish neighbors.

The day before, Nachman had left his place of concealment in a deep, dusty cellar in the Batei Machseh neighborhood, and went to the marketplace for something to eat to assuage his hunger. He was dressed as a woman, a veil covering his bearded face. As he walked through the narrow streets, he had an uneasy sense that someone was watching him. Affendi Mustafa, one of the regulars who sat near the coffee-house playing backgammon each day, suddenly leaped up and tore the veil from Nachman's face.

"Look, look!" he cried. "It's not a woman, it's Nachman!"

Nachman began to run, and Affendi raced after him.

Nachman's heart pounded with terror as he sprinted down the narrow streets. His eyes darted wildly from side to side, seeking a place to hide. Several times, passers-by tried to catch hold of him, but he always managed to avoid their grasping fingers. He was quick, and he was nimble. By the time Mustafa returned with a contingent of Turkish soldiers, Nachman had disappeared.

That same night, he parted from his parents and slipped hurriedly out of Jerusalem. His mother had managed to prepare a small bundle containing his *tefillin* and Shabbos clothes, including a *shtreimel* and frock coat (the customary Shabbos garb of young men in Jerusalem in those days, and among Karliner *chassidim* and others today). She added a loaf a bread and a few onions. In the dead of night, Nachman left his home and ran into the Judean hills. From that day, no one in the city heard or saw him again.

Alter and Mirel Schwartz did not know if their son was still alive, or whether they should mourn him. When the war ended, Alter Schwartz traveled the length and breadth of the country, seeking Nachman. From the bits and pieces of information he was able to amass, he learned that his son had reached Egypt. But from that point on, the trail grew cold. It was as though his son had vanished from the earth.

Nachman Schwartz arrived in Egypt disguised as an Arab peasant woman. He reached Port Said after a long, arduous journey, partly on foot and partly as a stowaway on board a train. A sharp-eyed Turkish officer, heading a regiment of Jewish soldiers who had been drafted against their will, noticed something unusual in the way the "Arab woman" was walking. Once again, Nachman was forced to flee for his life. His quick legs carried him back down to the harbor.

In a flash, he threw off his disguise. Before he could make another move, he heard the officer approaching. Nachman dived into a tall crate filled with oranges.

He heard the officer searching for him. After a while, the sounds grew fainter, and then stopped altogether. Nachman was just about to climb out of the crate, when he felt it being lifted into the air. Longshoremen had loaded the crate onto their strong shoulders, and they carried it into the dark cargo hold of a big ship.

Nachman lived on oranges for the next few days. At last, he gathered his courage one night and slipped outside, under cover of darkness. To his dismay, he found that the ship was sailing on an endless sea, and was filled with Turkish soldiers returning to their native land!

The journey was fraught with danger and adventure for Nachman. One night, he was caught, and thrown into the ship's prison, where he was to stay until the journey's end, in Turkey. All seemed lost. But he was energetic and he was able, and soon he was serving the ship's captain as a personal aide. In this way, he saved himself from being handed over to the military authorities on their arrival. He remained with the captain in Turkey for several months. At the end of the war, he was taken on a long, exhausting trip to France. In the port of Marseilles, he was transferred to a second ship, handed over to a second sea captain, who "bought" him from the first one in exchange for two packages of fine tobacco.

This time, the journey was even longer than the previous one. Several weeks later, Nachman reached the shores of America. His ship had docked in Newport, Oregon.

He seized the first opportunity to leave the ship, and never returned. Bundle in hand, he began to walk. Hunger chiseled the lines of his face as he hired himself out to work at different jobs, simply to

178 / TALES FOR THE SOUL

prevent himself from starving. From city to city and from state to state he wandered, until he reached Mills City, Montana.

Here, he found more respectable work: He became a salesclerk in a large department store. His job was to sell cleaning and household goods. He became friendly with the store's owner, a pleasant, observant Jew who took an immense liking to Nachman. In time, Nachman married the boss's daughter.

"My grandfather, Nachman Schwartz, wore these clothes in America until he was an old man. As a small boy, I would see him wearing them on Friday nights. It seems like a far-off dream now. Tonight, seeing you in the same clothes, I felt as though an electric current had passed through me. I was reminded of the whole story. I hoped that my father hadn't thrown out the clothes. I found them in a drawer." Mr. Black finished his long tale. "You realize that 'Black' is the translation of the name 'Schwartz'."

The lights had gone out some time ago, and Bob Black's face glowed in the golden candlelight of the long Shabbos candles in their silver candlesticks. Around them were fine china plates and flatware made of pure gold. Kirshman was silent. Black went on, speaking almost to himself.

"Look what clothes can do. I had made up my mind not to donate money to any yeshivah. The most eloquent speech would have failed to move me — but the sight of these Yerushalmi clothes has aroused all sorts of buried feelings —" He turned to face Kirshman. "I am changing my mind. I want to give *nachas* to the souls of my father and grandfather in *Gan Eden*. I want to be a worthy grandson to my grandfather, who was forced to leave home at the age of 18 and traveled so far, all the way to Montana, where he continued to scrupulously observe his faith and customs — even clinging to his traditional Shabbos clothes — all his life.

"With Hashem's help, I will continue in my father's footsteps," Bob Black said in a choked voice. "And since I've doubled my inheritance from my father, it's only right that I double his support for the yeshivah as well!"

# A Gaon in Sefer Devarim

THE FAMOUS GAON, R' ENZEL, *AV BEIS DIN* OF THE STREI community and a foremost student of the Ketzos Hachoshen, was a vigorous opponent of *chassidus*. In this new stream of Judaism he saw something alien, a collection of strange and different customs whose source was not explicit in the Torah, or — in the worst case — even stood in contradiction to its teachings. He viewed all *chassidim* as uneducated folk who did not know how to learn even a single chapter as it should be learned.

In his city lived a righteous and wise chassidic *gaon,* R' Ziskind Landau, a follower of the holy Rebbe, R' Uri of Strelisk. It was impossible to make fun of R' Ziskind: R' Enzel knew him personally and was well aware of his diligence and scholarship in Torah. However, R' Enzel heaped plenty of scorn on R' Ziskind's Rebbe, R' Uri. Though these taunts made R' Ziskind angry, he was a firm believer in keeping the peace and refused to answer even a single one of R' Enzel's scoffing remarks.

One day, R' Enzel doubled and tripled his usual quota of mockery against R' Uri of Strelisk. He cast the Rebbe as an empty-headed fool, poked fun at his teachings, and knowingly exceeded the limit. This time, he was sure, R' Ziskind's anger would get the better of him and he would strenuously counter all the mocking comments, one by one.

But, to his amazement, R' Ziskind held his tongue even now. He bowed his head and sat silently as his Rebbe was humiliated in the most degrading fashion.

R' Enzel could not understand it. Was R' Ziskind's patience really so vast? How could he listen to such insults to his Rebbe without reacting?

Seizing R' Ziskind's coat with both hands, R' Enzel demanded, "Why don't you answer? Why don't you say even a word?"

"What am I to say?" R' Ziskind said, with a sigh that seemed to come from the bottom of his soul. His head bowed even lower, as though it had grown heavier in his grief. "I have nothing to answer. You are correct in everything you've said!"

180 / TALES FOR THE SOUL

"*What?*" R' Enzel leaped up as though bitten by a snake. "What did you say? Did my ears hear correctly?"

"You heard me. And not only that, but I, too, laugh at him," R' Ziskind confided, head still bowed between his hunched shoulders.

Eyes alight with triumph, R' Enzel declared, "That means that you admit your rebbe is nothing but a boor and an ignoramus.. —"

R' Ziskind Landau raised his head with a dismissive smile. "Not necessarily."

"Then what do you mean?"

"The picture that you've painted so enthusiastically is not the image of my holy Rebbe, R' Uri of Strelisk," R' Ziskind said, and now he was laughing. "It's someone else, some clown, perhaps, at whom I, too, must chuckle. But someone entirely different lives in Strelisk — a man of G-d, holy and awesome, like an angel floating in the heavens. If you knew him, you would turn into his most fervent *chassid* and run to learn Torah from him even more than I do!"

For the first time, it was R' Enzel who had no answer.

The group standing in the town square, holding lit candles, attracted the attention of Gimpel, R' Enzel's *shamash*. Curiosity drew him to the square. As he approached, the mystery was abruptly cleared up. The men's heads were tilted back and their eyes were raking the sky for a glimpse of the moon.

"Look, the clouds are scattering," one of them cried out joyfully. "In another minute, the sky will clear and we'll be able to bless the moon!"

Gimpel could now recognize the figures: They were Strelisk *chassidim* who lived in Strei. He ran over to the group.

"*Kiddush levanah?*" he called out in anger. "*Now* you remember? The deadline for blessing the moon passed last night!"

The *chassidim* did not bother to answer. Their eyes were busily looking upward again, searching for the moon. Gimpel turned and ran like the wind, back to the *beis midrash*.

The *av beis din*, R' Enzel, was bent over a large volume, his thoughts immersed in the subject he was learning. At first, he did not grasp what his *shamash* was saying to him. When at last he understood, he scolded, "Why didn't you disperse them on the spot? You have the authority to do that. The *chassidim* are breaking all the rules of halachah, and you hesitate? Hurry back to the market square and tell those men, in my name, to return to their homes. Let us not allow even a corner of explicit halachah to be impinged upon."

Gimpel raced back to the square. To his shock, he saw that the *chassidim* had been joined by R' Ziskind Landau. How could he send such a man home? It was unthinkable. R' Ziskind was a paramount Torah scholar, and everyone agreed that his piety was even greater than his learning. He was a prominent figure in Strei, with a public stature that was not far behind that of the great R' Enzel himself.

Gimpel took a step backwards.

At that moment, the sky cleared completely and the moon shone out in its purity. The *chassidim* burst out in joyous recital of the blessing. Merry cries of "*Shalom aleichem*" echoed through the square. Soon all the *chassidim* were dancing in a circle, singing with joyous abandon.

Gimpel continued his retreat. The spectacle wounded him. Was it not enough that the *chassidim* were transgressing a halachic precept? Must they also sing and dance? In the distance, he heard the refrain float back to him. Derisively, he thought, "They're singing about 'this month,' when the time to bless 'this month' is over and done with!"

Without further ado, he retraced his steps to the *beis midrash*.

"*Nu*, Gimpel?" R' Enzel asked expectantly. "Did you send those rule-breakers home?"

"No, Rebbe. I saw R' Ziskind Landau among them, blessing the moon along with the other *chassidim*. I couldn't do it."

R' Enzel was stunned. If the learned R' Ziskind had been numbered among the group, the matter took on a different face. They were no longer talking about a group of ignorant men acting on a whim. Apparently, R' Ziskind had permitted himself to stretch the letter of the law. His association with the *chassidim* was leading him astray!

A look of fury darkened on R' Enzel's face. He ordered Gimpel to hurry to R' Ziskind's house and to demand where, in Heaven's name,

182 / TALES FOR THE SOUL

he had found a source permitting the blessing of the moon after the deadline stated clearly in the *Shulchan Aruch*.

Gimpel hurried to do as R' Enzel requested. R' Ziskind greeted both Gimpel and his question calmly. He picked up a piece of paper, dipped his pen in ink, and wrote one line: "This is what I saw from my teacher, the *gaon* of Strelisk."

When Gimpel showed R' Enzel the paper, R' Enzel burst out laughing. "The '*gaon*' of Strelisk? So, a new '*gaon*' has risen in Israel." He laughed louder. "If he'd written, 'the *tzaddik*,' I'd have understood. But — '*gaon*'? What does that word have to do with the Rebbe of Strelisk?"

The next morning, after *Shacharis*, R' Enzel showed R' Ziskind's note to all of his *misnagdim* friends. They, too, laughed uproariously.

They were still standing around, enjoying themselves at the expense of the *chassidim,* when R' Ziskind himself walked into the shul. R' Enzel approached him at once.

"Are we all fools here? Have you gone senile, Heaven forbid? Look at what you wrote in this note. Since when has your Rebbe turned into a *gaon*?"

R' Ziskind had not yet taken off his coat, but R' Enzel would not let him walk inside. He showered the other man with harsh critcism. "You know, it's you I am most angry at — precisely because you are a *talmid chacham*. If some ignorant *chassid* writes that his Rebbe is a *gaon* — well, I figure that, by his own standards, that's so. But you know better. You know what the word '*gaon*' means. How could you apply it to your Rebbe?"

"Excuse me," R' Ziskind said. He hung his coat on a hook on the old shul wall, placed his *tallis* bag on a table, and wiped his brow before turning to R' Enzel. "Do you want an answer? I have one for you!"

A number of other men had approached the two during this interchange, their prayer shawls abandoned half-folded in their curiosity to hear how R' Ziskind would answer R' Enzel.

"If we are talking about the term '*gaon*,'" R' Ziskind said, "perhaps your honor would explain to me how you, and all those like you, define the term."

"A person who is great in Torah," one worshiper called out.

"Why?" R' Ziskind shot back. "What's the connection between the literal definition of the word '*gaon*' and greatness in Torah?"

This time, a long silence reigned in the shul. No one knew precisely how to answer the question.

It was R' Ziskind himself who broke the silence. "Let me tell you what I've learned, from *sefarim* and from their authors. The term '*gaon*' is used to describe every *rav* and Torah scholar, because the word implies something tall and strong (as it says in *Mishlei*: '*Lifnei shever gaon*' — 'Pride precedes destruction'). In other words, Torah scholars raise and strengthen the ramparts of Torah.

"For example," he continued, "It says three times in the Torah, 'Do not cook a kid in its mother's milk.' If you were to ask a young child what this verse means, he would tell you the simplest meaning: that the holy Torah forbids us to cook a young kid in its own mother's milk. 'But perhaps you would be allowed to cook the lamb in a different sheep's milk and eat it?' you might then ask. The small child would not know how to answer, because his rebbi in *cheder* did not explain this idea any further. Our Sages have expanded and adorned the Torah, commenting on every detail of halachah until they derived, from this single verse, all the laws concerning meat and milk.

"Or take the laws of Shabbos. As it says in the *Gemara* [*Chagigah:*10], 'Mountains dangle from a thread; very little is written but many laws [are learned].' And so on, and so on. Our holy Sages are deservedly called by the term '*gaon*,' because they have expanded on the Torah and given it new height. A craftsman is known by his art."

"A very nice explanation," R' Enzel said appreciatively. "But what is there in your answer to tell us why you referred to your Rebbe as a '*gaon*' in your note? Does he, too, know how to explicate halachah from every letter and sign in the Torah?" He made no attempt to hide the mockery in his voice.

R' Ziskind's eyes flashed. "Certainly!" he cried. "The fifth book of the Torah, *Sefer Devarim*, states clearly a number of times, 'to love Hashem, to fear Him, and to cling to Him.' These three commandments are not mountains dangling from threads. They are not written in hints or secrets, but rather as clearly as can be: love of

Hashem, fear of Hashem, and devotion to Hashem. For you, these concepts are wondrous things. Your understanding of them is similar to that of the small child about the verse, 'Do not cook a kid in its mother's milk.'

"If you were to travel to Strelisk, however," R' Ziskind thundered at the *misnagdim* massed around him, "and you were to speak to my teacher and Rebbe, the holy R' Uri, about these three commandments — love, fear, and devotion — then you would discover the depth of his understanding of these three words. These are concepts for which every Jew was born and by which he seeks to serve his Creator all his life.

"Know this," R' Ziskind said sternly. "Were you to speak with R' Uri for months or even years about fear, love, and devotion to Hashem, you would never plumb the depths of his understanding. There is no limit to his wisdom where these three things are concerned."

He eyed the crowd and concluded. "You are '*gaonim*' in four *Chumashim*," he said, quietly now. "But my teacher and Rebbe is a *gaon* in the fifth — in *Sefer Devarim*."

If R' Enzel did not change his views after this piercing argument, he did put a complete stop to his mockery of R' Uri of Strelisk. Later, he stopped taunting chassidic customs in general.

In his old age, however, as he witnessed the way *chassidus* stood as a bulwark of defense against the Enlightenment, which had begun to make destructive inroads among the Jewish people and stole away the hearts of many young men, R' Enzel changed his tune completely. He began to befriend the *chassidim* of Strei, to welcome them warmly, and to speak to them at every opportunity.

"I have repented everything that I ever said about *chassidus* and its *rebbei'im*," he declared often. "May Hashem grant me atonement!"

# The Astonishing Arab Merchant

YOSEF ADAHAN WAS A GOOD AND SIMPLE MAN WHO SERVED as the *shamash* of his shul in the city of Fez, Morocco. He was no Torah scholar — not by any means. From the time he was a child, he had never merited being in the presence of great Torah minds, and as a youth he was forced to go out into the marketplace in order to help support his poverty-stricken family.

But, although he was not privileged to be counted among the learned ones, Yosef's heart beat with a pure fear of Heaven. His behavior was in the best Jewish tradition of modesty and piety. When he picked up a *sefer Tehillim* and began to sweetly chant its age-old words, the sternest hearts would melt. He always spoke to his Creator the way a child would speak to his father: simply and openly. He poured out his heart to Hashem and denied Him nothing.

It was after he had been blessed with a number of children that Yosef took on the position as *shamash*. The shul was headed by *Dayan* Yehonasan Seriro, a prominent figure in Fez. Throughout all of Morocco, R' Yehonasan was known for his wisdom and righteousness, his holiness and good deeds. His Torah knowledge was great, and his piety even greater. Everything that he did was directed toward the glory of Hashem, to honor the Torah, and to honor his fellow man.

For many years, R' Yehonasan was one of the first to enter the large shul in Fez every morning, and among the last to leave at night. In his old age, his many admirers — among them some fabulously wealthy men — built him a beautiful shul of his own near his home, to help him avoid having to make the long walk each day.

Yosef Adahan lived near the new shul, and he was among the first to begin *davening* there. His simple demeanor and radiant piety made him beloved of R' Yehonasan. He studied Yosef for a time, and when he determined that Yosef was indeed a fine, good man, a man who served Hashem faithfully and wholeheartedly, he decided to appoint him to serve as *shamash* in his new shul.

Yosef was the happiest man in Fez when the *dayan* approached him with the offer. He viewed R' Yehonasan as nothing less than an angel, and his shul as a *mikdash me'at* (a small Holy Temple). "I will serve this House of G-d with all my heart and soul," he promised fervently.

He kept his promise.

So great was the *dayan* in the *shamash's* eyes that Yosef treated him the way a servant would a master, with awe and humility. He tended the shul lovingly and faithfully, lighting the candles and polishing the glass oil dishes to a high gloss. He would prepare the water for hand-washing and arrange the *siddurim* and *sefarim* in their proper places. Each *erev Shabbos* and *erev Yom Tov*, he would clean the shul from top to bottom, until it looked as clean and new as the day it was built. And he did all of it with a joyous demeanor and endless patience.

R' Yehonasan loved his loyal and hardworking *shamash* dearly, and saw him as a pure and G-d-fearing Jew whose every action was for the sake of Heaven.

"My Yosef," R' Yehonasan would say from time to time, "you nourish my soul!"

In truth, the opposite was true. It was R' Yehonasan who nourished Yosef the *shamash's* soul.

Yosef had been blessed with numerous children — twelve in all, a dozen "tribes" of his own. His expenses were enormous — as was his poverty. Every day, Yosef had to rack his brains anew for a way to feed his family. Until the day he met the *dayan*, his children often went hungry. From that day, however, the *dayan* saw to it that Yosef's children had enough to eat. From time to time, he would press a small bundle of money into his modest *shamash's* hand, taking care that no one should see. He took extra pains before Shabbos and festivals. Had R' Yehonasan not stepped in, the poor *shamash* and his family might literally have starved to death, Heaven forbid. Thanks to his help, these were happy days for the family instead. They now had good food to eat on *Yom Tov*. And none of them had the slightest idea that the money was coming out of the *dayan's* own pocket.

R' Yehonasan's family satisfied themselves with a bit of bread and a drink of water, both on the weekdays and on Shabbos and *Yom Tov*, and no one knew. The selflessness and loving-kindness that he had sowed in his children's hearts was so powerful that they agreed to every sacrifice, and never complained to their father, "Why is the Adahan family more deserving than the Seriro family?"

They neither questioned nor grumbled. Love of charity had been fed to them with their mother's milk, along with a deep love of Torah — and a perspective that viewed this world as merely a hallway leading to the Palace: the World to Come.

For Yosef Adahan and his family, those were the "seven good years." From the day he first laid eyes on the worthy *dayan*, Yosef's family knew no want. As time went on, Yosef came to expect the charity, and even came to ask for help at times. R' Yehonasan knew that when his *shamash* came into his room and stood aside in awed and reverent silence, this was a sign that he had spent his last penny. The *dayan* would search his pockets for a bit of money and hand it over joyfully.

But the good times came to an abrupt end with the *dayan's* departure from this world. The city mourned his passing. They eulogized the man who had illuminated their eyes with Torah. The Jews of Fez felt like a flock that had lost its shepherd.

If everyone grieved, no one did so with greater sincerity than Yosef Adahan, the *shamash*. During the procession to the cemetery, he walked along behind the body weeping even more copiously than the departed *dayan's* own children. "My father, my father!" he shrieked bitterly. "Why have you left me?"

The community had been aware of the deep and abiding love between the *dayan* and his *shamash*, but no one knew just how deep it ran. Yosef fainted three times on the way to the cemetery, and had to be escorted, dejectedly, home, weeping in inconsolable anguish.

No one except for Yosef's own wife and children knew the hidden reason for his tears. Now there was no one in the world to care about him. He was a gentle soul, modest and shy. He could not have accepted charity from anyone but the *dayan*. Never could he walk the streets of Fez proclaiming his poverty and begging for alms. It was impossible.

He consulted with his wife. She advised him to go to the community's wealthiest figures, those who worshiped in the *dayan's* shul, and reveal to them his dire poverty. Without any other option, Yosef agreed to the plan. But his distress upon leaving the rich men's homes was even greater than his distress upon entering. Though the men welcomed him pleasantly enough, when he hinted at his reason for coming they abruptly fell silent. Sighing as though to commiserate with his pain, each ended by giving him a very meager donation. Yosef walked away, face darkened with sorrow.

It was the month of Adar. Purim came and went, and Pesach was soon approaching. This was the time of year when expenses mounted highest and quickest. Until this year, R' Yehonasan had seen to his family's needs. This year, Yosef and his family were orphaned.

Weighed down with worry and pain, Yosef went to pour out his heart to the one person who had known him well. He went to the cemetery, to visit the departed *dayan's* grave.

As if of their own volition, his feet took him to the right place. Casting himself down beside the grave, Yosef began to weep bitter tears. For a long time, he could not utter a word, so deep was his anguish. When he had calmed down a bit, he picked himself up and returned home. That was when he had his inspiration.

He would write the *dayan* a letter!

He sat down to do it at once. It was a long letter, and it opened with the words, "To his honor, the holy *dayan*, my rebbe and teacher, R' Yehonasan Seriro." In the letter, Yosef described the suffering he had undergone since the *dayan's* passing, and begged R' Yehonasan to come to his aid in his time of need. "I once heard from you that whatever a man engages in during his lifetime in this world will also engage him in the World to Come. Please stand by me now, as you did when you were alive..." During his lifetime, R' Yehonasan had supported Yosef and cared for him in times of need; now, Yosef pleaded with him to continue from *Gan Eden*.

It was late at night by the time he finished writing his letter. Reluctant to walk to the graveyard in the dark, Yosef waited impatiently for daylight. Immediately after *Shacharis*, he headed for the cemetery. Approaching R' Yehonasan's grave, he placed the letter on the tombstone, securing it with small stones lest it fly away in the wind. He wanted to be sure that the *dayan* would be able to read every word.

With a lighter heart, Yosef went back home. He was certain that, in R' Yehonasan's merit, his salvation would not be long in coming.

On *erev Pesach*, R' Massoud Seriro, eldest son of *Dayan* Yehonasan Seriro — and his successor — went to pray at his father's grave. Spotting the letter on the tombstone, he removed the stones and read the long letter from beginning to end.

"Yosef Adahan," he murmured. "He served as my father's *shamash* up until the end. What an ignorant man he is; he doesn't know that you don't write letters to the dead!"

During *chol hamo'ed*, Yosef paid the new *dayan* a visit. R' Massoud spoke pleasantly with him for a time. When Yosef rose to leave, R' Massoud said gently, "My friend, I went to the cemetery on *erev Pesach,* and I saw that you had written a letter to my father, may his resting place be in *Gan Eden*. That was not a good thing to do."

"Why not?" Yosef's face fell.

An expression of disapproval shadowed the *dayan's* face. "You asked my father for his help. Is he in place of Hashem? It is permissible to pray at the graves of *tzaddikim* — to pray to Hashem. Those graves are holy places, and our prayers may be more acceptable there, in the merit of those *tzaddikim*. But we don't write them letters. Please do not do such a thing again."

Surprised, the *shamash* asked naively, "Your honor shouldn't say such things. Did I write that letter to your dear departed father in vain? Who helped me, if not him?"

"What are you talking about?"

"Ah! Listen to this, and you'll see how much greater are the powers of a *tzaddik* after his death than during his lifetime!"

"I'm eager to hear," said the *dayan*, intensely curious.

"Here's what happened...."

The Jews of Fez had the custom of placing a certain type of grass, known as "*baboniz*," on their Pesach Seder plates, in symbolic reference to the verse, "I am *chavatzelet hasharon*, rose of the valleys," which is written in *Shir Hashirim* and read aloud each Pesach to express *Bnei Yisrael's* deep love for Hashem. But that year, no *baboniz* was to be found in all of Fez or its environs.

It was not easy for the pious to pass up this old custom, which had been handed down to them from their fathers and grandfathers. Anxiously, they searched high and low for the grass, combing city and village, prepared to pay any price. But all their efforts were in vain. *Baboniz* was not to be found anywhere that year.

On the thirteenth day of Nisan, at sunrise, Yosef Adahan woke to the sound of vigorous pounding at his door. Startled and afraid, he rushed to the door. "Who's there?"

"It is I, Abdul Hamid," replied an unfamiliar voice.

Yosef was even more frightened; it was a strange Arab, knocking on his door at the crack of dawn! "What do you want?"

"Open the door," pleaded the man on the other side. "It will be worth your while, you'll see."

Quickly, Yosef threw on his clothes, and then opened the door to the stranger.

The Arab appeared to be in his 60's. His hair was streaked with gray and his clothes carried the scent of earth and growing things.

"I've heard about you, my dear Yosef," the Arab said heartily. "I've heard that you are an honest man, and a hardworking and faithful one. You can be relied on."

Yosef lowered his eyes modestly to the floor.

Dispensing with compliments, the Arab went right to the point. "Listen, Yosef. I have a large quantity of the grass you Jews use on Pesach."

"What? You have *baboniz*?"

Laughing at his excitement, the Arab nodded. "Yes, and lots of it. Enough for all the Jewish families in Fez, and even for the Jews in the outlying villages."

Yosef was exhilarated. Still, he did not fully grasp the matter. Careful to keep the eagerness from his voice, he asked, "Why did you come to me — and so early in the morning, too?"

Again the Arab laughed. "I have only one donkey," he said. "How much can he carry on his back? If I overload him, the poor thing will collapse. I can't do two jobs at once. I thought that I would bring the grass from the fields to the marketplace, and you would sell it to the Jews for me. Afterwards, I'd pay you for your work. Don't worry, you won't lose out on the deal."

Yosef peered at him suspiciously. Was the Arab trying to lay a trap for him?

The shrewd Arab sensed his suspicion. He patted Yosef's arm. "Come on, Yosef, don't hesitate. I promise you, you won't lose by it."

On second thought, the affair seemed straightforward enough. As the man had said, Yosef had nothing to lose. They shook hands on the deal. Yosef went to shul, where he *davened Shacharis*. Afterwards, he headed directly for the marketplace.

The Arab was waiting for him there, standing beside a sturdy donkey. On the donkey's back were bags of the precious grass.

When he saw Yosef approaching, the Arab began to quickly unload the donkey. By the time Yosef reached him, the bags were strewn like pearls at Yosef's feet. Even before he'd finished calling out, "Who wants to buy *baboniz*?" customers began to flock eagerly around. The news spread like wildfire: Yosef the *shamash* was selling *baboniz*. Everyone wanted some.

Business moved with lightning speed. Yosef's head whirled as he sold *baboniz* to customer after customer. Sooner than he would have believed possible, his supply of the grass had dwindled almost to nothing — but the Arab appeared at once with a fresh load. Customers streamed toward Yosef from every direction, prepared to pay whatever price he asked. All were ecstatic at this chance to adorn their Seder according to their custom, after they had already given up hope. They paid Yosef's asking price without demur or hesitation.

The hours passed in a blur of sales. Yosef was the only seller of *baboniz* in the marketplace, and his customers continued to multiply throughout the day. From time to time, the Arab would appear with a fresh supply of the grass. The more Yosef sold, the more energetic the Arab became. Hardly had Yosef sold all of his stock, than the Arab returned with another donkeyload for him. Yosef was so busy with the hordes of buyers than he did not have time to exchange so much as a single word with the Arab all day long.

The money in Yosef's box — money that he would give to the Arab at the end of the day — grew and grew. The Arab left on another trip to bring more of the *baboniz*. He returned quickly, the donkey fully laden with a fresh supply.

And then, without warning, the Arab disappeared. Yosef was left with all the money — and the donkey, too!

Yosef turned over the marketplace in his search for the Arab. The man seemed to have vanished into thin air. He did not come to ask for his money or his donkey. Yosef went on to search for him in inns and taverns, but no one recalled ever seeing the fellow.

Finally, Yosef took his wages, as they had agreed, and put aside the rest of the money until the Arab should return for it.

"And I ask you, your honor," Yosef said, leaning forward intently. "Five days have passed, and the Arab hasn't come back. My heart tells me that he will never come. The money is mine — sent to me by Heaven. Did this miracle come about in my own merit? Wasn't it in the merit of your righteous father? Wasn't it because of the letter I left him, a letter whose every word was written with my heart's blood? This," he said, leaning back in triumph, "was his response to me. He answered my letter!"

R' Massoud Seriro had listened to Yosef's account in stunned silence, not interrupting even once. When the *shamash* finished his story, the young *dayan* said emotionally, "I was mistaken. I beg your pardon, Yosef. You have merited experiencing a miracle. Apparently, you met up with the 'merchant' mentioned numerous times in the *Gemara*, the *midrash*, and the holy *Zohar* (*Sanhedrin* 110 and other places; *Bamidbar Rabbah, Parashah* 18, *Zohar Shemos, Parashas Terumah,* et al.) — Eliyahu *Hanavi*! How happy is the lot of the pure of heart who follow the path of Hashem's Torah!"

# Three Who Cried

THE TELEPHONE RANG IN THE APARTMENT OF REPHAEL Abuhav, *mohel, chazan,* and *rav*. A hesitant voice asked, "Are you the *mohel* Abuhav?"

"Yes," answered R' Abuhav.

The speaker sounded as though he were choosing his words with care. "I wanted to invite you to a *bris* — that is, to perform a *bris* for our son. Will you do a *bris* in Holon [a surburb of Tel Aviv, not far from Bnei Brak]?"

If R' Abuhav was surprised at the speaker's strange manner, he hid it well. "Happily. What's the problem with Holon?"

"No problem at all," the man answered hastily. "Can you come tomorrow to perform the *bris* at 7:30 in the morning?"

"Certainly."

The man gave his name as "Golan," along with an address in Holon. He requested that the rabbi arrive punctually.

R' Abuhav hung up the phone. Up until that point, despite the slightly peculiar manner he had detected in the phone conversation, all was proceeding as usual. Another holy *bris* to perform, another mitzvah.

He could not have foreseen the bizarre events that were soon to unfold.

194 / TALES FOR THE SOUL

R' Abuhav woke early the following morning and went, as was his habit, to *daven* with the sunrise *minyan* in a shul near his home. At precisely 7:30, he stepped out of a taxi on a Holon street and looked around him.

It was a typically secular Israeli block. There were well-kept homes and gardens, just now blooming with color. An early-morning peace hung over the residential area. Nearby, a truck was parked in front of a grocery store, and workers were unloading cartons of bread and milk with the ease of long habit. Nothing was different today than yesterday, or the day before.

To his surprise, he saw no shul on the block. He glanced again at the piece of paper in his hand, on which he had written down the address the caller had given him. No, there was no mistake. He was exactly where he was supposed to be. Why, then, did he see no sign of preparations for a *bris*? No shul, no modest catering hall, no public building at all. What was going on?

At last, the *mohel* decided to try the house whose address was written on the paper he held in his hand, despite the fact that it was a residence and not a public building. There was no sign at all, outside, of any impending *bris*, but perhaps it was to take place inside the private home. That was unusual, but not unheard of.

He approached the house. A carved sign on the door read, "Golan Family." That was indeed the name the man had given him. He rang the bell.

The door opened. R' Abuhav found himself facing a tall, broad-shouldered man with a headful of curly hair. For an instant, he wondered if he had mistaken the address, after all, and took a step back. But the man's eyes lit up at the sight of him. "Are you the *mohel*?"

Smiling, the rabbi lifted his black bag slightly and answered, "Yes."

"Good! I'm very glad you came. Come in, do the *bris* quickly."

"Where will the *bris* be taking place?" R' Abuhav asked politely.

"What do you mean? It's taking place right here!"

"You intend to give the baby his *bris* here in the house?" The question hid a profound incomprehension. What, R' Abuhav wondered, was going on here? What kind of *bris* was about to take place? He saw no one at all in the house. It was all so strange.

THREE WHO CRIED / 195

"Well, come in already. Let's get it over with. I don't have much time; I have to get to work."

"Just a minute," R' Abuhav pleaded. "What do you mean, 'Let's get it over with'? We need a *minyan*. Where are ten men?"

"There's no *minyan*," the other said shortly. "I'm in a big hurry."

R' Abuhav was not prepared to back down easily. Going out into the street, he tried to draft eight more men to join them at the *bris*. To his distress, not only did he fail to snag even one person — but the baby's own father left, rushing off to work!

R' Abuhav was in a quandary. Seeing this, the baby's mother said, "I guess I owe you an explanation. To tell the truth, we didn't really intend to make a *bris* for our Yovel."

"Just a minute — you've already named him?"

"Yes, we call him Yovel."

The *mohel* rolled his eyes. "I don't understand. You didn't wait for the *bris* to give him his name?"

"Let me explain. We are very secular, you see. We have no connection to religion at all — absolutely none. We don't know a single religious Jew and we don't observe anything. As I say, we never planned on giving our son a *bris*, either. But Shagi and I weren't so comfortable with that —"

"Shagi?"

"Shagi is my husband," the woman explained. "Well, as I say, we thought it over again. Maybe it would be better, after all, not to be different from everyone. Maybe, when our Yovel grows up, he'd be embarrassed to be different, to be just like a gentile. So we decided to invite you down here, to make a *bris*."

R' Abuhav was at a loss — but his discomfiture was about to increase.

"I've got to leave the house now," the mother said. "That's why we asked that you come on time. I've got some shopping to do. We haven't invited any guests, because we didn't want to turn this into a party. In our view, a *bris milah* is just a minor surgical procedure. No one has to be present except for you — and the child, of course. Do whatever you have to. The babysitter will be here in half an hour. When she comes, you can leave."

The woman led the *mohel*, his mind reeling, into the baby's room. Little Yovel was sleeping soundly. The mother had her purse in hand; a moment later, she was out the door. R' Abuhav was alone with the baby.

Slowly, he recovered from his shock. Breathing deeply, he waited for his head to clear. From the time he had first begun his career as a *mohel*, he had never participated in such a strange *bris*.

A *bris milah*, all alone in an empty house! Who had ever heard of such a thing? If a *bris* was just a minor surgical procedure, as the boy's mother claimed — well, even an operating room has a staff standing by: doctors, nurses, orderlies …

He decided not to waste time in idle thought. He opened his bag and began arranging his tools on Yovel's changing table. As he worked, he glanced up once or twice to inspect the room.

It was a room that belonged, without question, to wealthy people. Yovel was an only son and his parents wanted to give him everything. His mother had shown no hesitation in leaving the child alone with a stranger; no doubt she trusted him as a religious man — an encouraging sign, he thought. Gently, the *mohel* reached down to wake the baby. He stroked and patted the child into calmness, and then began the "operation."

R' Abuhav placed the infant across his own lap; the child burst into tears. His heart was melting with pity for this poor child. Was this a *bris*? It was some time before he had himself under control again. He served as both *sandak* and *mohel* at this strange ceremony. As was his practice, he performed the circumcision quickly and efficiently. Holding the screaming infant in his arms, R' Abuhav stood up and recited the blessings. When he reached the words "and his name shall be called in Israel," he pronounced the name "Yovel," as had the boy's mother.

The baby broke into a fresh bout of crying. Bending over him, R' Abuhav murmured soothingly into his ear, promising that he would not leave until the babysitter came. But 8 o'clock came and went, with no sign of her.

R' Abuhav was upset. The woman had promised that the sitter would be there at 8 o'clock sharp, but the hands of the clock stood at 8:30 and the big, beautifully furnished house was still empty except for the *mohel* and the newly circumcised baby. He walked impatiently from room to room, glancing at the clock every few minutes. 8:40, 8:50 ...

He knew nothing except for the family's name, "Golan." He would never dream of looking through their personal belongings for more details. Instead, he paced the house like a lion in a cage, at a total loss. The baby woke up, hungry, and began to howl.

R' Abuhav began to search frantically for a baby bottle, but found none. He began to feel frazzled. The infant was crying pitifully, breaking the *mohel's* heart with compassion. He tried feeding the baby some lukewarm boiled water on a spoon, but Yovel was uninterested. His wails grew stronger along with his hunger pangs, until they pierced the *mohel's* heart like a sword. R' Abuhav burst into tears of his own, weeping along with the baby.

He did not cry over the predicament in which he now found himself, but for the unfortunate little Jew whose parents were planning to separate him from his link to his Creator, to the G-d of his people. R' Abuhav prayed fervently that, despite the antipathy toward religion that prevailed in this home, the child would grow up to study and keep the Torah and have fear of Heaven. And he wept for the unfortunate parents, two Jewish souls who had lost their way to the point that even a *bris milah* was no longer a given. He cried and cried. Along with him wept the baby.

He was still shedding uncontrollable tears when there came the sound of a key scraping in a lock. The door opened. A woman burst inside. "My sweet Yovel!" she cried, rushing breathlessly into the baby's room.

Her astonishment knew no bounds, when she spied the baby in the arms of an elderly, bearded, religious Jew who was trying, unsuccessfully, to hide his own tears.

"I'm the babysitter," she said, staring. "I'm very sorry, I got caught in the most awful traffic and I had some things I just had to take care of before I came here. That's why I was an hour and a half late. He's probably starving by now. Who are you?"

198 / TALES FOR THE SOUL

"I am the *mohel*."

"Ah, yes. His mother told me yesterday that a *mohel* would be coming here this morning. I'm sorry that I've held you up."

R' Abuhav left the house. The whole strange adventure, he believed, would be just a passing episode in his life — an odd story to recount at times. On his return home, he told his family about the strange *bris* he had conducted that day. The tale aroused amazement and strong emotion among his listeners. After a few days, however, it was all but forgotten.

Twelve and half years passed.

R' Abuhav, as a respected *mohel* who was in great demand, performed thousands of circumcisions during that time. He was not only a *mohel*, but also a well-known *chazan*, serving as chief *chazan* for the Tel Aviv Rabbinate. One day, a knock came at the door of his office at the Rabbinate. In the doorway stood a woman, a tall boy at her side.

"Are you the *chazan* and *mohel*, R' Abuhav?" she asked.

"Yes."

"I'm Mrs. Golan, from Holon. Do you remember me?"

For a moment, he didn't. "Remind me," he requested.

She laughed. "Twelve and a half years ago, you performed a *bris* on my son here, Yovel Golan." She pointed to the boy. "If you'll remember, you were alone at home with the baby, and the babysitter came late."

Twelve and a half years dissolved as though they had never been. "Do I remember?" R' Abuhav exclaimed. "How could I possibly forget a *bris* like that? I will never forget it, to my dying day! Well, I see that the boy has grown nicely, eh? How are you, son?" He smiled at the boy. Yovel had indeed grown into a nice-looking youth. He was tall and comely, and his eyes shone with a mysterious light, as though his entire personality was cloaked in secrecy.

The mother sighed. "It's because of him that I've come here."

"Has something happened?" R' Abuhav asked with concern. "Is there a problem?"

"Big problems!" Mrs. Golan burst into tears. "Something's happened to Yovel. For the past year, he won't learn a thing. There's only one insane idea in his head — to meet his *mohel*. I don't know where he got the notion from, but we have no choice. Yovel is our only son, and to make him happy we're prepared to do what he wants."

"How did you find me?"

"I remembered that your name was R' Abuhav. My husband and I searched for you, until we learned that someone by that name was also the chief *chazan* for the Tel Aviv Rabbinate, and that he has an office here. And so," she shrugged, "here we are."

She turned to her son. "Yovel, sweetie, have you seen your *mohel*? You can calm down now. Come on, let's go home."

Suddenly, the boy broke down in tears. "Imma, I want to talk to the *mohel* alone."

The mother was clearly in turmoil. As Yovel gazed at her pleadingly, she hesitated. Finally, she spread her hands in despair. "All right. I'm going out." She rose and left. The two were left alone.

Against his will, Yovel continued to sob. "Please, R' Abuhav, save me."

"What do you mean?" R' Abuhav asked in astonishment.

"I don't want to go to school because they teach heresy there. I want to be religious. I want to have a bar mitzvah, with *tefillin*. I want to keep Shabbos, to eat kosher — and mostly, I want to go to yeshivah, to learn Torah and serve Hashem!"

R' Abuhav was stunned. He had never witnessed such a thing before — such a young Jewish soul seeking a path to his Creator, all on his own initiative, and in the face of all obstacles. He called Mrs. Golan back into the room, and told her bluntly that her son wished to become observant. She did not appear surprised.

"I don't know where he got these ideas from," she said painfully, "but it's not new to me. We've already taken him to psychologists, to see if he has some sort of problem that's unsettling his mind. The experts talked to my son at length, and told us: 'The boy has no emotional problems. He is completely stable. Only one thing makes him unhappy: He wants to live a truly observant lifestyle. The choice is yours: either fight him, and worsen his condition until he may actually have to be hospitalized — or let him

200 / TALES FOR THE SOUL

have his way. We like your Yovel and have no desire to see him institutionalized in a mental hospital."

As he parted from the Golans, R' Abuhav reflected that the family had surprised him once, in the past — but it was surprising him far more in the present. Yovel shook his hand a long time and warmly, seeming reluctant to go. From that day on, R' Abuhav took the boy under his wing. He prepared him for his upcoming bar mitzvah. Yovel was not satisfied with learning the "basics" of Judaism and the laws of *tefillin*. He wanted to swallow the Torah whole, all at once. He wanted to go to yeshivah.

R' Abuhav consulted with the Golans. For the sake of their son's mental health, they were prepared to do anything. With his parents' permission, Yovel was enrolled in a yeshivah. His talents quickly came to the fore. In a word, the boy was brilliant. Though he started at the beginning, like a child in the first grade, in an amazingly short time he'd outstripped his friends in depth and understanding. But Yovel's talent paled beside his incredible thirst for everything holy. Within three years, he was a truly outstanding student, one who was always spiritually on the rise.

R' Abuhav was troubled. A question disturbed his peace, giving him no rest. One day, he visited one of the great Kabbalists of our generation. This was a hidden *tzaddik* whose every action was directed toward the sake of Heaven, and whose entire identity fled from honor and fame. R' Abuhav related the story of the marvel named Yovel Golan, beginning with the boy's unusual *bris milah* and ending with his fabulous yeshivah career. Then he asked his burning question:

"How is this possible? We struggle for years to raise our children to Torah and *yiras Shamayim*; sometimes we succeed, and sometimes we don't. And even when we are successful, our children rarely show a tenth of this boy's spiritual striving. This is a boy who was born and raised far from any holiness. Not only did his parents not seek to raise him with spiritual values, but they wanted just the opposite for him! And *he's* the one who looks like a candidate for *gadol hador*! How did it happen?"

The *mekubal* said, "Tell me, on the day you performed his *bris*, what happened?"

"I cried," the *mohel* said simply. "The baby was hungry, and I didn't know how to comfort him. I cried along with him."

"And you say that you were alone with the boy?"

"That's correct."

Emotionally, the holy man cried out, "You are mistaken. You were not alone! Eliyahu *Hanavi* was with you at the *bris milah*, and when the two of you cried, Eliyahu *Hanavi* cried with you. The weeping made a big impression in Heaven. The child was given a great soul, and so his path to *Yiddishkeit* was assured. Tears that are cried at a *bris milah*, as we ask that the child grow in Torah and *yiras Shamayim*, have a great effect. It's always worthwhile to *daven* during a *bris*."

Yovel Golan (his real name has been changed, for obvious reasons) is today a married Torah scholar, known for his piety. And it all began with tears wept at his *bris*, in an empty house.

# The Man Who Conquered the Ox

THE HEAT WAS UNBEARABLE. IT WAS ONE OF THE HOTTEST days of the summer of 5722 (1962), and the *shochet* R' Yosef Bender (names in this story have been changed) was bathed in sweat. Up in the sky, the sun blazed down, relentless.

R' Yosef glanced at his wristwatch: a quarter to two. In just fifteen minutes his shift would end, and he could travel home to Bnei Brak for a brief rest. He had been on his feet since early morning, slaughtering. His *davening* was always a rushed affair. He would dash out of the slaughterhouse together with a colleague, and head for a nearby

202 / TALES FOR THE SOUL

shul. Both of them would *daven*, without benefit of a *minyan*, at the outlandish hour of 11 a.m. What could he do? It was his livelihood. Truly, he was earning his living by the sweat of his brow.

How he longed to *daven* just once with a *minyan*, as he had done when he had been single and then newly married. But his working conditions were too difficult. In fact, they were nearly insufferable. Yosef frequently joked that, after 120 years of life, he would blame all his spiritual deficiencies on his employers. They were responsible for the fact that he did not have the time to pray as a Jew ought to pray, to learn a bit of Torah, and to engage in the kind of activities that the soul craves.

In his heart of hearts, he feared that excuses like this would be unacceptable in the Next World. But his work pressed on him until he hardly had time to think. How different was his own life from the lives of the beasts he slaughtered? The animals lived mindlessly, and he was doing the same. He was living like an animal and he would die like one, and that would be the end of that. Perhaps it was this reflection that led him to switch from slaughtering cattle to chickens. But his life was still the same, without a moment's leisure.

Just five minutes were left to his shift. The last of the chickens passed under his hand. The problem came with the last chicken of all. Isn't that always the case?

The chicken — a rooster — was especially large. Unlike other chickens, weak after several hours of being cooped up without food or water, this one lifted its head proudly. When R' Yosef tried to catch it by the wings, it slipped out of his hands and flapped to the floor with a triumphant crow. R' Yosef began to chase the rooster, to a good deal of laughter and mockery from his colleagues. Right and left he darted, finally lying flat on the floor, much to the others' hilarity.

Angrily, R' Yosef seized the rooster at last and held him tight. The bird rewarded him by scratching his hand deeply with a dirty claw. After a brief struggle, R' Yosef's knife did its work. The chicken was transformed into somebody's Shabbos meal, and the entire episode would most likely be forgotten in a day or two.

On the way home, R' Yosef studied his hand. The scratch was deep, and it was oozing blood. He briefly considered stopping in at the local clinic to have the hand looked at, but the pain soon stopped. At home, he dabbed on some gentian violet, wrapped the hand in an old rag, and went to work in Tel Aviv the next morning as usual.

He went, but he did not return.

As the noon hour approached, R' Yosef's head began to pound and black spots appeared before his eyes. He drank three glasses of water in quick succession, as he always did when he had a headache. This wonder cure had often helped him in such cases, and spared him the necessity of poisoning his body with all sorts of medicines.

But the cure did not help him today. His headache grew worse, not better. Then he began vomiting. His body doubled over and he broke out in a cold sweat. He felt very ill indeed. With great difficulty, he managed to stagger back to his workplace and whisper to the *shochet* next to him, "I don't feel well," before collapsing to the ground.

His friends rushed him to the nearest hospital. The doctors began to run various tests, and much time was wasted before someone made the connection between yesterday's scratch and today's symptoms. Hurried blood tests were conducted, confirming the suspicion: R' Yosef was a victim of blood poisoning! The rooster's claws had contaminated the *shochet's* bloodstream. R' Yosef had tetanus.

Unfortunately, precious hours had been lost before the diagnosis was made. By the time the doctors began antitetanus treatments, the patient's condition was critical. His life was in the gravest danger.

R' Yosef lay in bed, nearly unconscious, unaware of what the doctors were telling his friends. They gave him twelve hours to live, at the outside, with only a very faint chance of the treatment succeeding. "Pray hard," they advised soberly. "Only prayers can help him now."

One of the older *shochtim*, R' Shaul Weissbaum, sat down brokenly in the corridor and murmured several chapters of *Tehillim*. Suddenly, he stood up and returned to R' Yosef's room. He felt an urgent need to talk to him, to encourage him.

He approached the bed. "R' Yosef, can I talk to you?"

R' Yosef nodded weakly. Though very feeble and dazed, he tried to listen attentively. The older *shochet* sat down beside the bed and

204 / TALES FOR THE SOUL

began to try to strengthen the patient's spirit. After a few sentences, R' Shaul realized that R' Yosef's attention was wandering. His widened eyes were darting to and fro, filled with the fear of death.

"R' Yosef, I want to tell you a story," R' Shaul said. "It's about a *shochet*. Are you able to listen?"

"Y-yes."

R' Shaul began his story.

R' Yechiel Michel was raised in his uncle's home, the holy R' Klonimus Kalman of Cracow, author of *Meor VaShemesh*. His uncle's influence was stamped on the youth. R' Yechiel Michel was an extremely pious young man who learned Torah day and night. When he reached maturity, he was filled with Torah and fear of Heaven, and offers were made to appoint him as *rav* of some city.

But modest R' Yechiel Michel had no wish to adorn himself with the Torah's crown. He refused a rabbinical position and then, in order not to be dependent on others for his livelihood, decided to study the laws of *shechitah*. As soon as he received his *semichah* from his teachers — all prominent *shochtim* — he traveled to Hungary where he was appointed a *shochet* in the city of Kishlita.

R' Yechiel Michel prayed to Hashem to help him succeed in his chosen profession. Hashem blessed him. R' Yechiel Michel did his job faithfully and reviewed the laws of *shechitah* constantly, as he feared the *Gemara's* words: "If a slaughterer does not know the laws of *shechitah*, one is forbidden to eat of his *shechitah*" (*Chullin* 9a).

R' Yechiel Michel took infinite pains with the art of *shechitah*. The many improvements he made to the *chalaf,* the slaughtering knife, were unparalleled. He went above and beyond the letter of the law in his profession, though he conducted his personal life with tremendous modesty. Everyone knew him as an upright and pious man, a G-d-fearing man. Then an incident occurred that revealed to the entire city just how holy a Jew he really was. It was then that his praises began to be sung in earnest.

Here is what happened.

THE MAN WHO CONQUERED THE OX / 205

Benzion the butcher was certain that he had made the best deal of his life when he bought an ox in the marketplace that day. It was a giant animal, with sharp horns and fear-inspiring broad shoulders. But Benzion saw only the pounds and pounds of meat on the ox's flesh — meat that he would sell immediately after its slaughtering.

He led the ox directly from the market to the stable in his yard. Tying it to the wall by the neck, he left a generous supply of food to last the animal until it would be time for the slaughtering.

No one knew what it was that frightened the ox. With no one there to soothe it, the beast went nearly mad with terror. It bellowed repeatedly, eyes darting to and fro in a panic. Suddenly, it began to rampage. Terror lent the ox added strength, and it lunged forward until the rope around its neck pulled the wooden board clear out of the stable's side as though it were made of paper. The ox ran out of the stable and began to thunder insanely through the town's streets, the board trailing and bumping along behind. Its thrusting horns and powerful shoulders left tremendous damage in their wake, but the ox was not concerned with that. Within a few minutes, several people had been grievously injured in the marketplace.

The town went crazy. People fled in fear from the giant ox, though largely to no avail: Some of them, in the confusion, ended up running right under the rampaging animal's legs. The streets filled with screams and warnings, and the sound of fleeing footsteps. Those who had been unfortunate enough to be present in the market at the time ran for their lives to neighboring shops and homes, while those who were at home didn't dare leave for fear of the danger outside.

Finally, the news reached Benzion, the butcher. He ran out into the street, calling frantically, "Whoever captures the ox will get 500 silver rubles!" But in all the town, no one — neither gentile nor Jew — was prepared to risk his life, not even for a fortune.

The *shochet* was at home, *davening*, oblivious to the commotion outside. Then, abruptly, he became aware that something unusual was going on. Doors were slamming as though with the force of a storm, people were shouting and screaming in terror. Punctuating the noise were the groans of the injured. The sleepy little town sounded like a battle zone. The *shochet* walked out of his room and asked his family what had happened. They told him about the ox rampaging through the streets, strewing destruction in its wake.

R' Yechiel Michel immediately returned to his room, removed his *tallis* and *tefillin*, and picked up his *shechitah* bag. Before anyone could stop him, he had walked out of the house with a quick, sure stride. His family raced after him, but the *shochet* had already disappeared, and no one knew onto which street he had turned.

As his anxious family searched for him down one street, R' Yechiel Michel was walking up a parallel one. He stopped passers-by as they ran past, asking, "Where is the ox?"

Breathlessly, they answered, "He's on the street near the market square. But don't go near him, or he might gore you. That's one angry ox!"

The *shochet* had heard what he wanted to hear. Ignoring the warning, he continued his hurried walk in the direction of the street near the market square.

At the entrance to the street, he saw the danger. The block was empty of human beings; only frightened eyes peeked from windows. The eyes followed R' Yechiel Michel's calm progress up the street toward the ox, which was tossing its huge head and snorting violently. The ox was dancing furiously in place, raising clouds of dust and bellowing at nothing. From time to time, it lowered its head to gore at a nearby fence, turning it into a heap of rubble. It was a spectacle to reduce any onlooker to a quivering mass of jelly.

The *shochet* glanced about to make sure that no one was about. Lifting his eyes, he murmured a prayer beseeching Heaven's help. Then he continued walking lightly toward the ox.

When he was some little distance from the lunging beast, he took his knife out of its sheath and examined it. The blade glinted in the sun like pure silver. R' Yechiel Michel tested its sharpness with a fingernail, and found it perfect.

When he had completed his inspection, he approached the ox. Holding the knife up to the animal's furious eyes, he said calmly,

"Listen. Look at this pretty knife in my hand. It is worthy of slaughtering not only you, but even the *shor habor* in Jerusalem, our holy city, when *Mashiach* comes. With this precious instrument I come to fulfill the mitzvah of *shechitah*, as commanded by our Creator. Do not hinder me in my work. Accept Heaven's decree for you."

As soon as the words were out of the *shochet's* mouth, the ox ceased its snorting and lunging. Suddenly tame, it began to walk toward R' Yechiel Michel. Slowly, with a measured tread, it went to meet the *shochet* and his gleaming knife. When the ox reached him, it lowered its head submissively, in an almost-human gesture.

Heads began to pop out of windows up and down the street. People rubbed their eyes, unable to believe what they were seeing. The rampaging ox that, just moments before, had spread danger and alarm, had turned as docile as a kitten. The people witnessed the *shochet's* holiness and saw the way he had subdued the ox. Still, no one dared set foot out of his front door, lest the beast run at them, horns lowered.

Only one person came out of his house and began to move toward the *shochet* and the ox. It was Benzion, the butcher, the ox's owner.

Seeing him, R' Yechiel Michel called out, "Please tie the ox's legs before I *shecht* it." That was the usual procedure. But the butcher was terrified, and trembling too hard to be of any use to anyone. Only after the *shochet* assured him that nothing would happen did Benzion manage to come closer. The ox gazed at him peacefully, then lay down on the ground, offering its legs as though to say, "I am ready and willing to be slaughtered." With shaking hands, the butcher bound the ox's legs, and removed the rope and the attached board from around the beast's neck.

Then R' Yechiel Michel came up to the ox and stroked its neck. To Benzion's wonder, the ox looked up at the *shochet* with a gaze that was almost humanly affectionate. R' Yechiel Michel checked the position of the *shechitah* once more, recited the blessing, "*al hashechitah,*" and then — as the animal extended its neck willingly — he slaughtered the ox.

He conducted the necessary inspection immediately after the *shechitah*. The ox was found to be, unquestionably, *glatt* kosher.

Emotionally, the butcher stood by, slicing up the meat and handing it out to all the townsfolk. "From such an ox — an ox that stretched out its neck to be *shechted* — I wish to make no profit," he declared over and over as he stood for hours, passing out pieces of fresh meat to everyone.

Benzion wanted to give R' Yechiel Michel the 500-ruble reward he had offered for the ox's capture. But the *shochet* refused to accept a penny. "When I left my house to find the ox, I didn't know anything about the reward," he said. "I did what I did not for any reward, but to sanctify Heaven's Name in public."

R' Shaul Weissbaum stopped talking. He believed his story had fallen on unheeding ears. In the bed before him, R' Yosef seemed to be lying unconscious. Any moment now, the medical staff would come to chase the visitor from the room.

Then R' Yosef opened an eye. With difficulty, he whispered, "I heard the story. I heard it all. I was not asleep. I will learn its lesson. Like the *shochet* who conquered the ox, I, too, will conquer the 'beast' within me! I will recover from my illness. Afterwards, I hereby vow to set aside at least two hours a day for learning Torah."

"You will recover!" R' Shaul assured him unhesitatingly. He did not know where his certainty came from, but he sensed a wellspring of strength bubbling up from the depths of his soul.

A moment later, a nurse put her head through the doorway to ask him to leave the room.

All that night, R' Yosef battled for his life — and, with Heaven's help, emerged victorious. Almost miraculously, his body conquered the powerful poison that the doctors had despaired of subduing.

Years later, it was impossible to recognize R' Yosef the *shochet*, who transformed himself into one of the leading Torah scholars in his area. He learned not just two hours a day, but many more. Every so often he would add to his learning time, until he was regularly studying for six consecutive hours each day. He worked at his *shechitah* job only enough to support his family in a meager fashion. Until his last day on earth, he would tell acquaintances of how the story of another *shochet* saved his life — and how it prompted him to change his priorities and the way he lived that life.

# "Do Not Be Afraid"

THE FACTORY WAS FILLED WITH THE ECHO OF HAMMERS pounding on metal. Sparks flew from the thundering machinery. A stranger, walking in, would have felt himself in imminent danger of going deaf from the clamor. For the men working on the factory floor, these were normal working conditions. For those who managed the factory, the noise was like sweet music to their ears.

Thousands of workers labored throughout the giant hall, manufacturing railroad tracks. In the next room — equally large — hundreds more worked on building new railway cars. The workers were Arabs, as were the managers of the railway factory in Haifa during the British Mandate in Palestine.

In this sea of Arabs, there was just one tiny island. One single Jewish worker!

R' Avraham Chaim Spielberg, a pious Jew, had come through various life circumstances before he came to live in Haifa. One of the city's few religious Jews in those days, he had found himself a comfortable niche in the railway factory. His expertise at metalworking, along with his fluency in five languages (including Arabic and English), smoothed his dealings with his British employers as well as with his Arab co-workers.

210 / TALES FOR THE SOUL

As an observant Jew, R' Avraham skipped work one day a week. Six days he labored energetically, and on the seventh day he rested. Surprisingly, it was his Ishmaelite co-workers who made up his quota on Shabbos, in return for various favors that the talented R' Avraham was able to do for them. This arrangement lasted, to their mutual satisfaction, for a number of years. As long as the Mandate remained peaceful and stable, the lone Jew in the factory got along well with his hundreds of Arab colleagues.

But nothing lasts forever.

The Arabs in Palestine had never looked favorably upon the Jews' return to the land they had left more than 1900 years before. The more Jewish immigrants who made *aliyah*, the more incidents of murder and looting that took place in the land. Hatred rose up from its subterranean caverns, to erupt into the light of day in the form of massacres, like the terrible bloodbath in Chevron in the year 5689 (1929).

In general, these eruptions were spontaneous things, usually taking place after a fiery Friday sermon in the mosques incited the people to violence. From the year 5696 (1936), however, the Arab struggle began to take on a more permanent and consistent form. Egged on by their leaders, masses of Arabs attacked Jewish settlements. Shops were looted, stores were burned to the ground, and homes were invaded — but all these things were nothing compared to the loss of life. Armed Arab legions ambushed Jewish vehicles on the roads, shooting and killing those who wished to reach Jerusalem.

The Jewish community was not silent in the face of these attacks. Underground groups formed, and armed themselves for a guerrilla war against the enemy.

The general populace, both Jewish and Arab, watched these events with a sense of deep personal involvement. To R' Avraham Chaim Spielberg's dismay, the atmosphere in the factory began to change as well. Outside events were having their effect on the Arab workers' mood. If they had greeted him until then with a cheery "Good morning" and a friendly thump on the shoulder — not to mention the weekly help they gave him on Shabbos — R' Avraham suddenly became a *persona non grata*. The Arab factory workers lumped their Jewish colleague together with the rest of the "bad" Jews in their land. Every time they heard of a Jewish victory, their manner toward R' Avraham grew markedly colder.

Then came the morning when R' Avraham Chaim arrived at the factory to find his worktable overturned and his tools scattered. It was a hint of things to come — and not a subtle hint, either. His heart began to pound with fear, and did not let up that whole day. He sensed the undercurrents all around him, and was afraid to raise his eyes to meet those of his companions..

Two weeks later, the situation deteriorated even further.

One night, several Arabs — Haj Amin's men — were killed in the act of attacking a Jewish convoy. Unbeknown to the attackers, a well-armed band of Jews lay in wait in the dark hills. When the Arabs began shooting, the Jewish defenders swarmed down out of the hills and killed them all. R' Avraham Chaim knew nothing of this. He was to learn the hard way.

On his arrival at the factory the next morning, he was met by a sea of hate-filled eyes. His heart quailed. He tried to avoid the smoldering glances, but the whispers succeeded in reaching him: "May it be Allah's will that every Jew die!" R' Avraham Chaim played deaf. Then a tall, broad-shouldered Arab came close and thrust his face into R' Avraham Chaim's. There was no avoiding it this time.

"You think we're going to keep silent? We'll slaughter you like a dog!"

That Arab was just the first. Others — scores of others — followed close upon his heels. Men on whose friendship R' Avraham Chaim had depended until very recently walked up to him now, one by one, to earnestly assure the Jew that they intended to slaughter him like a dog.

Hiding his inner turmoil, R' Avraham Chaim did not reply. In the depths of his heart he prayed to Hashem not to let him fall prey to those who wished him harm. He fervently hoped that his prayers would be accepted, and that the threats being hurled at him would prove to be empty ones. Toward evening, when most of his colleagues had left for the day, R' Avraham Chaim approached the plant manager, Haj Ishmael Achbariya, and poured out his distress. "What do they want from me? Have I done anything to them? Why do we have to be influenced by what happens outside?"

Haj Ishmael Achbariya was a longtime friend. More than once, R' Avraham Chaim had offered his own broad technical knowledge and skills to help the plant manager. He was certain that Achbariya would listen to him now, and would order the others to stop embittering his life.

To his dismay, Haj Ishmael burst out laughing. With an evil gleam in his eye, he said, "What are you complaining about? If they'd threatened to slaughter you like a pig, I'd understand your feeling insulted. But they only said they'd slaughter you like a dog. That's not so bad!"

There was nowhere to turn. R' Avraham Chaim was forced to acknowledge this bitter truth. The Arabs had always hated the Jews. Even when that hatred had been temporarily subdued, it was a constant possibility, ready to erupt at a moment's notice. He was wasting his breath trying to win the Arab manager's sympathy or support.

To continue working under such conditions was impossible. He would take a vacation from his job. He would wait out the situation.

The following day, R' Avraham Chaim approached the "Captain," the chief manager in charge of the factories. This was a correct and polite Englishman who listened sympathetically to his story and then suggested that R' Avraham Chaim ask the doctor for a letter authorizing an indefinite medical leave.

"No doctor will give me a letter like that!" protested R' Avraham Chaim. "At most, he'd give me leave for a day or two off from work."

"All the better," returned the Englishman. "Any time you see your colleagues on the warpath, run for home at once. I will turn a blind eye to your absences and will mark on your record that you are taking a sick day. Your salary will not suffer at all."

And that was what they did. The days that R' Avraham Chaim spent at his workplace were filled with the bitterness of death. It was only a question of time before he would be physically attacked. The day was not far off when the Arab workers would finally attempt to carry out their threats, Heaven forbid.

When matters got so bad that he could stand the situation not even a moment longer, R' Avraham Chaim took the day off and traveled to Jerusalem. He visited one of the generation's *tzaddikim* and poured out his troubles.

The rebbe responded, "If that is the case, you must emulate your holy forefathers, Avraham, Yitzchak, and Yaakov."

"In what way?" R' Avraham Chaim asked, in surprise and trepidation.

"Run," the rebbe said simply. "Run away from a dangerous place. You must not place your life at risk. Saving a life takes precedence over the entire Torah — and it certainly takes precedence over your salary!"

It was a downhearted R' Avraham Chaim who left the rebbe's presence. This was not the answer he had expected. He had come for a blessing to take with him back into danger, to keep him safe from harm. In his secret heart, he knew that the rebbe's advice was absolutely correct. Was he waiting for a miracle to happen — for thousands of angry, hate-filled Arabs to undergo a change of heart? No, he had no other choice but to accept the ancient edict of the *Gemara*: "It is up to the damaged party to distance himself."

But the question of earning a living was no less frightening than facing a horde of violent Arabs. These were times of hardship and deprivation. A person without a job ran a very real risk of starvation. Today's blessed abundance of *chesed* organizations and support systems did not exist in those days, not even in one's wildest dreams. If he left his job, he might literally die of hunger.

R' Avraham Chaim was standing outside the rebbe's room, crying bitterly, when the rebbetzin passed by. The sight of the weeping man pierced her compassionate heart, and she asked him the reason for his tears. R' Avraham Chaim gave her a brief version of his troubles.

"Go to the Zhiviller *tzaddik*," she advised. "He lives not far from here. Go and see what he says."

R' Avraham Chaim wasted no time in proceeding to the poverty-stricken home of R' Shlomo Zhivil in the Beis Yisrael neighborhood.

R' Shlomo of Zhivil was famous throughout the land as a holy man, a *tzaddik*, renowned for the miraculous salvations he wrought.

R' Avraham Chaim found only R' Shlomo's wife at home. She

informed him that her husband always went to the *Kosel Hama'aravi* at that time of day, to *daven Minchah* and *Ma'ariv*. Thanking her, R' Avraham Chaim sped on his way.

He soon reached the Damascus Gate and crossed the Arab *shuk* to reach the narrow *Kosel* plaza. His eyes eagerly sought the Rebbe — to no avail. Questioning people as to the Rebbe's whereabouts brought the same negative results. With weary steps he trudged back and told R' Shlomo's rebbetzin that her husband was not anywhere near the *Kosel*.

"I have never spoken an untruth in my life," the rebbetzin said simply. "If I said that he is at the *Kosel*, then he is there!"

R' Avraham Chaim began to retrace his steps to the Western Wall. This time, however, the journey was more complicated. Passing through the Damascus Gate into the narrow, winding streets of the *shuk*, he found himself in the same situation that he had bemoaned back in Haifa: a lone Jew amid a sea of Arabs. As he walked past a group of Arab youths, he heard them discussing him in Arabic (a language in which he was fluent). To his horror, he heard one of the youths suggest to his friends, "Let's finish off that Jew!"

R' Avraham Chaim's heart began to pound. If they wanted to kill him, they could do it with ease. He began to run, taking long strides with mad urgency. His lips whitened and his head swam. To his relief, he heard another Arab, an older man, say, "Leave him alone. Don't you see he's running like a madman?"

With Heaven's grace, the older man's comment dissipated the youths' lust for blood. The danger — for the moment — was averted. R' Avraham Chaim at last reached the *Kosel* again, and immediately spotted the holy Rebbe, with his head close to the ancient stones of the wall.

He waited patiently for the holy *tzaddik* to finish *davening*, then approached him and told him his problem..

The Rebbe did not turn his head. He did not seem to have heard at all. He stood facing the wall, his lips moving.

*Perhaps the Rebbe did not hear me,* R' Avraham Chaim thought in confusion. He related the story once again.

Still, the Rebbe made not the slightest sign of having heard. He completed his prayers and started for home, R' Avraham Chaim trot-

"DO NOT BE AFRAID" / 215

ting anxiously at his side. For the third time, and then a fourth, R' Avraham Chaim retold his story.

The Rebbe ignored his companion completely. Reaching his small home, R' Shlomo went inside, sat down at his table, and opened a *sefer* as if he were alone.

R' Avraham Chaim's patience was at an end. He felt as though he had turned invisible, unheard. He could not understand why the Rebbe was treating him this way. Grasping R' Shlomo's sleeve, he tugged at it lightly, crying out, "Rebbe, save me, for the waters have risen up to threaten my life!"

For the first time, the Rebbe raised his eyes and regarded his visitor warmly. He glanced quickly into some holy book, his habit whenever he wished to quickly ascertain the Torah's stance on a particular problem. He sat lost in thought.

Suddenly, R' Shlomo slapped the table with his hand and turned to R' Avraham Chaim. "What are you afraid of? I don't see any reason to be afraid. Whoever touches you will come to a bitter end."

The words breathed fresh life into poor R' Avraham Chaim. This was the very blessing for which he had been hoping! He believed, to the core, that the Rebbe had marshaled the forces of nature on his behalf. Color rushed back into his face. Gratefully, he reached into his pocket, pulled out a one-lira bill — representing one-quarter of his monthly salary! — and handed it humbly to the Rebbe.

R' Shlomo refused to accept the gift. "Why do I need this paper of idol worship?"

"Please, Rebbe, take the gift," pleaded R' Avraham Chaim. "The Rebbe can use it to give *tzedakah*."

The Rebbe's reaction was unexpected.

"Thief!"

"*What?*" R' Avraham Chaim exclaimed, breaking into fresh tears.

"Yes, you are a thief," the Rebbe said forcefully. "When your day comes and you ascend to the upper world, you will be asked, 'Did you support your wife and children?' And what will you answer? You are stealing money from your children's mouths and giving it to me. I don't want it!"

With some difficulty, R' Avraham Chaim managed to persuade the Rebbe that his situation was not so dire; that it lay within his power to offer this gift and, at the same time, respectably support his family.

R' Avraham Chaim reported to work at the factory the next day, now calm thanks to the Rebbe's promise.

No sooner had he taken his first step through the doors than he was surrounded by a throng of his Arab co-workers. One of them, Mahmoud, thrust a powerful fist into his face. Blood began to stream from R' Avraham Chaim's nose, and an overwhelming fear filled his heart. Like wild beasts attracted by the sight and scent of blood, other Arabs came forward to add their share to the mayhem. They would make short work of this Jew.

*Rebbe! Holy Rebbe, you promised me. Master of the Universe, save me in the Rebbe's merit!*

The huge fist drew back. Perhaps Mahmoud was content to let the others finish the job he had begun. He began walking away — but did not get far. Mahmoud had taken no more than four steps when he began to sway. An instant later, he fell heavily to the floor.

His friends came running. They tried to lift him, but Mahmoud lay as though made of wood. They tugged him to the left and dragged him to the right, but there was no reaction. They poured icy water over his face and massaged his wrists, but Mahmoud did not budge. An ambulance was summoned and he was whisked off to the nearest hospital.

It was not long before the news reached the factory: "Mahmoud died of a massive brain hemorrhage."

The thousands of Arab workers understood that the Hand of G-d had struck down their colleague. They had not heard R' Shlomo's promise, but they had witnessed the miracle with their own eyes. No sooner had Mahmoud laid a finger on the Jew than he met his dark end — just as the Rebbe had said.

From that day forward, until R' Avraham Chaim Spielberg retired from work, no one ventured to harm as much as his fingernail. Moreover, they all made sure to always treat the Jew with the utmost respect and courtesy.

# "A Tzaddik Will Be Rescued"

*Yemen, 5693 (1933)*

THE SUN WAS BLAZING THAT DAY, AS IT DID EVERY DAY IN THAT arid land. And if it was hot everywhere in Yemen, it was doubly so in the southern portion of the country.

The city of Al-Bayda, in southern Yemen, was no different from any other city in that realm. Its homes were made of clay and crowded close to one another in the flat valley between tall mountains. A brownish-red color dominated the scene.

R' Zechariah Cohen sat in his back yard handling dried leaves. Some he crumbled with his fingers; others, which were moister, yielded a greenish liquid which he carefully gathered in small glass vials. His keen eyes inspected each leaf carefully to check for insect damage. R' Zechariah Cohen was a doctor.

He was well versed in the medicinal properties of the various leaves. He knew which leaf should be used for headaches, which worked best for stomach pain, and which was most helpful in treating inflammations of the skin. R' Zechariah's fame had spread throughout the area, and even the gentiles in the area related wonders that "Mori Zechariah Aron" was reputed to have performed. All Yemenite Jews who were *Kohanim* were called "Aron" after Aharon *HaKohen*, grandfather of all *Kohanim*. They said that Mori Zechariah Aron was an outstanding doctor whose medicines worked wonders.

218 / TALES FOR THE SOUL

Neither the Jews nor the gentiles knew —in fact, only his closest relatives knew —that R' Zechariah Cohen did something else after examining a patient thoroughly and dispensing medicine. As soon as the patient had left his office, the doctor would closet himself in his room, open a *sefer Tehillim*, and plead tearfully to his Creator, "I am doing what I can. But You, Father in Heaven, are the true healer, the healer of all creatures. Please, just as You sent an illness to this man, send him, too, a full recovery!"

These prayers, emanating from the depths of the doctor's heart, did more to help the patient than all the medicines he concocted. Usually it was only a matter of hours before the illness disappeared as if it had never existed. The patient felt as though he had been reborn. As he resumed his activities, healthy and whole, no one would have guessed that just a short time before he had been wracked with pain.

As Mori Zechariah's fame spread, people came streaming in to seek his services — and not only from the city of Al-Bayda. For the sake of good relations, he tended his Arab patients with the same devotion that he showed his own brethren. The local ruler, Ishmael, who governed Al-Bayda, greatly respected the Jewish doctor and recommended him to everyone who was in need of an expert physician's services.

A cloud of dust rose suddenly in the road. Mori Zechariah's eyes left his leaves for a moment and focused on the rapidly approaching cloud. In Yemen some seventy years ago, people did not usually hurry so. They covered long distances on foot or, if they could afford one, on the back of a camel or donkey. Fast-moving horses were generally reserved for members of the ruling family. *What can one of the royalty be looking for here?* he wondered.

Then, through the dust that the galloping hooves had raised in the road, Mori Zechariah identified the horse and its rider. In the saddle sat a man in military uniform. There was no room for doubt: The rider was heading for the doctor's house.

The officer dismounted and hurried into the yard. "Are you Mori Zechariah, the doctor?" he demanded.

Mori Zechariah nodded his head.

"His Royal Highness, the Imam, summons you urgently!"

"The king himself has sent you to me?" the doctor asked in amazement. "How can a small creature like myself help the mighty king of Yemen?"

"This is no time for modesty," the officer said impatiently. "The king's nephew, a young boy of 15 , is gravely ill. No doctor, not even the palace physician, has been able to find a cure. The boy is growing weaker by the hour. You must come at once! This horse is strong enough to carry both of us on its back."

"I must know what he is suffering from," the doctor said. "I will not be able to carry all of my medicines with me. If you will describe his symptoms, I will select the proper medicines to take along."

The officer sighed. "He is sick with fear! Fear of people — all people. All day long he sits in a darkened room, and when he catches sight of someone he is seized with a terrible panic. His entire body trembles as though he were about to be killed. His appetite has abandoned him. He has eaten so little for so long that he resembles a skeleton! If he is not placed in an expert's care, the doctors say, the boy will surely die."

Mori Zechariah sat sunk in thought, considering what he had heard. The officer broke into his thoughts.

"I know what is troubling you. You must be thinking about the prohibition for a Jew to enter the royal palace. But Ahmed, the royal steward, has warmly recommended you to the Imam, saying that you are the only man in all of Yemen who may be able to heal the sick boy. The Imam can't bear the suffering of his brother and his ailing nephew, and he has granted permission for you to enter the palace even though you are a Jew. Even more, the Imam has declared that, should you refuse to come, you are doomed to die!"

"No need to threaten me," Mori Zechariah said equably. "I would not refuse to help even the poorest man in the kingdom. I treat every suffering person, and I will certainly not refuse my help to our honored king, the exalted Imam."

Mori Zechariah fetched his *tallis* and *tefillin* and selected a generous supply of medicines from his stores. Bidding farewell to his wife and children, he climbed on the horse behind the officer. The officer pointed the horse's head toward the capital city, and the royal palace.

Mori Zechariah did not find it difficult to diagnose the boy's nervous ailment. The patient lay in bed looking as if he were at death's door. The Imam and his brother watched the doctor hopefully.

"Can you help him?" the Imam asked, his tone almost pleading.

Mori Zechariah lifted his eyes heavenward. "With the Almighty G-d's help, I think that I have the right remedy for what ails him. I will pour a few drops into his mouth, and repeat the process a few hours from now. By tomorrow morning he will be feeling much better. But no one must enter the boy's room all night."

"Very well. It shall be done at once," the Imam thundered. "We will come to see the boy in the morning. If there is no improvement in his condition, I warn you: You will suffer a bitter end!"

Mori Zechariah paled. The mighty Imam would not hesitate to carry out his threat and take his revenge if the medicine failed to work. Was the doctor at fault? He had not made the boy ill! But nevertheless, he knew well that he was in the ruler's hands, for good or for bad.

He poured several drops of liquid into the boy's mouth, waited in an adjoining room for several hours, and then administered another dose. Afterwards, he was escorted by two of the Imam's servants to quarters in a different wing of the palace. The door clanged shut behind him, and was locked. The Imam was leaving nothing to chance. Tomorrow morning, he would check on the boy. If there was no improvement in his patient's condition, the doctor's life would be worthless.

Immediately after the door was locked behind him, Mori Zechariah began to pray. This time, he knew that it was not only the boy's life that hung in the balance, but his own as well. He *davened* with all his might, begging the Creator to take pity on them both. He did not sleep at all that night, but prayed and said chapters of *Tehillim* until dawn.

"A TZADDIK WILL BE RESCUED" / 221

The early morning brought with it the rattle of a key in the lock. A servant walked in, beaming.

"The boy is feeling much better today!" he announced jubilantly. "It looks like a miracle — the bringing of the dead back to life!" In the same breath, the servant went on to relate, "All night long, the boy kept crying, 'Water, water, bring me water! I'm thirsty, I'm hot — I'm sweating!' and similar things. We wanted to enter the room to give him a little water to drink, but you had given strict orders not to go in. With difficulty, we managed to get through the night without disobeying your instructions. And now it looks as if you were right!"

Soon Mori Zechariah Cohen was able to verify the servant's account. The boy's eyes, which the day before had been closed and lackluster, showed a new sparkle this morning. His pale cheeks now held a faint splotch of color.

The Imam and his brother entered the room behind the doctor. When they saw the change in the boy's condition, they nearly broke into a dance.

"Bring me a jug of boiled water," Mori Zechariah said. When the water was brought, he sat alone with his patient, feeding him boiled water by the spoonful until the jug was empty and the patient's thirst had been slaked. The boy's eyes closed and he slept for three full days. When he awoke, his physical and mental well-being had undergone a radical change for the better. Just hours later, he got up from his bed and went outside, smiling and happy.

The Imam was beside himself with joy. He paid the doctor handsomely for his services, and insisted on giving him a diplomatic pass that would enable him to travel easily from place to place. Yemen's Jews in those days were severely restricted in their travel, but Mori Zechariah the physician would henceforth be permitted to go wherever he wished.

Several years passed.

Relations between Ishmael, the regional ruler, and the Imam, king of Yemen, worsened dramatically. Ishmael reigned supreme over his own territory, and he and his army of loyal soldiers plotted to rebel against the king. They were armed and ready to follow Ishmael into battle against the Imam whom they hated fiercely.

Like Mordechai the Jew in his time, Mori Zechariah uncovered the plot against the king. Just as Mordechai's knowledge of the seventy languages enabled him to understand the conspirators' talk, so Mori Zechariah was fluent in all the languages, idioms, and dialects of Yemen. One day, as he stood in a field collecting his medicinal herbs and grasses, his sharp ears caught the secret talk of several of the local ruler's soldiers as they plotted to poison the Imam's well on the following night. They saw the Jewish doctor but were not alarmed by his presence. They were from a different part of Yemen and were certain that no one nearby understood their language. They arranged the details of the plot — where and when to meet to carry it out — and separated.

Very shortly afterwards, Mori Zechariah set out on a fleet-footed horse, headed for the capital city. His diplomatic pass gained him access to the Imam's palace, where he revealed what he had overheard.

"Are you certain that Ishmael wants to poison me?" the Imam asked, his brow darkening in fury.

"Could I have imagined such a thing?" the doctor countered. "I came here with all possible speed in order to save Your Highness' life."

When darkness fell, the palace guards positioned themselves in ambush among the bushes surrounding the well. An hour after midnight, they captured several of Ishmael's soldiers red-handed, holding vials of colorless, odorless poison, powerful enough to have taken the life of every person living in the palace.

That same day, the poisoners were hanged in the capital city.

Back in Al-Bayda, Ishmael conducted a secret investigation, which unearthed the fact that the Jewish doctor had galloped away to the capital city on the previous day. "Why did the doctor hurry so?" the ruler fumed. "He must be a spy!"

Mori Zechariah's home was quickly surrounded by soldiers. He was dragged off to jail and sentenced to death by hanging!

The execution date was set for the seventh day of Pesach.

It was the hectic week before Pesach, but Mori Zechariah's home resembled *Tishah B'Av*. His family's voices were raised in lamentation.

The head of the household was gone and there was no one to help them. Towards the end of the holiday, he was slated to climb the scaffold.

Only Mori Zechariah's wife, Shoshana, did not abandon hope for a moment. "They will not kill Zechariah," she declared over and over with complete faith. "*Hakadosh Baruch Hu* will make a miracle, you'll see!"

On *erev Pesach,* the menfolk set out to bake their matzos. Singing as they worked, they kneaded the dough, then rolled and baked it. In their traditional robes and turbans, *peyos* swinging to the rhythm of their swaying bodies, they seemed engaged not in baking but in prayer.

Only Shalom Cohen lacked the joy that shone from the faces of the other men. His father, Mori Zechariah Cohen, was missing today. Tonight, everyone would sit on the floor and recline on cushions like royalty at the Pesach Seder, singing songs of praise. Only his father would not be there. He would be languishing in a prison cell, without matzos or wine, counting the hours left until his execution.

Shalom, Mori Zechariah's firstborn son, had been blessed with many talents, including a sweet voice and an outstanding ear for music. When he sang, people stopped and listened, transfixed. Right now, however, singing was the last thing on his mind. He was frantically turning over ideas, trying to find a way to rescue his father from the fate that loomed over him.

And at last he found it.

One *chol hamo'ed* day, Shalom set out for the capital city. In nearly miraculous fashion, he managed to reach the hill facing the Imam's palace. There he opened his mouth and began to sing, loud and strong and sweet. He sang a song filled with feeling, a song that related how his father had been snatched away by the king's enemies after saving the king's life. The song concluded tearfully that, in a few days, his father was to be hanged.

The Imam was relaxing in his room when he heard the song. He forgot everything as he listened to the melodious voice. The song enchanted him, but he could not make out the words. Going to the window, he saw the youth standing opposite his window, singing emotionally.

"Who is that singer?" he asked his servants. "Bring him here. I wish to enjoy his music at closer range."

The servants hastened to do the king's bidding.

"What is that lovely song you sang just now?" the Imam asked.

"Would His Majesty like to hear it again?" Shalom asked, eyes sparkling.

"Certainly."

Shalom Cohen's sweet voice filled the room as he sang the song again, from the first verse to last, telling the story of what had happened to his father.

"Is that so?" the Imam asked, brow creased. He thought for a moment, and then smiled. "You are a clever lad. You have saved your father! Have no fear — Ishmael will not hang Zechariah."

On the seventh day of Pesach, Mori Zechariah was taken out of his cell and brought to the special gallows that had been erected for him in the city square. A great crowd of Arabs had gathered to watch the spectacle. Their eyes flitted back and forth, from the Jew with the constantly murmuring lips, to Ishmael and his cronies seated opposite.

Al-Bayda's Jews were not idle. They climbed up the hill behind the scaffold and spread their *talleisim* in a broad canopy over Zechariah to create a large shady area over the condemned man's head. If all they could do in the doctor's final hour was ease his discomfort in the bright sun, then that was what they would do. As they stood there in despair, Shoshana Cohen's words kept echoing in their ears. She had refused to attend her husband's hanging. Up until the very end, she kept asserting, "Hashem will make a miracle. Wait and see!"

"What is that shade over the Jew's head?" Ishmael asked suddenly. His eyes narrowed as he scanned the opposite hilltop. In a flash, he saw what was happening. "The Jews want to make shade for their friend? Well, I won't let them!"

He sent a troop of soldiers up the hill to disperse the Jews and their *talleisim*. But at that moment, from the horizon, came a small white cloud. It floated to a spot over Zechariah's head and remained there, as though tied by invisible ropes. The cloud shielded Zechariah from the sun — much to Ishmael's chagrin. Heaven itself, it seemed, was battling on the doctor's behalf.

The hangman climbed up onto the scaffold and prepared to slip the noose around the Jew's neck.

Suddenly, the hangman let out a high-pitched scream. He flung himself to the ground, clutching his middle. "Someone help me! My stomach is exploding!" His screams were terrible to hear.

From his vantage point, Ishmael looked on with mounting fury. "Why is the execution delayed?"

"The hangman is lying on the ground wailing about a stom-achache," one of his men explained.

"There's a second hangman," Ishmael said impatiently. "Let him take the other's place at once!"

But when the second hangman approached the Jew, he, too, fell to the ground with unearthly wails. He clasped his arms around his middle as his face turned green. A third hangman came in next to carry out the hanging — only to join his friends writhing on the ground.

And then, as Ishmael was dancing about, enraged at the ineptitude of his hangmen, down from the hills swarmed the Imam's soldiers. They burst into the square, taking Ishmael and his men by surprise. Not many minutes later, the petty ruler's body was carried up to the gallows and hanged in place of the Jew.

The only one who was not amazed by this turn of events was Shoshana Cohen, the condemned doctor's wife. "What have I been telling you all along? I said that *Hakadosh Baruch Hu* would make a miracle. After all, it says explicitly that a *tzaddik* will be rescued from trouble and the wicked will take his place!"

[My friend, R' Mordechai Cohen of Jerusalem's Mekor-Baruch neighborhood, heard this story in its entirety from his father, R' Moshe Cohen of Bnei Brak, son of Mori Zechariah Cohen *zt"l*. R' Moshe Cohen remembered the story from his childhood.]

# Sweetening the Judgment

The normally quiet Tel Aviv street was stirring. An important visitor — the holy Karliner Rebbe, R' Avraham Elimelech Perlow — had come to the elderly rebbe, R' Yisrael of Husyatin, who welcomed his young guest with honor.

The youthful rebbe's face was uncharacteristically melancholy. Though normally he epitomized the injunction to, "Serve Hashem with joy," today things were different, and the host's grave countenance mirrored that of his guest.

Waves of heat beat down on the pavement, and people threw open their windows in the hope of catching a breath of air, a faint sea breeze from the west. But despite the oppressive heat, the moment his guest entered the room the old rebbe closed the window tightly and made sure that the door was securely locked. Those *chassidim* who tried to eavesdrop on the conversation between the two *tzaddikim* were doomed to disappointment. They couldn't hear a word.

Actually, the two rebbes were not alone. Mr. Leiber, a Tel Aviv resident staying in the Husyatiner Rebbe's house, was the third person present at that extraordinary meeting.

R' Avraham Elimelech's eyes widened in surprise. This meeting was supposed to be completely private. What was this fellow doing in the room?

R' Yisrael understood the unspoken question. His silent answer was a simple nod of the head, as though to say, "He can be trusted to keep a secret."

And the conversation began.

This was not the Karliner Rebbe's first visit to Eretz Yisrael. On previous trips, he had traveled to the graves of his ancestors, paid his respects to living *tzaddikim*, and engaged in various communal activities. But this visit, in the summer of 5699 (1939), was unlike the others. The moment he stepped off the small boat that had borne him from the large passenger ship, the *chassidim* who had come out in great numbers to welcome him erupted in a joyous dance. The rebbe stopped them, crying out brokenheartedly, "We haven't come here merely to pay a visit. We have come to arouse pity for our Jewish brothers in Europe, upon whose heads the enemy's sharp sword dangles by a thread!

"Know this," R' Avraham Elimelech continued soberly. "Dark clouds are gathering over European Jewry. The Jews of Poland, in particular and of Europe in general are in grave danger. We have come to pray, and to beseech mercy from the Guardian of Israel at the graves of *tzaddikim* and other holy places. May He have compassion!"

The rebbe prostrated himself at the graves of the *tzaddikim* and shed copious tears at the Western Wall. But he felt as though the words were being torn from his lips. With a heavy heart, he came to hold a private conference with the Husyatiner Rebbe, to see if there was any way at all to sweeten a very bitter situation.

At first, Mr. Leiber was astounded at the respect that the elderly rebbe accorded the guest half his age. Listening to their conversation soon made him change his attitude.

"The Poles will not be able to stand firm. They'll fall immediately," one said.

"Galicia, too, will fall into their hands like a ripe fruit," said the other.

"France, and Greece, and Italy —"

"And what will happen to the Jews?"

A long silence followed, and then the sound of weeping.

"But when they start up with Russia, the downfall will begin!"

"'*U'behar Tziyon tihiyeh peleitah*" ('And on Har Zion there will be refuge')...' "

Mr. Leiber was dumbfounded by their discussion. Fragments of their sentences were completely incomprehensible to him. They were talking like a pair of military strategists about possible battlegrounds. Names of various countries were mentioned, one after the other, as the rebbes examined their strengths and weaknesses from every angle, calculating which would fall and which would stand. The talk continued for a long time. When it was over, the Karliner Rebbe left the room with resigned and sorrowful eyes. The decree had been made, and there was no changing it. He remained in Eretz Yisrael for some time longer, consulting with the great men of his generation, who urged him to stay.

The Karliner Rebbe sailed away on the last ship that left for Europe before the outbreak of World War II. He clearly knew the fate that awaited him there, but like a faithful shepherd he did not want to abandon his flock — his family and his *chassidim*. He preferred to share their destiny.

Mr. Leiber was known among his friends as a thoughtful, intelligent person, a man who took every step based on logical reason. Therefore, they were very surprised at his behavior.

He seemed like a different person after he had sat in on the discussion between the two *tzaddikim*. He was fully aware that the entire world stood at the edge of an explosion. For days, he went around like a sleepwalker. To concerned inquiries — "What's the matter? What happened to you?" — he merely shrugged.

He tracked world events. From the international news, it seemed as though tragedy might still be averted. Various heads of state were making great efforts to extinguish the flames before they blazed out of control. There were numerous diplomatic meetings.

But Mr. Leiber was not convinced. He knew what it meant to believe in *chachamim*, and understood that the two rebbes had spoken of matters that would certainly come to pass.

His business instinct told him to invest his economic future in sugar. "If a world war breaks out, the international trade routes will be closed and the price of food will soar. Flour can become wormy — but sugar, if stored properly, will last," he decided.

Mr. Leiber began to race from one city warehouse to another, buying out almost the entire supply of sugar. After two weeks of this, he totaled his purchases and realized that he still did not have enough.

He then traveled to the big ports of Haifa and Atlit and bought tons of sugar straight off the ships on which they had come.

His family was certain that he had gone mad. Mr. Leiber borrowed money from every possible source, rented huge warehouses and filled them with bags of sugar to bursting.

Germany's invasion of Poland marked the outbreak of the Second World War, and it took nearly the whole world by surprise. But Mr. Leiber was not surprised at all. He was prepared. His warehouses held hundreds of tons of sugar, and he owed an astronomical debt that might have brought him to bankruptcy, or jail — or even both together.

Communication between ports ceased almost at once. Shortages in the shipment of basic food supplies quickly followed. The country was left with hardly a single grain of sugar to be found.

This was the moment that Mr. Leiber had been waiting for. He opened his warehouses to the suppliers and sold his sugar at reasonable prices. Even so, his profits were enormous. He became a very wealthy man.

# What R' Elisha Learned

Even in his worst nightmares, R' Elisha Brandes never dreamed that he would be forced, at his advanced age, to travel abroad on yet another fund-raising trip. But life is full of unexpected twists, some of them most unpleasant. His young grandson, Shimshy, who was only 10 years old, had been stricken with a serious illness. To save his life, the boy required an urgent and very expensive operation. R' Elisha had worked as a fund-raiser in the past and was experienced in raising money outside of Eretz Yisrael.

But the situation was different this time. This time, his grandson's life hung in the balance. Shimshy was a sunny-tempered boy, full of sweetness and charm, and an excellent student besides. The thought of something horrible happening to Shimshy was the goad that drove R' Elisha on. He was ready to do anything to help Shimshy beat his illness. He could do nothing for the boy medically, so he decided to take it upon himself to collect money, something he had not done in years.

On the day before his departure, he went to see one of the *gedolei hador*, to ask advice and receive his blessing for success. The *gaon* spoke with R' Elisha briefly. At one point, the discussion touched upon the *daf yomi* that R' Elisha learned each evening.

"I have a request to make of you," the *gadol* said. "On the day of your trip, do not learn the *daf yomi* at night, as you usually do. Learn it on the morning of your flight instead." He did not explain.

To R' Elisha, this was more than a suggestion; it had the ring of an order. Early the next morning, on the day he was to travel, he abandoned all the many things that needed to be done and sat in front of his *Gemara* instead. The day was the beginning of the month of Iyar 5760 (2000), when *daf* 41 of *Maseches Kesubos* was being learned.

The words of the *Gemara* refreshed R' Elisha Brandes's soul. Removed from the bustle of daily activities, he sat enwrapped in sprituality. There was a tangible pleasure in his learning that day, as he turned the page from one side to the next, and even came up with an original thought on the material.

"R' Nosson says: From where do we know that a person should not raise a bad dog in his home?... Because it says, 'And you shall not place blood in your house.' "

A question occured to R' Elisha as he learned this section. "A bad dog? Why doesn't the *Gemara* say that a person should not raise a dog — any dog — in his home? It only refers specifically to a bad dog — a killer Rottweiler or a bulldog, for example. It is forbidden to raise those kinds of dogs in one's home, because the dog might kill someone. But a good dog, a dog that is not in the habit of chewing people up, is apparently acceptable for raising in one's home, as it poses no danger."

WHAT R' ELISHA LEARNED / 231

He wanted to discuss the issue with a friend and hear what the halachah had to say about it, but time was pressing. He zipped up his suitcases and hurried to the airport to catch his plane.

The flight passed uneventfully. He landed around noon, New York time, and did not waste a minute. After depositing his bags at a relative's home, where he would be staying, he went straight out again on his first round of fund-raising. "Every minute is precious," was his motto. Each day that he spent here in the United States was worth a fortune in gold.

He went to an exclusive New York neighborhood where very wealthy people lived. In the past he had tried his luck here, mostly unsuccessfully. He had heard, however, that there had been some improvement of late. In places where collectors had previously been turned away in humiliation, it was now possible to leave with some hard cash in one's pocket. R' Elisha decided to see for himself.

The houses were set on spacious lots. The entire area boasted wealth. Every home was surrounded by a huge lawn and garden, which in turn was surrounded by a tall iron gate. The homes themselves were three stories tall, and generally housed no more than five or six people. R' Elisha approached the first mansion, tested the gate, and inspected the *mezuzah*. Experience had taught him that you could tell who lived in a house by its *mezuzah*. Finally, he pressed the intercom button under the name "Cooperman."

"Who is it?" asked a voice in Hebrew. R' Elisha was encouraged. At least he would not be forced to break his teeth trying to speak English, after ten long years in which he had hardly spoken the language at all.

"A collector from Eretz Yisrael. I am here on a matter of life and death."

"What happened?"

R' Elisha found himself telling the voice on the intercom all about his grandson, Shimshy, and the illness that had laid him low. He spoke of Shimshy's chances of recovery if he could have the necessary surgery.

"All right," the master of the house said. "I'm sending out the money."

R' Elisha waited, expecting a child or servant to emerge from the house. What came out instead was something completely unexpected.

Down the winding path from the front door to the gate came a huge brown-and-white dog. The dog carried an envelope in its mouth.

232 / TALES FOR THE SOUL

R' Elisha felt the blood rush to his head. He was furious. Was it necessary to humiliate me to such an extent? he thought. They sent the money with a *dog*?!

He wanted to turn around and stalk away in open affront. Then, suddenly, he remembered what he had been learning only that morning. "Where do we learn that it is forbidden to raise a bad dog?" In other words, the *Gemara* was teaching that it is permissible to raise a good dog. A dog that came bearing *tzedakah* was not a bad dog.

He waited for the dog to come closer, and studied it with interest. It was a very large dog, the kind known as a Seeing Eye dog, whose job is to guide its blind master. Apparently the master of the house was blind, and was using this big dog to fulfill the mitzvah of giving *tzedakah*.

The dog pushed its head through the bars of the gate and thrust the envelope at R' Elisha, who opened it. Inside were two ten-dollar bills.

"Thank you very much," he told the dog, and turned to leave.

"Wait a minute!" shrieked a voice over the intercom. "Come inside."

As R' Elisha stood there in astonishment, a buzzer sounded. He pushed the gate open and followed the dog, who breathed warm, damp air on him.

The master of the house was waiting in a large, beautiful kitchen on the ground level. He was a man of medium height, wearing a small yarmulka, and as his guest entered he was pouring hot coffee into a mug. R' Elisha saw that his assumption had been incorrect. His host, Mr. Cooperman, was definitely not blind. He had guessed as much when he had been paged on the intercom as he had been on the point of leaving, and now he saw his host's open and seeing eyes.

"Listen," Mr. Cooperman said. "I was watching on the closed-circuit camera, and I saw the way you hesitated before taking the envelope from my dog. I saw you overcome your disgust and take it from him. You surprised me. I was sure you would leave, the way so many others did — and lose out. Instead, you won!"

"I had a reason." R' Elisha explained what he had learned that morning, in which he had understood that it is permissible to raise a good dog in one's home. His host's eyes sparkled, and his mouth turned up in a smile. "You don't say!" he exclaimed. "It says that in the *Gemara*? Very nice!"

Still chuckling, he sat down at the kitchen table and wrote a check for one thousand dollars. "For your grandson's operation."

"I — I have no words," R' Elisha thanked him emotionally. He hesitated. "Can I ask you a question? I thought that you must be blind, but now I see that your eyes are fine. Why do you use a dog to give *tzedakah*? It's a humiliating feeling to take money from a dog."

It had taken more than a little courage to ask the question, but Mr. Cooperman seemed to appreciate that. "I will tell you a secret about Ginger, my dog. As you see, she's a Seeing Eye dog, and she used to belong to my father, *z"l*, who was blind. It was hard for my father to get around, so he used to send an envelope of money with Ginger. When my father passed away a few years ago, I inherited the dog and decided to continue his custom as well. Let the dog that used to give *tzedakah* continue to give *tzedakah*!"

In other circumstances, R' Elisha Brandes would have burst out laughing. But Mr. Cooperman's expression was serious. Thanking him again, R' Elisha took his leave. He had certainly begun his fundraising tour on the right foot.

As he left Mr. Cooperman's house, R' Elisha heard a chorus of birds chirping from the decorative trees with their rich, green foliage. He closed the iron gate behind him and walked along, his heart filled with hope, to the next house, which stood some fifty yards away.

This lot was similar to the first, but much more lavish in appearance. The garden was lush and meticulously kept, nestled behind a vast expanse of emerald lawn dotted with shade trees. From behind the house came the blue sparkle of a private swimming pool. A sign on the door at the gate read "Yoram Saidi." Inspecting the *mezuzah*, R' Elisha found some of his ebullience evaporating. The *mezuzah* was tiny. In other words, the homeowner here was not very religious. He pressed the intercom button, and waited.

Suddenly, he stopped breathing. Stalking up to the gate was a huge, powerfully built man with long hair and muscled arms ending in lethal-looking fists. As if this were not enough, at his side trotted a dog nearly as large as a mule. The two wore identical expressions of near-murderous rage. R' Elisha wanted to run for his life, but the man's shout immobilized him. "What do you want?"

"I - I - I'm c-c-collecting m-m-money for my s-s-sick g-g-grandson," R' Elisha stammered in terror.

"Aha! You must be coming from my neighbor's house, that blasted Cooperman. He has a reputation for giving charity, and they all come straight from his house to mine. We've been fighting over it for years. It's your good luck that I was taking my dog for a walk just now, or he'd be standing by this gate barking at you to get lost, the way he does to everyone coming from Cooperman's place. This is one serious dog, let me assure you. Right, Max?" He glanced lovingly at the enormous dog. "You'd probably say that he is antisocial and even a killer, like everyone who maligns my Max."

R' Elisha's thoughts raced. He didn't know whether to laugh or to cry, but his facial muscles, frozen in fear, had been rendered incapable of doing either one. With all the kindness that he could muster, he replied, "What do you mean? Max looks like a good, well-trained dog. Besides, if he was raised by a man like yourself, he must surely have a heart of gold. Our Torah says that it is permissible to raise a good dog in one's home."

A surprised look crossed Yoram Saidi's face. "I don't know about that, but my wife likes Torah. Maybe you should tell her what it says." Abruptly, as if coming to a decision, he said, "Come inside the house with me." He actually smiled. "My wife, Temima, will be happy to hear what you have to say."

To R' Elisha's astonishment, for the second time in an hour he found himself entering a mansion whose threshold he had never dreamed of crossing.

"Temima, come here!" Yoram called. "We have a guest who has things to say about the Torah."

The mistress of the house, originally of Yemenite origin, came almost at a run. She welcomed him enthusiastically, offered him some refreshment, and then asked eagerly if he could tell her a *devar Torah*, for which her soul thirsted. "I have some holy books here in the house," she confided, "and I even understand them a little."

For the second time that day, R' Elisha Brandes related what he had learned that morning, which felt like months ago. "... And it would seem that we learn from this that it is permissible to raise a good dog in one's home."

The Saidis nearly howled with joy. "You have to tell that over to my father!" Temima exclaimed in great excitement.

Yoram explained that his father-in-law — a wealthy Yemenite Jew who had moved to New York from Israel — lived nearby. He refused to visit them because of their dog. "It's either Max, or me," he had said resolutely.

"He has to hear what you just told us," Yoram said. He picked up the phone, punched in a series of numbers, and handed it to R' Elisha.

R' Elisha waited politely until someone picked up at the other end. Then he struck up a conversation with Yitzchak Tzubari, Temima Saidi's father.

He quickly gave the background of the call, telling of his grandson who needed urgent surgery. Then he related what he had learned in the *Gemara* that morning.

"*Really*?" Tzubari exclaimed in surprise. "I wouldn't have believed it. Thank you for opening my eyes and sparing me further quarrels with my only daughter. Tell Temima and Yoram that I'll come see them this very evening, now that I see that I was mistaken and that it is permissible to have a dog at home. Please ask my son-in-law to give you a check for $180 in my name. May your grandson have a speedy recovery. Tell Yoram that I'll return the money to him this evening."

"Only $180? That's all he's giving?" Yoram Saidi complained. "He's a millionaire!" He thought a moment. "I'll tell you what — if he's giving you $180, I'll add $500 to that, for the health of Shimshon, your grandson."

R' Elisha now had an additional check for $680 in his pocket. In his wildest imaginings he had never thought he'd have such amazing success on his very first day — and in only half an hour's time! And it was all thanks to the *Gemara* he had learned early that morning, and the ideas it had raised.

He could have taken his leave then, with words of thanks. But he followed the example of Yaakov *Avinu* where it says, "*Vayavo Yaakov shalem.*" Our Sages explain that Yaakov was *shalem* (complete) financially, but he remained to rectify the city's spiritual deficiencies.

"Before I go, I have three requests," R' Elisha told the couple.

"Even up to half my kingdom," quipped Yoram. It was impossible to recognize the furious man who had met him at the gate a short time before.

R' Elisha saw a window of opportunity, and plunged in head first. "First, I would ask you to replace the *mezuzah* on your gate."

"Why? Isn't it a good one?" Yoram asked, stung.

"I didn't say that. But, in general, such small *mezuzos* often prove problematic."

"We'll change it," Yorom promised. "What else?"

"With all due respect to Max — I hope he's not listening — please don't let him stand at the gate and frighten away visitors with his barking. You have no idea what kind of *Gan Eden* you'd be preparing for yourselves, if you would only open your doors and give each charity collector even one dollar."

"A dollar is nothing," Yoram said jovially. "Very well, Max is hereby banished from the gate. From now on, every collector will get ten dollars from me. What was your third request?"

"That you make up with your neighbor, Mr. Cooperman."

Yoram's face darkened all at once. "No! Whatever you said before, I can accept. But I can't honor this request. We've been on bad terms for years."

"Why?" R' Elisha pleaded. "What brought about your quarrel?"

"All the *shnorrers* come here directly from his house —" Yoram's expression suddenly lightened. "Actually, you're right. If I also start giving charity, then what does it matter if I patch things up with Cooperman? — But I can't do it. It would humiliate me."

"Don't worry about that," R' Elisha said quickly. "If you'll permit me, I'll go right back there and execute a peace treaty between the two of you!"

Straight from the Saidis' home to the Coopermans' ran R' Elisha, to pass on the good news that his neighbor was willing to mend fences after all these years.

How powerful is a *gadol's* suggestion — and how powerful are just two short lines of *Gemara*!

[Thanks to the sender of this story, R' Dovid Goldschmidt of Kiryat Sefer, on behalf of the Swiss newspaper, the *"Yiddishe Tzeitung,"* where the story was first printed in the winter of 5760 by the story's protagonist.]

# Fifty Secret Signatures

In the home of the Mattesdorfer Rebbe, R' Yisrael Toisig, who departed this world in Tishrei 5728 (1968), there was a secret cupboard that no one had permission to open except for the rebbe himself. Everyone knew that no one was permitted to touch the secret cupboard, and no member of the rebbe's family dared disobey

One day, near evening, the rebbe left home to conduct a wedding for one of his students. One of his grandsons, who remained behind in the house, was suddenly overcome with a burning curiosity to learn the secret hidden in the cupboard. His curiosity gave him no rest. Looking all around to see if anyone was watching him, he went to the cupboard and opened it with trembling hands.

At first, because of the gloom that filled the house at dusk, he saw nothing. He thrust his hand inside and felt about on the shelves. His hand touched a paper that lay in a corner of the cupboard. The boy removed it, but could not read a word in the dimness. Moving closer to the window, he smoothed out the paper.

238 / TALES FOR THE SOUL

The page held scores of signatures, all crowded together so that they looked at first like meaningless scribble. Only when he looked closer did the grandson see that they were the names of Jerusalemites, some well known and others less so. They were people who had lived in the city some sixty years before. The signatures filled the page without order or organization. And in the margins, beneath each signature, was this line:

"I hereby pledge myself as a guarantor that no harm will come to them. Gedalia Moshe Goldman, the Rebbe of Zhivil."

The boy recognized this name: He was the Zhiviller Rebbe, son of R' Shlomo, better known as R' Shlom'ke of Zhivil. After his father's passing, R' Gedalia Moshe of Zhivil led his flock for less than five years, until his own death on 24 Cheshvan, 5710 (1950). But why all these hasty signatures? What was the meaning of the guarantee that the departed rebbe had signed — the promise that no harm should befall them?

Before anyone in the household could find out what he had done, the boy returned the mysterious document to its place, closed the cupboard as he had found it, and left the room. He guarded the secret, not telling anyone else about his discovery, but he quietly began to ask questions within the family circle, to see if anyone knew the secret of the document and its signatures.

And then, one day, an uncle told him the story.

It was the year 5708 (1948), at the height of war.

Shells shrieked over Jerusalem. The Jordanian Legionnaires aimed their cannons, perched in the nearby hills, directly at the Jerusalem neighborhoods that contained the most Jewish homes. Jerusalem's finest citizens were in the enemy's gunsights.

When a shell exploded, hundreds of shell fragments scattered in every direction, sowing death and destruction. Jerusalem's Jews cowered in their air-raid shelters, listening fearfully to every incoming whistle, which was inevitably followed by a fearsome explosion and the unavoidable question: "Did it get anyone? Who did it get this time?"

It was at the height of this terrible period that R' Yisrael's only daughter, Hindel, was stricken with a grave illness. Hindel's husband, the *gaon* R' Chaim Brim, who passed away only recently (on Shabbos, 25 Adar, 5762 [2002]) was already recognized as a genius in Torah. He left his *Gemara* briefly to run to the city's *rav*, R' Yosef Tzvi Dushinsky, and beg the rabbi to pray for his wife.

"She is a young woman, and we have young children at home. What would I do without her? What would I do?" R' Chaim's throat choked up and tears poured from his eyes. The more he tried to suppress his weeping, the stronger it became. At last he gave in, his entire body shaking with the force of his sobs.

R' Dushinsky sat lost in thought. He seemed to be calculating what needed to be done in the face of the woman's critical situation. Hindel already had one foot in the grave.

"I have only one suggestion," he said at last. "Hurry as fast as you can to the holy rebbe, R' Gedalia Moshe of Zhivil. Beg him to pray for your wife. Who knows, maybe the Merciful One will take pity on her."

R' Chaim flew to the rebbe's home like an arrow from its bow. The rebbe was living in Katamon at that time, which was farther away from the shelling.

The rebbe's father had been the well-known *tzaddik*, R' Shlom'ke of Zhivil, one of the previous generation's leading lights. Jerusalemites were not the only ones who knew of his greatness; people flocked to him from everywhere. After his father's passing, the son, R' Gedalia Moshe, took his place. He was great in Torah and a giant in *tzedakah*, but he hid his greatness behind simple behavior. Hashem helps people in the path that they wish to follow; R' Gedalia Moshe managed to keep his secret well. Only a few knew his true worth, while the rest accepted him at face value.

R' Chaim had reached the rebbe's door. He knocked lightly, and entered. There were no *gabbaim* here, no assistants. Anyone could come right in and see the rebbe.

The Zhiviller Rebbe listened as R' Chaim told of his wife's illness, and how he had just been to see R' Dushinsky. R' Gedalia Moshe look astonished. "*Vus vill ehr fun mir? Ehr meint az ich bin der tatteh?*" ("What does he want from me? Does he think I am like my father?")

No one who knew of the relationship between R' Dushinsky and R' Shlom'ke of Zhivil would find the question surprising. The *rav* was in the habit of sending various difficult cases to other *gedolim*, but when it came to a delicate and complex matter, one that touched the essence of the soul and entailed changing a person's name, he would send people only to R' Shlom'ke. Surprisingly, after R' Shlom'ke's passing, R' Dushinsky continued to send people to the same address — this time, to the rebbe's son and successor. The *rav* had deeper insight than the average person, and he saw that the apple did not fall far from the tree.

R' Chaim, hearing this sharp comment, understood that there was nothing more to say. The rebbe had absolutely no intention of performing a name change for his wife.

He left dejectedly, stepping out into a street that churned with danger.

Every few minutes, the shriek of an incoming shell rent the air. The very sky seemed filled with menace. But the young man, whose wife's life hung in the balance, spent no time caring about danger. He began to run through the street, taking shelter from time to time when the blood-chilling shriek came. Reaching R' Dushinsky's home at last, he recounted his meeting with R' Gedalia Moshe.

The *rav* of Jerusalem listened attentively, then declared with great firmness, "Go back to the Zhiviller Rebbe's house and tell him that I command him, in the name of the *mara D'Asra* [the community's spiritual leader], to bring salvation for your sick wife!"

An electric current seemed to pass through R' Chaim. Could his ears be deceiving him? Could the *rav* actually decree that the rebbe bring salvation? He could not imagine approaching such a great man and repeating such harsh words.

But the memory of his poor wife, hovering between life and death, infused him with strength. He went out again into the menacing street and made his way with all possible haste to the rebbe's house. He passed on R' Dushinsky's message.

This time, the rebbe relented. He stopped refusing to help. Turning to R' Chaim, he said, "Your wife is in a state where adding a name won't make a difference, in any case. What I need is fifty signatures, each of them from a man willing to donate one year of his own life for the healing of Hindel, daughter of Sarah, may Hashem send her a speedy recovery. When I have the necessary signatures, we can, with Heaven's help, do something together with a name change."

One cannot argue with *gedolei Yisrael*. With their Torah wisdom they see things that ordinary people do not. Sometimes, however, one must ask a question, especially in such an instance. R' Chaim Brim, who was already considered an outstanding Torah scholar of Jerusalem, did not understand what the rebbe had just told him.

"The rebbe surely knows that many people have been breathing their last here in Yerushalayim, a city under seige. Some die of hunger, others of thirst, some from illness and others from the shells that our cursed enemies, may their names be blotted out, keep raining down on our heads. Everyone wants to cling to life, and each holds on like a drowning man clutching at a straw. Who will agree to sign on for such an obligation — to donate a year of his life?" The distraught husband burst into tears.

The rebbe stroked his hand warmly, calming the tears that arose from a broken heart, and said something that only a man of "broad shoulders" can say:

"You can tell them, in my name, that I guarantee that anyone who signs up to give a year of his life on behalf of your wife will emerge from this war unharmed."

"I need fifty signatures," R' Chaim mumbled to himself as he left the rebbe's house. Fifty Jews willing to contribute a year of their own lives for the sake of a young woman's recovery. His brilliant mind struggled with the question of where to find fifty such Jews all at once. The streets were desolate and the homes were empty. People were in hiding — in air-raid shelters!

With a sudden spurt of energy, he raced to the nearest shelter.

In those days, most bomb shelters were nothing more than the ground floor of a two-story building. The first floor was considered relatively protected, as the upper story would bear the brunt of a shell landing on the house from above. Occasionally, the shelters were actually proper ones built beneath the ground, in a cellar. These shelters were usually crowded to bursting, because anyone seeking genuine protection would go there rather than huddle in a first-floor apartment being used as a makeshift shelter.

It was to one of these underground shelters that R' Chaim proceeded now. Every minute was precious.

A thick atmosphere hit him as soon as he opened the door. The shelter was filled from wall to wall with people, packed in like sardines. Babies wailed loudly. One child wanted a drink and another wanted something to eat. One slept with his head on his mother's knee, while his brother, just a year older, tugged at her sleeve and begged to be allowed to go out to play in the fresh air. The men sat and recited *Tehillim* in unison, verse by verse. Hope shone from their eyes, mingled with a deathly fear. No one knew what the coming day would bring; everyone feared for his life.

R' Chaim entered the shelter and cried aloud, *"Gevald!"*

Silence fell. The *Tehillim* ceased. Even the babies were surprised and stopped crying. R' Chaim seized the temporary lull to plead, "My wife is very sick. You know her, she is the daughter of holy people, a modest and righteous woman, a young flower that has not yet opened her petals and is already in danger of withering away. Please, take pity on her. I need fifty people to donate one year of their lives for her. Here is a page in my hand. Please, I beg of you, fifty signatures. Save her!"

At first, the silence continued. His words had stunned his listeners. Then the huddled crowd began murmuring.

"Have you lost your mind?" a woman asked him with a bitter smirk. "We are all in the same boat. Is your wife the only one in danger? The Angel of Death is picking us off day by day, without pity — and you come here with such a strange request?"

R' Chaim dropped his bombshell. "The Rebbe of Zhivil, *shlita*, guarantees that anyone who signs will survive the war unharmed!"

A tumult burst out. The shrewd Jerusalemites sensed the truth at once: The son was just like the father. The Zhiviller Rebbe would not say such a thing lightly. His word was his bond. A promise was a promise.

They forgot what they had been saying just a moment earlier. The bitter smirk was transformed into a hopeful smile. There was a sudden surge in the crowded shelter, as everyone tried to reach R' Chaim at once. "Let me sign! Let me sign!" Everyone wanted the security that the rebbe had promised — to emerge from this terrible war unscathed.

The tables had been turned. A moment before, R' Chaim had been certain that he would have to leave without a single signature. Now, he had to scold those who pushed others out of their way. "Just a minute! Not everyone can sign; the amount is limited to fifty signatures. I can't let the whole city sign!"

No one listened. Who would not want to merit the *tzaddik's* protection? Who didn't want to be saved from the war that had already exacted such a high toll among the city's Jewish population?

R' Chaim let them sign and sign. Abruptly, he snatched back the page and began counting signatures. He cried, "Enough! I already have more than enough signatures. I thank you all. I must hurry back to the Zhiviller Rebbe now."

R' Gedalia Moshe took the page from him and read it carefully. Yes, there were fifty (and more) signatures of people agreeing to donate a year of their lives on the sick woman's behalf. Beneath the signatures, the rebbe wrote, "I hereby pledge myself as a guarantor that no harm will come to them. Gedalia Moshe Goldman, the Rebbe of Zhivil."

He turned to R' Chaim. "Now we can add a name to your wife."

The rebbe added the name "Ruchama" (from that day forward, she was known as Ruchama Hindel) and blessed her with Hashem's compassion and a speedy recovery, a long life and good years.

And that is what happened. 'The young woman recovered from her illness. Within a short time, she left her sickbed. She lived fifty-one years longer, until her death in the year 5759 (1999), leaving behind her illustrious husband, R' Chaim Brim, and a fine family of children, grandchildren, and great-grandchildren.

As an addendum to this story, here is another tale about the *tzaddik*, R' Gedalia Moshe of Zhivil. Two years after this incident, in the month of Cheshvan 5710 (1950), the wife of R' Yaakov of Chakova fell gravely ill. Her son, the *gaon* R' Moshe Halberstam, a member of the *beis din tzedek* of the *Eidah HaChareidis*, was only a youth then. At his father's bidding he ran at once to the Zhiviller Rebbe, bearing the news that his mother was very sick and pleading for the rebbe's prayers on her behalf. The rebbe glanced at him sorrowfully, as though to say that he could not help. R' Moshe understood the look, and burst into bitter tears. The rebbe wept along with him.

A few days later, on the 12th of Cheshvan, Rebbetzin Halberstam passed away. And twelve days later, on the 24th day of the month, the rebbe himself departed this world and was buried in the old cemetery at Givat Ram.

Two weeks before the rebbe's passing, R' Aharon, the Belzer Rebbe, had come to see him. As was his custom whenever he spent the month of Tishrei in Jerusalem, before his return to Tel Aviv R' Aharon would pay a return visit to the various rebbes and *rabbanim* who had visited him during his stay. During the course of their talk, the Belzer Rebbe suddenly asked, *"Vi alt zent ihr?"* ["How old are you?"]

The Zhiviller Rebbe trembled all over. "Rebbe, rebbe, *ich hub nuch tzeit. Ich hub nuch tzeit!"* ("I still have time!" In other words, I still have more time on this world to improve and accomplish.) R' Aharon's *gabbaim*, who were present at the meeting, were very surprised at their rebbe's question, which was not at all in his usual style.

Indeed, the Belzer Rebbe — as the Zhiviller Rebbe understood — did not ask questions idly; he had some definite intent. At that time, the rebbe of Zhivil was still in good health. Only a few days later, however, he suddenly fell ill, and departed this world for the Heavenly Yeshivah on the 24th day of Cheshvan, as mentioned above.

Several hours later, the Belzer Rebbe heard that his own brother, R' Mordechai of Bilgoray, the father of the present Belzer Rebbe, had passed on as well. He died on the 25th of Cheshvan and was buried in Teveriah. These two *tzaddikim* were cousins: R' Mordechai of Bilgoray's mother, wife of R' Yissachar Dov of Belz, was a sister of R' Shlom'ke of Zhivil. After R' Mordechai of Bilgoray survived the

Holocaust, the two great men, R' Gedalia Moshe and R' Mordechai, were inseparable. Together to the end, they left for the Next World within a few hours of one another.

[Special thanks to a son of the family, who wishes to remain anonymous, who sent us this moving story.]

# By the Light of the Bonfire

Meiron was crowded with people that year, 5718 (1958), as it was every year. The old Egged buses parked on the slopes of the hill to discharge their passengers. These were Jerusalemites who had traveled seven or eight long hours to arrive at their destination. They stepped onto solid ground, stretched, and breathed in relief; the long trip was over at last.

They began the trek up the hill toward their goal: the yearly celebration at the tomb of the great *Tanna,* R' Shimon bar Yochai. The klezmer musicians, Avremele Segal ("shpieler") and Eliyahu Kuperman ("clarinetist"), were already in place at the cave's mouth, together with their instruments. Along with all the others, they were waiting for the signal: the lighting.

With nightfall the stars began to twinkle in the sky, which darkened from minute to minute. In the cave and out of it, *minyanim* formed to *daven Ma'ariv.* Then came the great moment, when *sefirah* was counted: "*Hayom shloshah u'shloshim yom, sheheim...*" ["Today is thirty-three days, which is..."]

Crowds of merrymakers were already on the roof, surrounding the lighting stand. The burning torch was extended over the stand, which was filled with cotton and linen garments and rags dipped in

246 / TALES FOR THE SOUL

olive oil. The flames lit the people's faces as joyous song and dance broke out to honor "bar Yochai."

The dancing lasted many long hours. From time to time a dancer, weary and thirsty, would break away from the circle to fetch a drink of cold water from a barrel. If he was hungry, no need to worry: Yitzchak-Chaim Taubes was circulating through the crowd with pita halves filled with pickled vegetables and bits of salted fish. He had able assistants for this task. Cartons of filled pita halves were distributed by his crew of helpers, each a well-known charity-collector in her own right: Gittele *"da frumer,"* Savta Miriam, and Chanala "the Karliner." These good women did not rest until every hungry person had eaten his fill and could go on dancing energetically.

The amenities then were very different from what is available in our times. There were no fountains dispensing fruit drinks, no hot coffee and tea handed out in amazing quantities by the good people of "Yad Ezra" and the many other charitable organizations. And who could have imagined in those days the rivers of wine and grape juice that now flow for the celebrants? Over forty years ago there was not even a hint of the abundance that we take for granted today. On the contrary, most people knew only poverty and privation. But goodwill and the desire to help exists in every generation. Yitzchak-Chaim Taubes was such a *chesed*-loving Jew.

Yitzchak-Chaim Taubes was a simple man. He had been born and raised in Tzefas, and was typical of the residents of that city. Taller than average, with large hands and feet, Yitzchak-Chaim walked with long strides and was very strong. He could swing a heavy sack of potatoes over his shoulder with ease. He dressed simply, his clothes hanging on him loosely. But his external appearance belied his inner self. While he bore a simple and even slightly coarse exterior, inside he was pure and good. A pleasant-spoken and kindhearted man, he was ready to help anyone at any time, even at his own expense. He found it difficult to earn a livelihood; though he was always switching jobs, bad luck seemed to follow him everywhere. And yet he always looked cheerful. His mood was cheerful and his manner pleasant all year round, but at no time was it as joyous as on Lag Ba'Omer night — the highlight of Yitzchak-Chaim's year.

༄༅

Sometime during the long stretches of the night, the clarinets faltered a little. The klezmerim and the dancers rested for a few minutes from their strenuous labor. Yitzchak-Chaim sat surrounded by a group of young feasters, their mouths filled with his pitas and pickled vegetables.

"Yitzchak-Chaim," they asked, "how did you come to do this? Why is it that you provide us with this meal every year on Lag Ba'Omer night?"

Yitzchak-Chaim looked as though he had been waiting for just that question. He loved relating the story of the miracle that had happened to him on this great night. But he never launched into the story on his own. He always waited for someone to ask. It was easier for him to speak when requested to do so, knowing that he was not imposing himself or his tales on an unwilling audience, for he did not wish to be a bother to other people.

Yitzchak-Chaim waited until the group finished eating, washing the food down with drinks of cold water. They eyed him expectantly. He greatly enjoyed spinning out the suspense, so he waited a little longer, until every ear in the circle was his. Then, with a deep breath, he began to speak.

"You know," he said, "I haven't rested today. Since morning, I've been working without a break. I have to worry about feeding this huge crowd. Early this morning, I *davened*, and then immediately ran to get the vegetables and everything else. That's exactly the way it was 25 years ago — only then I didn't have the car to carry the food all the way to Meiron. Back then, we used donkeys. Things were very different."

As he spoke, a haze of memory veiled his eyes. He was far removed in time, but not in place. Yitzchak-Chaim had returned to an older Meiron, a Meiron that was no more.

Two days before Lag Ba'Omer that year — it was 5693 (1933) — Yitzchak-Chaim rose very early. He was a young man then, his posture still erect and his strength at its peak. After he finished *davening*, he went to the homes of his Arab neighbors to borrow their donkeys. Then he began loading up the animals.

He took empty barrels to fill with cold water, for slaking the thirst of the dancing hordes. He brought baskets filled with fruits and vegetables, and flour for baking pitas and rugelach. When he'd finished loading the donkeys, he made his way to the righteous charity-collector Nechama, whom everyone called by the nickname "Nechomkil" or sometimes just "Chomkil."

"Yitzchak-Chaim, *shalom aleichem!*" Chomkil cried joyfully. "How is your mother, my good friend, may she live and be well?"

"My mother isn't feeling very well," Yitzchak-Chaim answered briefly, and sadly. "You know, the usual."

Yitchak-Chaim's mother, Tova, was a sickly woman who suffered greatly from pains that sometimes made her cry aloud. In order to distract her from her suffering, Chomkil would visit her from time to time and relate stories to her to distract her from her pain for a while.

"Is everything ready?" Yitzchak-Chaim asked.

"'Is everything ready?'" Chomkil mimicked in mock-anger, though a warm light glinted in her eye. "Do you think I started working just today? I've been preparing for Lag Ba'Omer since last summer! I haven't rested a minute, to make sure that everything will be ready on time."

During the summer months, when vegetables were plentiful and cheap, Chomkil would buy great quantities of cucumbers and pickle them in barrels that had originally been used to store kerosene and then thoroughly scrubbed for their new purpose. After she had pickled the cucumbers in salt, garlic, and spices, the tinsmith, R' Sholom, son of R' Mordechai Mesh'l Segal, would solder the barrels shut, sealing them hermetically. He also prepared handles for the hundreds of cans that were collected all year long, to be used as drinking and washing cups.

Chomkil kept all these barrels and cans in the yard of her home. Now Yitzchak-Chaim lifted them in his strong arms and piled them onto the donkeys' backs. Then off he started for Meiron.

BY THE LIGHT OF THE BONFIRE / 249

When the caravan of donkeys had reached its destination, Yitzchak-Chaim began the job of unloading them: empty barrels for water, primus burners, charred old wicks, sacks of charcoal, sacks of flour, cans of preserved vegetables. A crew of women baked pita breads with the flour, along with *pletzlach* (fried, salted cookies) and rugelach. They kneaded the pita dough with fruit juices — especially fig juice; water was a precious commodity in Meiron. For boiling tea and coffee, there were women who volunteered to drag water in large cans from a nearby spring.

After Yitzchak-Chaim finished unloading the donkeys and arranging all the things he had brought, the "welcoming committee" of good women set about the job of preparing food for all the expected comers. Meanwhile, Yitzchak-Chaim strolled through the area with his hands in his pockets.

Nechomkil, seeing that he was idle for the moment, requested his help. "Yitzchak-Chaim, there's still time. We should use all the precious daylight hours. None of the women are free to go down to the spring for water, and there's not a single drop of water to be had for drinking or washing. Please take the donkeys down to the spring and fill the empty cans that you brought from Tzefas. It's hot already, and I expect that this year's Lag Ba'Omer will be a scorcher. There'll be a huge crowd coming to celebrate tonight, and a lot of people will be thirsty."

Being the good-hearted man that he was, Yitzchak-Chaim did not refuse this woman, who never thought of herself and cared only for others. He went at once to the donkeys, untied them from the iron spikes to which they were tethered, and led them downhill to the small spring in the valley. He walked carefully, with the four donkeys following along behind. Each descent and return climb would allow him to bring up eight large cans of water. If he hurried, he'd have time for two round-trips to the spring and back. That meant sixteen cans of water — a veritable treasure! How much tea and coffee for the thirsty crowd could be boiled up with that amount of water!

The path down to the spring was really no path at all. It wound among boulders and thorns, and the footing was treacherous for the donkeys. At times, the beasts refused to move. But clever Chomkil had promised Yitzchak-Chaim that he would receive payment for the dif-

250 / TALES FOR THE SOUL

ficult job, apart from the merit of the mitzvah he was doing. In addition, she had added a blessing that his mother have a speedy recovery in the merit of this mitzvah. Yitzchak-Chaim loved his mother and could not bear to watch her suffer so terribly. If this arduous task could possibly help her, he was ready to do it. And, apart from all this, he found it hard to say no to Chomkil.

So Yitzchak-Chaim went down to the spring. Access to the water was difficult, and required much physical agility and strength. Leaving the donkeys on a slight elevation above him, he bent over to reach the water, which he began to draw up with the help of a small copper pail. Carefully, he poured each bucketful into the larger cans strapped to the donkey's backs. Over and over, he bent and filled, rose and poured. Time passed quickly, but he was unaware of the gathering shadows.

At last — eight large cans filled to the brim with water! He swiveled the lids to close them tightly so as not to lose a drop on the way up. Then, leading his pack of donkeys, he started up the narrow path, hemmed in by the trees crowding in on either side.

Suddenly, he caught his breath in fright.

A gigantic hyena was standing right in front of him, its mouth open to expose its teeth, its tongue hanging out. The donkeys began to yammer and bray in fear, and fled in all directions. Yitzchak-Chiam was left alone facing the animal.

He had never seen such a large hyena in his life. It was the size of a big wolf, and its yellowed teeth were sharp as knives. He remembered hearing Arab peasant-farmers tell stories about hyenas, which they called, singularly, "*deva*".

"The *deva* is very dangerous," the peasants had said, as they sat around the campfire sipping strong Turkish coffee from the *finjon*. "When it sees a man alone, easy prey, it casts a kind of spell on him. The hyena begins wailing, with a sound almost like hysterical human laughter. The victim is drawn to that cursed laughter as though he were under a spell. Like a hypnotized man, he'll follow the animal to its lair. There, in the dark cave, the hyena will fall on him with its sharp teeth."

Yitzchak-Chaim had listened to this description scornfully, dismissing it as an "Eastern fantasy." Now he was standing face to face with a *deva*. The hyena broke into a wail that sounded exactly the way the Arabs had described it: like rolling, hysterical laughter. And Yitzchak-Chaim (as he later told the tale) found himself following the hyena as if he were under a spell!

*Why am I not running away?* he tried to ask himself. *Here, I'll stoop down and find a big rock to throw at the animal's head. Then I'll run.*

But these thoughts were not translated into action. The hyena continued walking, and Yitzchak-Chaim continued unwillingly in its wake. He seemed to have lost his senses. The frightening stories he had heard from the peasants were coming true right before his own eyes! He was gripped with a deathly fear. One part of his brain called for him to flee, but another part seemed to lock him in, forcing one foot to follow the other after the mesmerizing animal.

From time to time, the hyena let loose another eerie wail of "laughter" and turned its head to see whether its prey was still following. Yitzchak-Chaim walked on, completely powerless to stop, all the way to the beast's den.

Dusk had fallen, stretching its long shadows over the Galilee mountains. The lights that had been set up to illuminate the cave of R' Shimon bar Yochai seemed like a distant dream. All around was joy and light, but darkness was upon Yizchak-Chaim. In just another moment or two he would meet his end, and no one would ever know how or where he had disappeared. They would not even find his remaining bones.

Suddenly, he found himself falling to the ground. His voice rose in a great, hoarse cry:

"G-d of R' Shimon, hear me!"

At that very moment, up above, the fire was being lit in the stand on top of the *Tanna's* resting place, directly over the one in the cave below.

252 / TALES FOR THE SOUL

The fire took hold of the garments soaked in olive oil: used and worn-out yarmulkas and *talleisim katanim*, as well as fluffy cotton balls. The flames flared up into a huge blaze, forcing the surrounding crowd to step back.

As Yitzchak-Chaim cried out, "G-d of R' Shimon, hear me!" a powerful north wind sprang up. From the pile of oil-soaked clothes, a *tallis* flew up into the air. The wind carried the burning *tallis* directly down to the thorny patch where Yitzchak-Chaim lay like a stone at the mouth of the hyena's cave. The hyena stood ready to seize its prey with its teeth.

The *tallis* fell between Yitzchak-Chaim and the hyena, and the thorn patch began to burn.

"The *deva* is a dangerous animal," the Arab peasants had warned. "But there is one thing you can use against it: Fire! The *deva* is mortally afraid of fire."

When the hyena saw the flames that seemed to have fallen from the sky engulf the thornbushes, it burst into a frightened wail and ran as though it was pursued by a thousand evil spirits.

Pale and trembling, Yitzchak-Chaim stumbled to his feet. Around him, tongues of flame licked at the thornbushes, but he was not afraid of the fire. He knew that it had been sent from Heaven, straight from R' Shimon bar Yochai's bonfire, to save him.

On his way up the crooked path, he was suddenly besieged by a terrible thirst. His encounter with death had dried him up inside. "Who will give me a drop of water?" he whispered with parched lips.

Hardly were the words out of his mouth than his donkeys arrived, laden with their full water cannisters. Yitzchak-Chaim recited a grateful "*Shehakol*" and drank. The merit of the mitzvah, which had saved him from the hyena, had also spared him from his excruciating thirst.

By the light of the dancing bonfire, he made his way up the hill. Under his breath, he hummed along, "A *tzaddik,* the foundation of the world, who revealed what was hidden, who can acquit the world, our master, Bar Yochai!"

"Who can acquit the world!" He, Yitzchak-Chaim, had just witnessed this with his own eyes. The holy *Tanna* had acquitted him from a harsh decree, and the violence of the menacing beast.

"From that day on," the elderly Yitzchak-Chaim told the ever-growing crowd around him on Meiron, "I celebrate Lag Ba'Omer as a personal holiday. And, because I was saved in the merit of the public for whom I had gone, how better to celebrate than in a similar way, by performing acts of *chesed* for the public!"

This volume is part of
THE ARTSCROLL SERIES®
an ongoing project of
translations, commentaries and expositions
on Scripture, Mishnah, Talmud, Halachah,
liturgy, history, the classic Rabbinic writings,
biographies and thought.

For a brochure of current publications
visit your local Hebrew bookseller
or contact the publisher:

## Mesorah Publications, ltd

4401 Second Avenue
Brooklyn, New York 11232
(718) 921-9000
www.artscroll.com